COMPLETE BOOK OF

HOME REPAIRS
AND
MAINTENANCE

COMPLETE BOOK OF

HOME REPAIRS

AND

A POPULAR SCIENCE BOOK

MAINTENANCE

Jackson Hand

POPULAR SCIENCE PUBLISHING COMPANY
HARPER & ROW
NEW YORK • LONDON

Library of Congress Catalog Card Number: 70-167603

Designed by Jeff Fitschen

Manufactured in the United States of America

CONTENTS

CONTENTS

INTRODUCTION

THE POET SAID it takes a heap o' livin' to make a house a home, and he was right. His pragmatic next-door neighbor might have made it even more truth than poetry by adding: *it takes a heap o' fixin', too.* Every day the homes we live in become more complex. They're better structures, better designed, better equipped by far than anything built even a scant twenty-five years ago. The materials, construction methods, and finishes are all superior. But things go wrong. And sometimes when things go wrong, fixing them involves techniques and materials not always as familiar to most of us as things like good old nails and putty and faucet washers.

Along with the increases in complexity has come the well-known and much-lamented shortage in what was once referred to as the "services." It is no longer funny to joke about how many days it took to get a plumber to come and fix a flooding bathroom. Not long ago I went to an electrician with one of my problems and spent an hour or more talking sympathetically with him about his problems, mostly involving personnel procurement. I ended up doing the repair work myself.

You may have to do the same thing, and that is why this book was written.

TO DO—OR NOT TO DO—IT YOURSELF

You are probably fairly handy—or willing to learn—or you wouldn't be reading this book. Chances are that you can take care of most of the things that go haywire around the house, especially with a little guidance. You know something about tools. You can figure a thing out, if you spend a few minutes studying it.

On the other hand, there are some class-A foulups you shouldn't try to take care of, either because they involve so much work and time that it's inefficient for you to tackle them in your spare time, or because they involve tools and materials and skills that most of us don't ordinarily possess.

In the preparation of this book, considerable research, observation, and experience were devoted to a differentiation between repair-and-maintenance problems that are possible and those that are likely to become bigger problems if an amateur starts monkeying with them. The author and the editors decided upon a more or less foolproof method of letting the average guy know if he should take on a given job: *If it's too tough for the average pair of hands, we just don't cover it.* As a consequence, if you run across something that needs fixing around your place and you *don't* find it covered in this book, probably you should get on the phone and see if you can't locate a professional to do the job.

On the other hand, we have taken careful pains to include just about everything that might go wrong that you *should* take care of on your own.

WHAT THIS BOOK DOES FOR YOU

The words "home repair" in the title of this book are the key to its objectives. The basic assumption is that *something has gone wrong.* Something needs fixing. Don't look here for ideas or methodology needed to add on a porch or furbish a basement gameroom. Here we're *fixing* things.

In each case, we try to tell you what probably caused the trouble. We try to tell you what should be done about it, with what tools and materials and tricks. We try to tell you how to keep it from happening again, or at least from happening again too soon. The methods we suggest may not be the same as those a professional would use, because there are often amateur procedures that are easier than those the experts use.

The results, however, will be as good, as permanent, perhaps even better.

Although this is not a book about home maintenance — that is, things you do routinely like painting — there is a certain attention to preventive maintenance. Every attempt is made to help you prevent the recurrence of a problem; the book helps you, also, to recognize trouble that is imminent so that you can correct it before it gets too far out of hand.

In order to be most helpful, the book is "what-and-where" oriented, rather set up like a dictionary or reference book. If you have trouble in a basement, see the chapter on basements. If you have trouble with a window, there's a chapter on doors and windows. Turn to the chapter on masonry if you have troubles involving concrete or bricks. And, of course, there's an index. If you know the name of the trouble — or the name of the thing that's broken — the index will tell you where to hunt for the solutions in the book.

TOOLS AND
WORKING FACILITIES

A round-up of the tools that work best in home upkeep, tips on how to use them most effectively, and some ideas for finding efficient working areas without devoting excess space to them on a permanent basis.

1

HOME REPAIR
GETS EASIER EVERY DAY

IN THIS AGE OF CONSTANT technological change, it seems as though everything we own is becoming a little too difficult to understand. There are so many mysterious gadgets, built-in computers, and other combinations of science and magic that few of us are clever enough anymore to enjoy one of mankind's oldest and most pleasurable activities: fixing things.

Happily this applies less to our houses than to our possessions. Not that technology is leaving us behind; in fact, few aspects of day-to-day living have enjoyed as much honest and useful improvement (not mere gadgetology) as houses. One of the major reasons for this is that houses are still built board by board, brick by brick, shingle by shingle. When an improvement comes along it usually means a better board, brick, or shingle. But it also means a board, brick, or shingle that is easier to install in the first place, and easier to fix if something goes wrong.

While a great many of the basic improvements are aimed at making the job faster for the men who build a house, much of the good rubs off on those of us who live in the houses and want to keep a roof overhead, a floor underfoot, and walls in

3

between. A good example is apparent in one widely used category of materials: tile.

In the bathroom, tile once had to be set in plaster. Mark that idea as long gone. Now easy-to-use plastic-mastic adhesives are absolutely waterproof, and have the extra advantage of a certain elasticity. A quick switch from hot shower to cold may cause dimensional changes in the tile, but the adhesive goes along with them.

On ceilings, tile was once the symbol of ugliness—what you'd expect overhead in a cheap roadside restaurant. Today's tile is one of the most beautiful things you can put on a ceiling no matter how wealthy you happen to be. Gone are the polka dots. Now the textures are lovely, not mechanical, even in effective acoustical materials. As a result, if you finally reach the point where you're sick of patching and painting a plaster ceiling every year or so, you can stick up ceiling tile, again by spreading a mastic, and pushing the tiles in place. Moreover, the use of less moisture-vulnerable materials makes ceiling tile eligible for use on porches, where once we had little choice other than narrow, grooved boards called "ceiling"— certainly one of the least lovely materials ever devised.

On the floor, you've got to include tile among possible replacements for deteriorating hard-surface sheet materials, because it is so easy to put down. Some of it is self-sticking; all of it utilizes simple mastics. Much of it is so ingenious in design that you can't tell it's tile. None of it is as mundane as the checkerboards that were the only choice a short time ago.

And with tile as popular as it is, we have the paradox of excellent sheet materials for floors and walls that look like tile. These include hardboard with super-finishes in tile patterns and vinyl floor materials with the look of exotic imported ceramic tiles. Even wood flooring takes on the characteristics of tile, in unitized parquets or plywood squares that go down at the rate of a room a day.

Many of the materials and components we work with are approaching tinkertoy simplicity. There are electrical switches and outlets with no screws; you can just shove the ends of the wires in a hole. For a long time now much plumbing has been done with copper tubing that is easy to assemble, and entirely leakproof, with solder and a Bernz torch. Now they've expanded that to iron pipe as well. Some new faucets have no washers; they're dripless. Lumberyards sell weather stripping that combines plastic gaskets with a wooden member much like a doorstop, making it a simple brad-and-hammer job to tighten air leaks around entrances. Surely the circuit breaker, inevitably taking over for the routine fuse, is easier to reset than the fuse is to replace, particularly if you include the horrible nuisance of having to run downtown to buy the new fuse.

Adhesives are another world. Time was, you could glue two pieces of wood together fairly easily and permanently. Now you can use adhesives to fasten just about any material to any other material, except for a few plastics whose greatest value lies in the fact that nothing will stick to them. There are adhesives that are set hard in one minute to five minutes, sticking to glass, ceramics, metal, pottery, wood, leather, and many other materials. Strong? In many home repair situations, you can use glues that dry hard and fast in half an hour or less and forget mechanical fasteners, unless you need them to hold the parts together while the glue dries.

Tools become more efficient all the time and cost less in proportion to other products we buy. Sears and Ward's catalogs show excellently performing tools called "utility" or "medium duty," or otherwise marked for the kind of intermittent use we'd find for them around the house. Stanley has duplicated almost the entire line of professional tools in a slight scale-down called "Handyman." They all meet the requirements of quality, but at less cost.

As you wander through the tool department at a hardware or department store, you see many new special-use tools. Plier-like rigs that set grommets or eyelets in fabrics. Wire strippers that zip the insulation off the end of a wire of any size and include cutters as well as, in some models, special crimpers to lock electrical fitting on the end of the wire. Combination sets of wrenches, screw drivers, and sockets, put up in the sizes you need most. Kits including all you need to do electrical soldering. Double clamps that position two pieces of stock perfectly for miter-cutting. For nearly any job you run into, you can augment standard tools with time-saving specialists, if you want to.

All of these things and many more combine to make life simpler for the man who finds that he must do his own home repairs. They help us all to be handier than we think we are, putting many jobs within reason which would have been too hard to do—or too time-consuming—a few years ago.

THE TOOLS YOU NEED

FORTUNATELY, MOST HOME REPAIR and upkeep chores can be done with a minimum of tooling up. And, when the objective is keeping a house running, the ideal becomes not how *much* equipment you can accumulate, but how *little* you can get by with and still be acceptably efficient at what you've got to do. Then, you need a place to store the tools where you can find them.

And, you need a quick and handy method of transporting certain tools to the job. The reason for this, of course, is that a great deal of home repair work is done on location — where the damage exists. For instance, you fix a leaky faucet where it is; you patch a cracked ceiling where it is. You replace a broken window where it is, but a broken storm window you might want to take to a work area, not only because it would be more convenient but also because possibly it's 20 below zero out there where the broken storm window is. You'll find some ideas for portability later in this chapter.

THE ESSENTIAL HOME UPKEEP TOOLS

Nearly everybody has at least a shoebox full of tools, a starter in tooling up. There are two ways to put yourself in business full scale.

• You can buy tools as you need them. This way, you will probably find it less of a budget burden to buy the best, since the total purchase program is spread out. However, a repair job is all the more bothersome if, in addition to fixing something, you have to run out and buy a tool to do it. Bothersome becomes impossible if it happens to be late at night, with stores closed.

• You can take the list which follows and visit a hardware store (or Sears or Ward's catalog). Either way, avoid bargain-table tools. They don't perform, even for the handiest man in the world, and by the time you replace them with tools worth owning, you haven't enjoyed any bargain. When you begin to look at tool selection from the standpoint of efficient mini-mums, you move sometimes toward a bigger, better, more professional tool, and other times toward smaller, less professional, but entirely adequate equipment. Examples are plain in the first category below: You get more work done faster with a bigger, heavier 12-foot pull-out rule than with a light 8-footer. On the other end of the scale, a small but good torpedo level will do as much for you in home maintenance work as the bigger, more cumbersome level you see professional builder-carpenters using.

• Follow-up shopping for tools is an excellent way to fill in the gaps. As you walk through tool departments in hardware and other stores, run your eye over the displays. Now and then you'll see exactly the tool you wished you'd had the

Bigger, longer pullout rule with locking device handles more jobs than smaller rules.

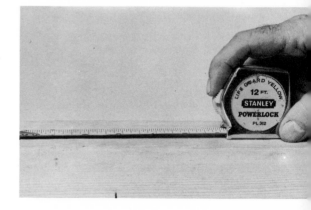

last time something needed fixing—or the tool you know you'll need when you finally get around to some job you've been putting off.

Here is a listing of tools selected for their particular suitability to home repair work in the hands of a typical home owner. They are broken down into arbitrary categories.

Measuring tools. Buy that wider, heavier, 12-foot rule. Avoid the kind that is marked in feet and inches only. Most of us are better accustomed to thinking "seventy-five inches" than "six feet, three inches."

Square. A combination square is generally handier than a carpenter's square. You can use it for squaring, for mitering, and as a marking gauge, since the head slides on the blade and can be locked in any position. Some models even include a useful level. The standard carpenter's square is less handy, often cumbersome. Buy it later—when the need makes itself felt.

Level. The level built into a good combination square will handle a lot of problems, but a good little "torpedo" level is handier. Find one that will give you horizontal, vertical, and 45 degree readings.

Cutting tools. In this category the warning about bargain tools is particularly important. You'll never be able to keep them sharp, because a great deal of their cheapness is due to poor steel.

Saw. The smaller 24″ size is big enough for any job, and it not only costs a little less but takes up less storage space. Don't buy a ripsaw under typical home upkeep conditions, because most lumber you work with will be in the form of moldings or standard widths. In other words, you'll be replacing something standard, and the length is the main consideration. You'll find a "10 point" saw (it means teeth-per-inch) best. It cuts smoother than coarser saws, and its action is fast enough for work around the house.

Chisels. As a set or purchased individually, get the ¼″, ½″, ¾″ and 1″ sizes. Actually, with a ¼″ chisel you can do any-

Look for a number stamped in the blade of a handsaw, near the handle. It means teeth per inch. "Ten tooth" is best for most work.

Two planes that give you widest working range are a low-angle block plane (*bottom*) for light work, edge grain, etc., and a foreplane for planing true, straight edges.

thing you can do with the 1″ size. It just takes longer and probably won't be as neat a job.

Plane. A block plane does most of the jobs you'll ever run into. Be sure to get the "low angle" kind. It is easiest to handle, more versatile than any other kind.

Knife. A linoleum knife or a utility knife beats trying to work with a razor blade or something out of the kitchen drawer.

Sharpening stone. Get the aluminum oxide (Carborundum) variety that is about 2″ by 7″, fine on one side and coarse on the other. Actually any stone only takes care of fine honing. If a tool is very dull, it must be ground, then honed. As soon as you can work it into your program, buy a motor-driven grinder.

Joining tools. These are the tools you'll need for all kinds of assembly work, and for the ripping apart of old joinery which often precedes it.

Hammer. For most homeowners it is easier to use the 13-ounce hammer than the 16- or 20-ounce sizes the fulltime carpenter uses. Get the curved-claw kind called a "nail hammer." You'll never need a ripping hammer for ordinary use.

Wrecking bar. You'll need a small wrecking bar or a "pinch"

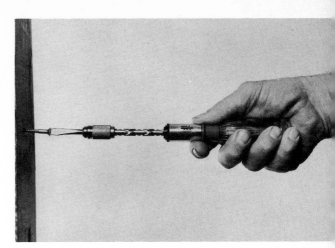

Ratchet screwdriver speeds up the job. You merely push and an inclined plane on the shank produces the twist— in or out.

bar, to handle the tear-apart that so often precedes the put-together of repair and maintenance.

Screwdriver. You'll never regret buying a good "ratchet" screwdriver, the kind with a spiral shank that twists the screw in or out while all you do is push. The ratchet variety is so much faster and easier to use than the regular variety that you'll quickly forget what it costs. Get three bits for it—small, medium, and large—plus a couple of sizes of Phillips drivers. (The Phillips is the screw with a slot in the form of a cross that grows more and more popular.) If the ratchet job you buy doesn't come with a selection of bits, you may need to buy auxiliary screwdrivers in small and large sizes. Buy shorter and longer models as you need them.

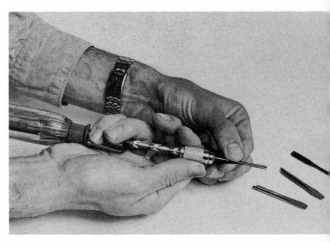

Small Stanley ratchet driver has accessory bit sizes, plus some drills for predrilling screw holes. If you do a lot of work, the bigger ratchet model (130A) is faster.

Team up an electric drill with a hand drill, one to drill deep holes, the other to countersink for screw heads. Electric drill handles holes up to about 1", with special types of "spade" bits, and will drive masonry bits up to about ½". Small bit shown is "ScrewMate," bores holes for core, shank, and countersink in one pass.

Hole making. By far the most common power tool in the world is the electric drill, and this is entirely proper. With it you are faster and more accurate not only in hole-drilling but in a variety of other home upkeep functions made possible by attachments, which will be discussed in full in the chapter on power tools.

However, for drilling of small holes up to ¼", a hand drill will handle most work around the house. It will also drive a countersink and in that role it teams up perfectly with the electric drill you may get later on, for speedier drilling.

Brace and bit. If you decide to forego the electric drill for the time being, you can bore holes larger than ¼" with a brace and bit. Large holes are not the only virtue of this old standby tool, however. It works also to drive big screws, when you chuck in a heavy screwdriver bit. You can buy sockets that make a wrench of it. You can bring it into the drill-and-countersink team if you wish. Some braces are made with a ratchet device in the chuck end, so that you can operate the tool with a series of short strokes. This is often imperative when you work in close quarters, so be sure the brace you buy has this feature.

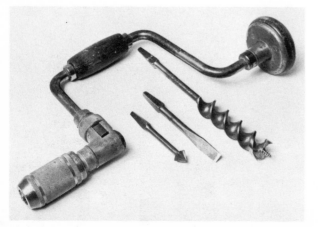

Good old-Fashioned brace and bit does more than bore holes, as you'll find when you enlist its aid with heavy screws. Brace takes over hole sizes too big for electric drill, also teams up as countersinker in many jobs.

Bits and drills. Twist drills up to ¼″, along with auger bits on up to an inch or more, complete the hole-making equipment for most work around the house. You may want to buy some special bits which drill for core, shank, and counterbore of screws, although these are usually more useful in new work than in repair and maintenance.

Clamps and vises. You need, many, many times, a third hand to hold things while you use the other two for tool manipulation. Vises and clamps do it.

Vises call for a permanent workbench (see the next chapter) but there is a "portable" vise, typified by the Stanley 700, which clamps to any temporary working surface and can be stowed away between jobs.

Clamps. Web clamps are a fairly recent addition to the "third hand" world. They can be used to hold a wobbly chair together until the glue dries—they work for a lot of edge-gluing—for any sort of a job which is too bulky or widespread for ordinary clamps.

C-clamps in 4″ and 6″ sizes hold many typical assemblies together, either for gluing or fastening with screws.

Spring clamps are extremely handy, quick and easy to squeeze and release in place. They hold "the other end" for you in many situations, and are the fastest and simplest of all clamps for small glue jobs.

Spring clamp holds work while you assemble it with screws, and will work as gluing clamp in many operations. There are three sizes, so inexpensive you'll want several in all three.

Web clamp is a loop of strong nylon braided tape with a tightening device. It does many jobs ordinary clamps would find diffcult or cumbersome.

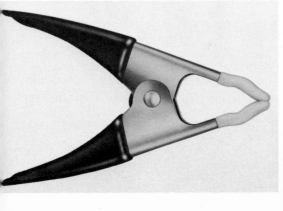

Wrenches. The adjustable wrench, often called "Crescent," is ideal for the home upkeep man. With the 6″ and 10″ sizes, you can handle just about any nut size around the house.

Locking pliers are handy because you can close them on a nut, or on a round object, and they snap tight in place with a grip far greater than you could apply with ordinary pliers. But you also need a pair of standard slipjoint pliers to do the kind of work the locking type bungles because of its size.

TOOLS FOR SPECIALTY WORK

You should have, all in a kit and ready to go, the working units for certain kinds of home repairs which require tools so specialized that they aren't used for anything else. These areas include:

Plumbing. You need two pipe wrenches; one is just about worthless. Buy a 10″ and a 14″ wrench. They work together, one holding the pipe while you tighten a fitting.

Much modern plumbing is copper, assembled with soldered joints. In fact, the iron pipe industry now produces pipe and fittings of a close enough tolerance to allow soldered joints. For this work you need a propane torch, with some solder, flux, and coarse steel wool. Cutting iron pipe is hardly man-around-the-house work, but it is easy to cut and fit copper tubing, if you have a tube cutter—preferably one with a reamer attached.

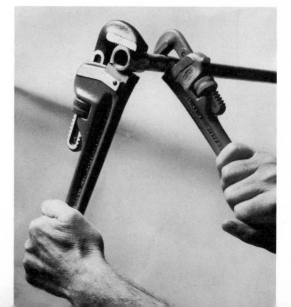

Pipe wrenches always work in pairs, one to turn the fitting and one to hold the pipe from turning.

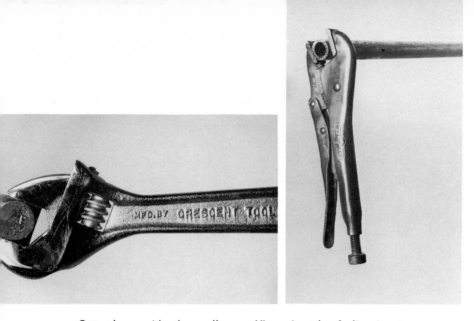

Get along with the well-known crescent wrench as long as you can, but when the time comes buy a set of sockets, a set of box and open-end.

Vice grip style of pliers is extra-rugged and extra-handy, since the jaws will clamp on and stay there. Screw adjusts tool to required size.

You can borrow the Crescent wrench and a screwdriver from your regular tool box and take care of the rest of the plumbing requirements.

Electrical. You do most of the electrical maintenance around the house with a screwdriver, which removes switch and outlet plates, disconnects and replaces wires, mounts and demounts electrical fittings. Also very handy: a special tool for cutting wire and stripping insulation. If you get into very serious electric work, you need a pair of linesman's pliers. The type with the square nose twists wires together better than any other kind. An electric soldering-iron is handy, but you'll use it more on things that plug into the electrical system than on the system itself.

Masonry. When you decide to do something about deteriorating masonry, you usually need a chipping chisel, a tuck-pointing trowel, a small patching trowel, and a finishing trowel. The latter can be used as a "hawk" for a small amount of tuckpointing, although the section on masonry repairs suggests more businesslike methods.

MISCELLANEOUS TOOLS YOU CAN'T WORK WITHOUT

There are many tools that don't classify but work for you on many different jobs.

Tin snips. The shorter kind, called "aviation snips," has a double lever system which makes it easier to cut heavy metals and effortless to cut ordinary tin and aluminum.

Standard tin snips handle typical work with sheet metals. With the "airplane" snip (*lower*) there is a double-lever in the handle, letting you work with heavier metal.

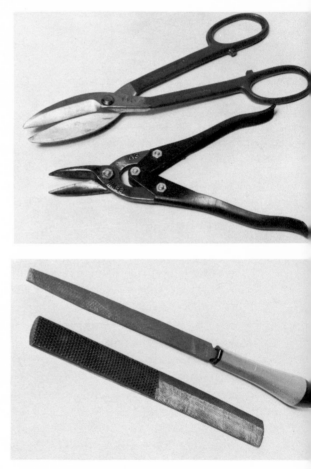

Flat file (*top*) handles most work with metal, although you'll want to get three-cornered and round styles eventually. Woodworking rasp with most versatility is the "four-in-hand" style (*bottom*), combining both coarse and fine teeth on flat and half-round faces.

Files and rasps. Get an 8″ mill file and an 8″ four-in-hand rasp. This tool has a fine and coarse flat side, a fine and coarse rounded side. A rat-tail or slim-taper file is handy too.

Scratch awl. For marking points and lines on lumber, and for making precision starting points for screws.

Nail set. You'll need this tool when doing a fine-finishing job and want to drive nail heads just a bit below the surface of the wood and then fill them with putty or plastic wood.

Putty knife. No sense soiling a screwdriver or some other tool when working with putty. Get a putty knife; you'll see how much easier it is to work with one.

Joint knife. This is the tool you'll need for plastering spots in walls and ceilings. It's usually bigger than a putty knife because of the larger surface it has to tackle.

Hacksaw. There are plenty of jobs around the house that require cutting metal. A good hacksaw is the only tool that will do the job quickly.

STORING AND TRANSPORTING TOOLS

The specialist tools you use for one kind of work only are best stored in some manner that also provides portability. Since the number of tools in each case is small, and the required supplies are limited, store-and-carry units do not have to be big or complicated. For instance, you could put all your electrical specialty tools in a one-pound coffee can, and stick it away on a shelf. A ten-quart galvanized pail would take care of all the plumbing equipment, providing you with a convenient carrying handle.

The tools in the basic list may be teamed up on this job or that, but since the teams are not often the same, it is handy to hang them up on display so you can see them all and pick the ones you need for a job. Put them in a small tote box and make off for the problem area. Nothing beats a sheet of perforated hardboard as a hanging place, and the main reason why is the wide selection of hangers you can buy, each designed to hang a different type of tool. However, you can hang just about anything on nails driven into a piece of plywood. If you have a specific work center with or without a bench, your hanging board belongs there, of course. Otherwise it can go on a garage or basement wall.

The drawings and photographs on the following pages suggest a few tote box ideas that have proven their worth over the years, plus a brand new idea: the tool drum built on the lazy susan principle.

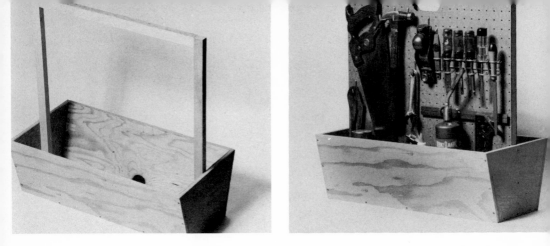

Many of the most-used tools in a home upkeep setup can be stored and transported in this tote box. Make it by nailing together a splayed-top box of ½″ plywood, with a frame screwed to the ends as shown in the photo at left. Nail on two pieces of pegboard with a cutout at the top of each for a handhold. Dimensions are shown in plan below.

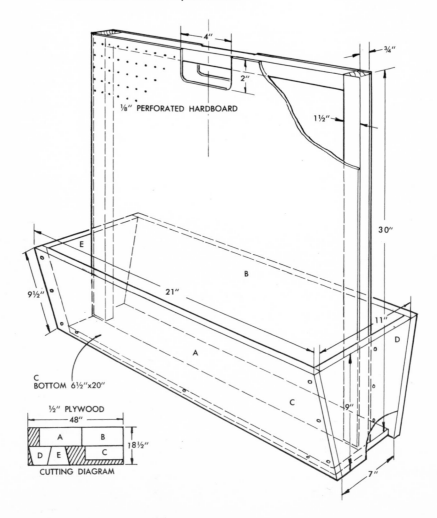

⅛″ PERFORATED HARDBOARD

4″

¾″

2″

1½″

30″

E

B

21″

9½″

11″

D

A

C
BOTTOM 6½″x20″

C

9″

½″ PLYWOOD
48″

A	B
D	E	C

18½″

CUTTING DIAGRAM

7″

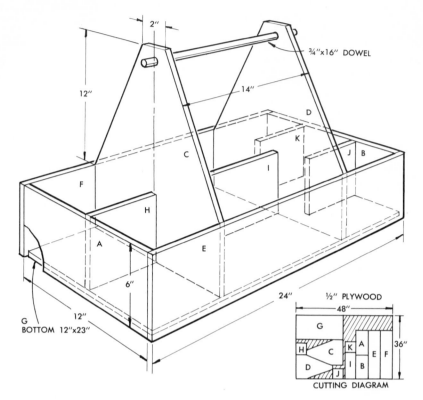

2"

¾"x16" DOWEL

12"

14"

D

K

C

J B

I

F

H

A

E

6"

24"

½" PLYWOOD

48"

G

H K A

C E F

D I B

36"

J

CUTTING DIAGRAM

G
BOTTOM 12"x23"

12"

This tote box with compartments for tools and supplies is dimensioned to hang up between jobs on two overhead joists.

Handiest tote box for a small complement of tools is a ten-quart pail. Use it for jobs in far corners of the house.

The smaller of the tote boxes is intended to hold the tools you need for two or three specialist jobs. You might, for example, keep your plumbing and electrical tools and supplies in the box, ready to go at all times. It is shown with seven different compartments. The purpose of these is to save the time you waste rummaging around in a box for small tools or materials. You simply assign each category of tool, material, and supply to one of the little bins. The box is designed so that you can hang it between two ceiling joists, for storage completely out of the way in space useless for other purposes.

With its two-faced pegboard construction, the other tote box is a combination of carryall and hanging board. On its hanging surfaces and in its bins, you can store as much of your tool complement as you feel like carrying, and you'll find that's most of them. The same features apply to the portable tool drum. It's superb hanging space, portable, but you might prefer to pick a few tools off it to make a lighter load to carry.

HOW POWER TOOLS
EARN THEIR KEEP

THERE ARE THREE quick reasons why you may want to take advantage of electrical power for some of the jobs hand tools can do quite well. Power tools are *faster*. Power tools, relieving you of the need for physical strength and leaving you only the job of guiding a tool, are *more accurate*. Power tools, as companions on a job you may not look upon with joyful anticipation, are *more fun*.

Because of the last factor, it isn't always possible to make a decision about buying a power tool on a strictly practical basis. Certain portable tools are called into action so often that it seems contrary to common sense to pass them up. The electric drill is the obvious example. Others gather dust for months, then perform some tasks in minutes that you'd spend hours at with hand tools. Leaving the factor of fun up to the individual, let's look at the relative usefulness of power tools as a means of determining which you need first, which to buy later, which possibly to rent, which to get along without.

THE GRINDER-SHARPENER

It has been, for years and years, the sage advice of men who know about tools and working with them that the first piece of power equipment anybody should own is a grinder with which to *keep the hand tools sharp.* There is no other way than with a grinder to put the slightly concave bevel on a cutting tool which you can then hone to a perfect cutting edge. Attempts to keep tools sharp with just a stone always produce a rounded bevel, increasingly blunt, increasingly difficult, and finally impossible to bring to sharpness.

A good grinder is nothing more than a double-spindle electric motor, with some simple additions, and the motor doesn't have to be big. A quarter horse or even less will do it. As a result, you don't have to spend much for a grinder, but be sure that what you buy has these features:

• Grinding wheel, medium grade, with at least a ½″ face. Diameter is not critical; 6″ is a standard size, but for light work you can use a smaller wheel.

• Wire wheel, medium grade, on the other spindle.

You can buy, as your need for them arises, coarser and finer grades of both wire and grinding wheels.

• Metal wheel guards over both wheels, covering them completely except for the opening in the front, where you apply the object being worked on.

• Transparent shield (usually Plexiglas or a similar plastic) to protect your eyes and face from flying debris.

• Tool rest—a stop on which you support the material being ground- or wire-brushed, as a means of making sure it doesn't slip.

The grinder industry, working with experts on safety, has arrived at a set of standards aimed at making grinders as safe to use as possible. The tool rest, wheel guards, and eye shield are a part of this program. Make sure the grinder you buy meets these requirements for safety, to protect yourself.

First power tool any man should own is a good grinder to keep his hand tools sharp. Modern grinders double their value with wire wheels, buffing pads, and other work-saving features.

THE ELECTRIC DRILL

More people own electric drills and get more useful service from them than any other powerized tool. To meet the challenge of this popularity, manufacturers have been improving drills at a rapid rate, bringing in such features as these:

• Variable speed, which lets you run the drill at the speed best suited to the job. For instance, you start drilling a hole at slow speed, then rev up to top speed after the drill has penetrated a sure distance and isn't likely to skid. Most variable speed drills have an adjustable stop, so you can preselect a speed and automatically return to it time after time. Nearly all of them are engineered so that a slight pressure on the trigger starts a slow rotation of the shuck, and as you squeeze harder, the speed increases. If the load on the drill causes it to slow down, you naturally squeeze a little harder. This delivers more power to the drill and it picks up speed.

• Reversible drills (usually the same models that have variable speeds) can be set to rotate in the normal clockwise direction, or in the opposite direction. This feature serves to loosen a drill which may become clogged and stuck deep in a wooden member. It also makes the drill truly useful when it is put to work driving screws or tightening small nuts. The reversible model will *un*drive and *un*tighten too, and just as fast.

• Battery-powered drills, of course, set you free from the need for electric lines. This means no extension cord when you go up on the roof to work on a TV antenna. It means availability of power at the far corner of the lot—up in the tree house, in the attic—where nobody thought of putting an electrical outlet. Batteries are rechargeable.

ATTACHMENTS FOR DRILLS

As an instrument purely for boring holes, an electric drill would barely earn its keep. In a normal home repair operation, there are too few holes to be drilled. But, ever since the drill leaped into popularity with the do-it-yourself movement of the 1950s, there have been accessories which increase the utility of the drill. Among the most useful of the attachments are:

• A drill stand for mounting the drill in a vertical position, with a handle that makes the tool work just like a regular drill press. Naturally, this provides greater accuracy, but more than that, it makes it possible to apply the precise and uniform pressure you need for drilling in steel and other metals.

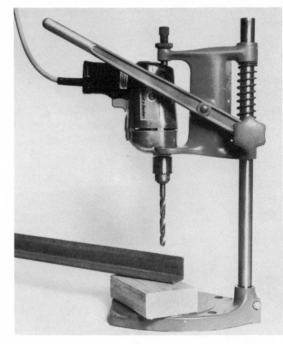

Electric drill expands in precision and usefulness when a drill stand converts it into a drill press. The stand is valuable if you must drill metals accurately.

• A bench mount which accepts the drill in a horizontal position, where it functions like any other electric motor. You can chuck a variety of attachments into the drill. The serious drawback of this accessory is the absence of guards, tool rests, and other essentials of safety. Using a drill mounted in one of these stands, you run a considerable risk of getting hurt by flying debris thrown by the rapidly spinning attachment.

• Chuck-in attachments include grinding wheels, wire wheels, and a variety of sanders, buffers, and polishers. All of these make their kind of work easier, particularly buffing and polishing with sheepskin bonnets over a rubber pad. However, the aspects of danger from flying debris are even greater when you chuck grinding wheels and wire wheels into a hand-held electric drill. A good deal of skill and a great deal of care are important if you use such attachments.

• A speed reducer, one of the less-known gadgets, is one of the most useful. It is an enclosed gear box which goes between the drill and the chuck, cutting the rotation speed to perhaps an eighth of the motor speed. This, of course, increases the torque eightfold, more or less. You can put a 1/2" chuck on a 1/4" drill and have plenty of power to run the larger size. With a screwdriver bit in place, you can run big, heavy screws—even bigger than those a variable-speed drill could handle.

• Screwdriver attachments, working on a variety of mechanical principles, are handy if you happen to run into a job involving a great deal of screw assembly. One of the most effective operates somewhat in the manner of an "impact tool" such as the one mechanics use changing tires at your filling station. The attachment drives the screw rapidly at first, when the going is easy. As the resistance builds up, however, the driver starts "slipping a cog," then regaining linkage with a light but continuously repeated tapping. These attachments handle screws up to about No. 8. Above that, a mechanical screwdriver would be costly; your screwdriver bit in a brace does the job quickly enough.

Capacity of the standard 1/4" drill is doubled with "geardown" devices which increase effective power of the tool, making holes up to 1/2" in steel. Slower speed is good for driving screws and other twist-power jobs.

Advances in electrical insulation. With an electric drill, as with all other electric powered tools, there is always the chance of electric shock. The records are full of fatalities due to failure of the insulating system of such tools. Many years ago, manufacturers took a step toward eliminating a great deal of the danger by wiring tools so that all parts of them you touch, handles, housing, chuck, etc., are grounded *when the tool is properly plugged into a proper electrical circuit.* These tools have a three-wire cord with three prongs. Two of them are the regular flat metal prongs which make the contacts necessary to run the tool. The third is a round prong. It makes contact with the grounding system of the wiring. If there should be an insulation failure in the tool, the electricity takes the path of least resistance through the ground wire. The user is spared the shock he might otherwise absorb if the electricity were to pass through his body.

However, not every home is wired in a way that can take advantage of this advance in electrical safety design. Adapters have proved to be a nuisance. Most home owners who bought power tools with three-prong plugs finally ended up breaking off the grounding prong, or using a "cheater" which made the third prong inactive. The result, of course, was a tool no safer than the old two-wire variety.

If any power tool you buy has only two prongs (1) be sure that it is "double insulated." The nameplate will tell you. The three-prong cord (2) means that the tool is grounded against electrical shock. The worst mistake in the world is (3) to remove the grounding plug from a three-prong cord, because it leaves you exposed to electrical shock which could be fatal.

1   2

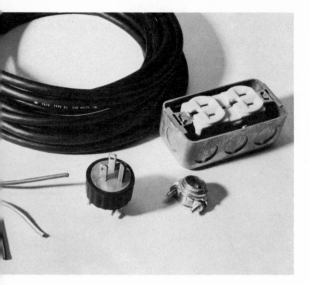

Make yourself an extension cord better than most you find offered for sale, using 16/3 or heavier cord, a three-prong plug, a three-hole outlet, and a metal utility box. The fastener is the kind normally used for Romex wiring.

To remedy this potentially dangerous situation, manufacturers began to use another safety system, called "double insulation." What this means, in simple terms, is that the electrically motivated parts of the tool are insulated in one "capsule," separated electrically from the handle and the housing of the tool. The second insulation covers cord, plug, and so forth. In addition to this insulation, the body of double-insulated tools is usually made of a non-conductive plastic material. As a result, it would take a rare combination of interlapping and overlapping coincidences to produce electrical shock, particularly since the insulating materials used for one phase of insulation are not subject to failure from the same causes as the materials used for the other phase.

The advantages of double insulation are that the plug has two prongs and will fit into any outlet or extension cord, and that it does not rely for safety on third-wire grounding which may or may not function.

Experts in tool safety agree that when three-prong is properly used it is as safe as double insulation. They point out, however, that double insulation does not offer the temptation to bypass safety the way three-wire does when it is deliberately used improperly, or when the wiring actually does not accommodate it. That is why the move toward double insulation has become all but universal—and that is why the tools you buy should have it.

PORTABLE ELECTRIC SAW

Sawing by hand is hard work. It's slow. If you have much cutting to do, you get tired of it in a hurry. Add to this the fact that few of us can saw really straight with a handsaw. The portable electric saw solves both sides of the problem. It cuts fast in thick wood or thin, and it is easy to guide with excellent accuracy in ripping and crosscut operations — even at an angle or a bevel.

The 7″ blade size is big enough for work around the house. It will handle 2″ lumber with ease — even set for a 45-degree bevel. On rare occasions when you might be working with stock thicker than that, you can make two cuts, one on each side. On the other hand, a saw much smaller than 7″ won't handle hardwood when the time comes.

There are usually three or four grades in any manufacturer's line of saws, labeled with such terms as "industrial," "heavy-duty," "standard duty," and "utility." You may not need the extra quality of the top model, considering the intermittent nature of your work, but you'll find the features of the upper end of the line worth their cost. Adjustments are more convenient and more accurate. Handling is easier. Safety features may be more effective.

There are several different blades on the market for portable saws, and you may find it handy to have two or three. First, a *carbide-tip* blade will last for years and years without being sharpened, in ordinary use. Since it's a nuisance to take saw blades out to a sawsmith for sharpening, and the expense runs up toward $2, many home craftsmen find the carbide blades worth the $8 to $10 they cost. *Teflon coated* blades run with less friction between blade and wood, and work better in wood that is wet or pitchy. *Plywood* blades have very fine teeth, and tend to cut with less splintering, an important feature if much of your work is with plywood. *Hollow ground* blades, when they are properly sharpened and properly used, produce a cut so smooth it may need only sanding before you put on a finish. These blades are more effective on stationary power saws than on portables, however, since much of their performance depends on the precision of the table saw.

To get the maximum use from a portable electric saw, you can mount most brands on specially designed tables. The saw goes upside down, with the blade and retractable guard rising up above the surface of the table. The bevel feature of the saw can be used, and the table comes equipped with rip fence and miter gauge. The rig is not as accurate or as convenient to use as a good table saw, of course, but in home repair situations it will do most of the work you run into. And, it gives you the advantage of a table saw when you need it, without the space requirements of a full-time saw.

POWER SANDERS

Three different forms of power sanders are available for home use, each with its own advantages and disadvantages. These are the disk, vibrating and belt.

• Disk sanders, also called sander-polishers, are built somewhat like an electric drill, but are a bit more rugged. They drive a wide variety of "heads" and it is often most convenient to buy them in kit form. A typical kit may include a rubber back-up pad, lamb's wool bonnet for buffing, pile fabric pad for applying polishes and compounds, a fabric wheel, wire wheel, grinding wheel, and a variety of abrasive disks. In some cases a handle is provided, long enough to let you use the tool as a floor polisher. Some kits have a bracket for mounting the sander-polisher as a bench tool.

The disk sander is often more useful in its role as a polisher than as a sander, except for quite rough work. The whirling action of the tool produces swirl marks that are often too severe to remove with conventional sanding techniques. However, you often see a complete house sanded clean and bare with a disk sander—often the only answer to a dismal-failure paint job. When you want to *sand away* rather than *sand smooth*, it's the tool that does it. A disadvantage is the need for sandpaper disks, instead of convenient, conventional sheets.

• The term "vibrating" is used to cover a small family of sanders that operate on the principle of a rapidly vibrating pad, usually the size of about a third of a sheet of sandpaper.

You clamp the paper over the pad and although you move the sander slowly over the work, the vibrations multiply tremendously the amount of actual sanding action.

The pad may be driven in an endless series of tiny circles as on the sander called "orbital." Or, it may be driven forward and backward in straight line vibrations. The best models produce either movement of the pad, at the flick of a lever. This is handy. The orbital action cuts fast. You use it to take a rough surface down to a fair degree of smoothness. Then you switch to straight to remove the tiny circular scratches made by the orbital action.

A definite advantage for the vibrating sander is that it can work into corners, which other mechanical sanders cannot do because of their size or design.

• The belt sander is the best of the three, all factors considered. It will produce an extremely smooth surface. You can use it, also, when you want to remove a lot of surface material—paint or roughness. It will not work into corners. You can't use it for buffing or polishing. But it is the most effective sander. Even though the belts are relatively expensive, they last a long time, and a belt will often out-perform other forms of abrasive, penny for penny.

You can buy sanders with belt widths ranging from 2″ up to 4″. Some models have vacuum bags that pick up sander dust as fast as it appears; in other versions, the vacuum is an accessory.

PORTABLE SABER SAW

The portable saber saw is, in form and function, a jigsaw. It can be used to cut a straight line, but that is the least of its accomplishments. It can also cut a crooked line, as a jigsaw can (among stationary tools), or as a coping saw can (among hand tools). When a portable saber saw is small, a minimum tool, it must be thought of mainly as a powered coping saw. However, the more rugged models can take over some of the efficiency and convenience of a portable circular saw. Although the blade design does not help insure fairly straight travel, as a circular blade does, the overall design of the saw is businesslike enough so that it will do pretty much what you ask it to do. If you direct it on a straight line, it will cut a straight line. If you direct it along a curved line, it will follow that line, without temperamental wandering if the density and resistance of wood change.

The newest and by far the best performing of the saber saws are those with a rotating head, typified by the top saw in the Sears line. With this saw, you do not turn the entire tool as you describe a curve. Rather, the body of the saw maintains its position, and you turn the spindle, using a knob atop the forward part of the motor housing. Then, you merely change the direction of "feed," following the turning of the spindle. Since this style of saw will cut forward, backward, to either side, or at any angle around the entire protractor, it gives you advantages impossible with stationary-spindle models. In fact, it gives you advantages no saw of any kind provides, if you take advantage of all the varieties of blades available.

Whether your requirements call for the features of the big, rotating spindle saw, or can be met with smaller and less sophisticated models, one thing is critical: the *length of the stroke*. The better saber saws have a stroke about an inch long. This distributes the cutting load over a useful length of the blade. If the stroke is short—regardless of the length of the blade—the cutting must be taken care of by just a few teeth. When the stroke is longer, more teeth share the cutting load.

There are tables in which you can mount saber saws, much in the same manner as you mount a portable circular saw. With the blade sticking up through the table, you have a small version of the standard jigsaw. Instead of following a curve by maneuvering the tool, you maneuver the stock. A great deal more accuracy is possible this way, and the saber-saw-in-a-table has one great advantage over even the finest standard jigsaw: There is no "throat." You can turn the biggest piece of stock any which way without striking the upright support of the saw, because there isn't any upright support.

Store and carry an extension cord on a rack like this. Two heavy dowels are mounted at opposing angles in a length of 1 x 6. Wind cord in a "figure-8" and it won't twist.

All these features recommend the saber saw as at least the third most useful power tool, and many home owners who do their own upkeep rate it almost equal to the portable circular saw.

There are other portable electric tools you might find useful from time to time, including:

A *router*, which accepts cutters of various shapes and can be used to produce moldings. A *reciprocating saw*, a horizontal cutting, outsize version of the saber saw, useful for fast cutting big stock—even logs. *Impact tools*, for tightening nuts or driving lag screws, etc.

Except for special work, portable tools other than drill, sander, saw, and saber saw rarely earn their keep. Your most efficient approach to them may be rental when you need them.

STATIONARY POWER TOOLS

There are only a few things you can do with big, stationary power tools that you can't do with portable tools and their accessories. However, you can do everything more accurately, more rapidly, and in bigger scale. And among the few additional things stationary tools can do are some fairly important functions. For these reasons, if you have the space for them and the budget, give some thought to these tools.

Saw. There are some differences in performance between the two popular types: table saw and radial arm saw. Fundamentally, it is easier to *crosscut* on a radial arm saw because you merely hold the stock in place and draw the arm across it, whereas you must push the stock across the blade on a table saw. If the stock happens to be a length of 2-by-stuff, and if you happen to be cutting it near one end, it is close to impossible to handle the board on the table saw. (You'd be better off with your portable electric saw.) On the other hand, it is easier to rip on a table saw, because you are moving the stock lengthwise, in plain sight, in the clear, against an easily adjustable fence. On the radial arm saw, you have to rotate the head, adjust the blade guard, set the width of cut, and be sure everything is tight, before you can cut. Then if you must make an ensuing crosscut, you have to loosen everything and set it back to the original position.

Taking all factors into consideration, the table saw gets the nod for a home upkeep tool. If you decide to go for one, figure on the 10″ size, tilting arbor, *bench* model. This will cost you less than the *floor* model because you don't spend any money for the stand. Instead, you make your own stand out of plywood, and build some features into it—such as a dust bin, accessory storage cabinet, etc.

Jointer. Altogether too few home shops are equipped with a jointer, despite the fact that almost every time you saw a board you end up with an edge that must be smoothed. If your aim is to set up a home maintenance shop that really saves you time and does the job right, team up your saw with a jointer. (Some companies produce them as a unit, mounted on a single table, operating from a single motor.)

Other big tools include bandsaw, jigsaw, shaper, sander, drill press and lathe. Except for the lathe, these tools are duplicated in function by excellently performing portable tools. Do you need a lathe? This much is true: When you *do* need a lathe, there is no substitute. Suppose the task is to replace a broken spindle in a porch railing, and the spindle is a turning. Fortunately, a lathe is a simple hunk of iron, you can buy one for less money than almost any other big power tool, and it is almost always simple to power it with a motor that serves dual duty on some other power tool.

As with hand tools or portable electric tools, there are attachments and accessories designed for use on stationary power tools. The best way to buy them is as you need them, either from a good hardware store or by mail order.

HOW TO GET THE MOST
OUT OF YOUR TOOLS

IN THE CHAPTERS that follow this one, you'll find scores of tool-use tricks that apply to specific problems and specific situations. The purpose of this chapter on *how to get the most out of your tools* is, therefore, a roundup of suggestions for the proper use of basic equipment—plus warnings about improper use. If you're an old hand with tools, fine. But if you are one of those householders who finds that the average hammer handle is 8″ too long—that you only really need those 3″ or 4″ right next to the head—see if you don't find some ideas here that make you handier.

The emphasis in this chapter is almost entirely on hand tools. You get no instruction booklets with them, generally, while power tools are usually accompanied with literature that tells you how to get the most out of the equipment, in the safest manner possible. Now and then, however, you'll find an idea for power tool use. When you do, it will quite likely be an offbeat gimmick that has proved useful on the job but doesn't warrant coverage in the manufacturer's own how-to instructions.

Start a cut with a handsaw by pulling the tool toward you, after it is precisely positioned at the cutoff point.

SAWING

Your crosscut saw does most of its work on the downstroke, because the teeth are slanted upward. Thus, on the downstroke you exert slight pressure, so the points will dig in. Not too much pressure, however, or you just make sawing too much of an effort, without cutting any faster. Normally, the angle of the handle of the saw is designed so that when you tighten your grip a little, the teeth automatically bite in harder. Tilting your wrist forward slightly increases the pressure. Hold the saw at an angle of about 45 degrees to the surface when you cut typical one-by-stuff. Working on two-by-stuff, make the angle a little steeper. With thin wood and plywood, a flatter angle cuts better, with less chipping at the bottom.

When you start a cut, *use gentle upstrokes only,* until the kerf is deep enough so you can be sure the saw won't jump out and mar the work. Then begin very gentle downstrokes, gradually increasing pressure as the cut deepens. Use full-length strokes whenever possible for fastest cutting and to make sure you don't end up with a saw that's dull in the middle.

A hacksaw blade's teeth slant forward to an even greater degree. There is practically no cutting action on the upstroke, and it is best to lift the saw slightly as you pull it back. This avoids the possibility of breaking teeth and dulling them unnecessarily. Since the cutting is all on the forward stroke, start a hacksaw cut with virtually no pressure; gradually press the saw against the work, until it starts to cut. Use full strokes, once the kerf is deep enough to keep the blade from skidding.

36

Always use the coarsest blade that will handle the material you are sawing. Here are basic teeth-per-inch recommendations for typical materials:

• Solid metal—steel, brass, copper, aluminum, ¼″ thick and up—18 teeth to the inch.

• Thinner metals and iron pipe—24 teeth to the inch.

• Thin metals, thin-wall tubing—32 teeth to the inch.

(When metal is quite thin, galvanized or aluminum sheet, sheet steel or thinbar or rod, you may find it easier and faster to cut with aviation snips.)

When you cut thin metals with a hacksaw, keep the angle of blade to stock quite flat. Otherwise, there is a chance that teeth may be scraped off by the edge of the metal.

Coping saws cut on the opposite stroke from hacksaws. The teeth point backward, and virtually all the cutting action comes as you pull the saw toward you, through the stock. The reason for this is the springiness in the coping saw frame. If it cut on the downstroke, the frame would bend, and the blade would tend to buckle. However, when it is pulled, the force is direct from handle to blade. Use gentle pressure, full strokes.

Blades for coping saws come in a range of teeth-per-inch, as well as in varieties of thickness and width of the "body" of the blade. For typical work, about 15 teeth is right. (The number of teeth is usually marked on the packaging.) The smaller

Coping saw teeth must point backward; the tool cuts only on the backstroke. That way the handle, rather than the springy frame of the saw, pulls the blade.

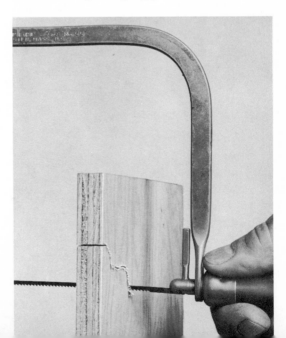

blade sizes are intended for extremely tight curves, bigger blades for gentler scrolls and curves.

Most coping saws have a means of turning the blade in the frame, so that it cuts down, up, to either side, or any angle in between. This permits a greater range of scroll work without having the frame of the saw hit the stock. You'll need a little practice sawing with the blade turned away from its normal up-and-down position, until you learn to forget the frame and watch only the blade and the direction of its teeth.

To make a "pocket" cut with a coping saw — that is, one that starts inside the perimeter of the stock, instead of at an edge — first drill a hole in the scrap near the line to be cut. Then, unhook the blade at one end. Insert the blade in the hole, and rehook it. At the end of the cut, unhook the blade to remove it.

MAKING HOLES

All types of hole-making devices require two things from the operator.

• You must provide pressure or "feed," to take the bit through the stock. No type of bit or drill pulls itself. The little threaded cone at the tip of an ordinary auger bit is intended merely to guide the cutting edges accurately to the surface, and when the cutting begins, you must apply pressure.

• You must guide the bit so that it enters the stock at right angles to the surface or at some preselected off-angle. Once the hole is as deep as three or four diameters of the bit, it will usually continue straight and true.

With all hole makers except electric drills, you must also provide power.

To guide a drill accurately, reverse one hand and rest your wrist on the surface to be drilled. Guide the bit with this hand, and gradually lower the tip to the surface.

It is not always easy, at the beginning, to apply the three types of forces hole-making requires. It is easy for most of us, however, to hold a hand drill as if it were a sword being used to thrust, rather than as a dagger being used to stab. If you keep your elbow at right angles and close to the body, you'll find that you direct the drill most accurately, while at the same time you hold it steady as you turn the crank.

The brace and bit is at best a cumbersome device—big, heavy, demanding a lot of space. Most home upkeep experts prefer to cup the stationary handle in one hand, then lean into it with the natural pocket just in front of the shoulder.

Easiest way to handle brace and bit is with the top cupped in your hand and the pressure applied by leaning your body on the back of your hand. You must maintain pressure to keep the tool cutting.

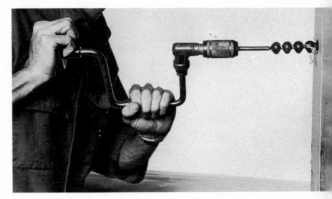

You may find it easier to push against your cupped hand with the middle of your chest. If you have a hole to bore in an awkward place, stand on a chair or step-ladder—or lie on your side—or by whatever means possible, get yourself as nearly as possible behind the brace.

SCREWS AND NAILS

There is a *right* way to drive a screw. There are several wrong ways that in many cases work just as well.

For maximum strength—the ideal—you must go through a fairly complex predrilling operation. First, you bore a hole the length and the diameter of the "shank" of the screw. (That's the smooth part, between the head and the threads.) Then you switch to a drill that is the size of the "core" of the screw at that point where the tip of the screw starts to taper sharply to the point. A glance at the photograph of a screw on

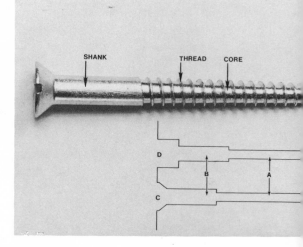

For maximum strength, a screw should go into a pre-bored hole as shown in the drawing. Section A should match the diameter and length of the core; B the diameter and length of the shank. To leave the head flush with the wood surface, countersink the hole (C). To set the head below the surface, for concealment with putty, plastic wood, or a wooden plug, counterbore the hole as at D.

this page will show you how this works. Finally, if it is a flat-head screw, you use a countersink to provide a beveled seat for the head of the screw. When you do this, the threads of the screw cut their way into the hole and at the same time exert a wedge-like action. Driven home, the screw combines the strength of the threads with that of the wedge action. To tear apart this sort of union, you've got to destroy the wood.

At any hardware store, you can buy a shortcut to all this sold under the name of "Screw Mate," a name selected no doubt because the drilling device exactly matches the specifications of given screw size. For example, you buy a Screw Mate called 1¼ No. 8, and it will drill for you a hole that is shank-size, then *tapered* core-size, so that a 1¼ No. 8 screw you drive snugs up at full strength, and is countersunk. You can buy these special drilling bits to match any screw size you're likely to run into.

Wrong way to hold a screwdriver, making it impossible to keep the tool from wobbling and slipping out of the slot.

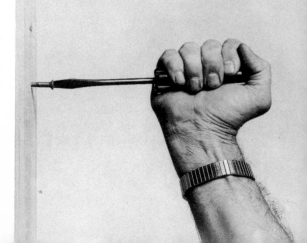

With forearm in the same line as the screwdriver, you have complete control.

But either way, it's somewhat of a nuisance if you just want to fasten two things together. What are simpler approaches?

If you are working with a hardwood—maple, birch, true mahogany, walnut, and some others—you have no choice. These woods are so resistant that you cannot drive a screw into them if you do not predrill properly.

In softwoods, those that we encounter most often in home upkeep, you don't have to be so pure in your procedures. Although it is best to drill through the top member, you can usually force the screw into the lower piece. This spreads the wood fibers, and their tendency to spring back helps grip the screw. The screw head will normally pull in flush, although for the best appearance, you must use a countersink.

Finally, if you are interested primarily in the extra holding

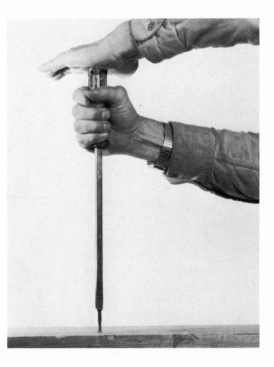

When you cannot line up forearm and tool, use this trick. One hand steers and applies pressure, while the other applies the torque to drive the screw.

power of a screw and its ability to pull two members together, you can adopt the following crude practice: Use a hammer to drive the screw in part way, leaving about ½″ above the surface. Then give it a few turns with a screwdriver. This works only in soft woods. The only reason you'd do it is that it's almost as fast as nailing, although the situation demands a screw.

Nailing is so simple that how-to-do-it tricks are scarce—but there are some. Many now-and-then nailers hold the hammer too close to the head, and as a result might as well be driving the nail with a hand-held stone. You may grip the handle midway to *start* a nail, or to produce the gentle impact you need for small brads or tacks. But to drive a nail, hold the hammer with about ½″ showing beyond your little finger. The pounding action combines the action of both elbow and

The absolutely wrong way to hold a hammer. That handle is on there for a reason.

With the hammer gripped this way, you can apply gentle taps to start a nail merely by flexing your wrist. Then, turn on the pressure by swinging your entire forearm plus the wrist action.

wrist, and it is the position of the elbow that determines your accuracy. You start missing the nail when you start to get tired, and you work longer without fatigue if you hold the hammer right and swing it right.

The most-used nail size is the one called 8-penny — or 8d, in the language of the trade. It's about 2½″ long, ideal for nailing 1″ lumber to 2″ framing. A 10d nail is about ½″ longer; a 6d is about ½″ shorter, and there are sizes on about ½″ intervals up to as long as you'll ever need them — and down to about an inch. Below that, nails are labeled by their length, and are usually called brads.

There are differences in diameter, too. "Common" nails are a bit heavier than "box" nails. For your purposes, you'd use box nails when there is a chance of splitting.

And there are differences in heads. The common nail has a relatively large head, roughly three times as big in diameter as the body of the nail. The "finishing" nail has a head barely larger than the body. (There are some refinements in head

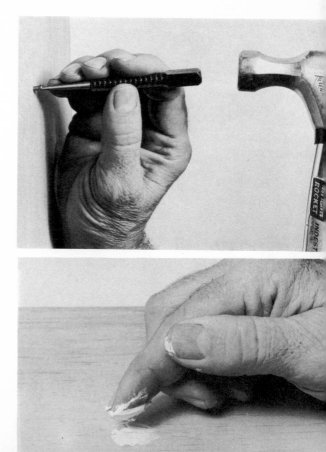

When you do careful nailing, stop when the head of the finishing nail is about ¼″ above surface. Then drive it home with a nailset.

A dab of vinyl patch or plastic wood or rock-hard putty fills the hole. When you sand it smooth, the joinery is invisible under paint.

size and shape, few of them of interest in home repair work.) Basically, you use a common nail for rough work, where appearance is not critical and you need strength. For fine work, you pick finishing nails, set their heads slightly below surface, and fill the hole so that they are invisible.

For maximum strength—and for resistance to corrosion— you may pick galvanized nails. The zinc coating is always rough and toothy; it holds better than a plain smooth, shiny steel nail. Another tough holding nail is the kind called "coated box." It is covered with a layer of resin which acts almost as an adhesive between the nail and the wood when it is driven.

Since there are a dozen or so specialist nails (roofing, siding, sheetrock, flooring, etc.), the best way for you to buy them is to tell a knowledgeable hardware or lumber dealer what you want them for. Since lumber dealers often know more about on-the-job-problems, they may be able to give you the best advice if you pick up nails at the same time you buy lumber.

In the context of home repairs, you may find yourself *re*nailing more often than not. In that case, a simple and frequently used trick of the professional is to remove the original nail and replace it in the same hole with one that is slightly larger. When a nail has been in place for a period of years, the wood around it has usually given up its elasticity, and is no longer clinging to the nail. When you drive in the next larger size—or a galvanized nail where a plain nail was used before—you again stretch the wood fibers and regain their help in making the nail secure.

A block under the hammer head when you pull big nails means more leverage, easier withdrawal, and no damage to the wood.

MEASURING AND MARKING

A great deal of the measuring you do around the house on repair work is to establish the dimensions of something you must replace. Whenever possible, use the old part as a ready made gauge. When this is not possible, bring on your measuring tools. One important fact to keep in mind, however:

Nine times out of ten you don't care what a dimension is, in feet, inches, and fractions. All you want to know is a distance, a length, a space, a height.

It is difficult to remember such weird dimensions as "three feet, five and five-eighths inches plus a scratch." Yet, most things we measure come out something like that—never in any exact, easy figure like "three feet six inches." To avoid the problem of carrying a computer-load of information around in your head, you can use a standard procedure among professionals that is rarely thought of by home craftsmen.

Forget the inches. Take a scrap of wood long enough to cover the situation. Put one end of it at one side of the distance to be registered. (Not measured, but simply registered.) Make a pencil mark on the wood at the other side of the distance. There is your dimension, and you don't have to clutter up your mind with figures and fractions.

Another way to do this is with two scraps of wood. Put an end of one at one point, and an end of the other at the other point, and let them lap somewhere—anywhere—in between. Use a clamp to hold the two pieces of wood in position until you are finished with that dimension. This trick is particularly useful when you need the distance between two surfaces, as for instance across the back of a closet where you want to nail a shelf, or between the floor and the top of a door. So useful is this trick that many professionals carry what they call a "ten-foot pole," made as shown in the accompanying photographs.

Another sometimes difficult dimension to establish is the depth of a hole or groove. The job is made easy if you use your combination square as a depth gauge. Merely loosen the blade, place the head on the surface, push the blade into the hole or groove until it touches bottom, then tighten the head in that position. The combination square makes a good marking gauge too. Set the blade so it protrudes the proper distance, then run the head along the edge of the stock while you hold a pencil at the end of the blade. This method of running a line along an edge is ideal when you want the line to be parallel to the edge although not necesarily straight. If you want a straight line, you must use a straight edge, of course. And for this purpose, nothing beats a length of aluminum bar 1" wide and ¼" thick, sold at hardware stores.

CUTTING TOOLS

The basic key to success with any edged tool is a sharp edge. Learn how to sharpen chisels, knives, and plane irons. They'll work better, cut smoother, and be safer to handle if they are so sharp that you don't need a great deal of force to make them cut.

Chisels are, in effect, hand carving tools. A great deal of the work you do with them involves physical pressure, plus karate-like thumping the handle of the chisel with one hand while the other guides the blade. Only when you must remove a great deal of wood or when you are working with hard woods should you need the force of a mallet. When you do, save the cost of a tool you'll rarely use by converting a hammer into a mallet by slipping a crutch tip over the face.

When the job calls for the removal of a lot of material, always start work with the chisel well inside the final margins of the cut. Gouge out the hole in the middle, and gradually enlarge it toward the edges. When you get close, put the mallet away and continue by hand. Remember that a "shear" cut—with the blade at an angle—is as useful and as workable with a chisel as it is with a safety razor on your face. And, that a slicing cut with a chisel is as workable as it is when you take a knife to a roast of meat.

A plane is the safety razor of the tool lineup. It cuts smoothly, easily, and under controls that keep you from cutting too deep. You'll find it easier to set the blade for a medium cut, and make more passes, than to set it for a heavier cut. And it's easier if you hold the plane at a slight angle, so there is a degree of shear action in the cut.

Sharp tools work better and are safer to use than dull tools. First step in sharpening is (*top*) rough-grinding. Keep tool rest at proper position to maintain the tool's original angle. Then switch to a flat stone (*center*). Rock the tool gently until it seats at the proper angle. Then make strokes forward only. Finally, turn the tool over and make a few strokes forward on the flat, to remove the "burr" (*bottom*). With a two-side stone like that shown, sharpening is possible without the grinder, if the tool is not too dull. Do the bevel on the coarse side of the stone. Then flop it to finish the job the same as you would after initial grinding.

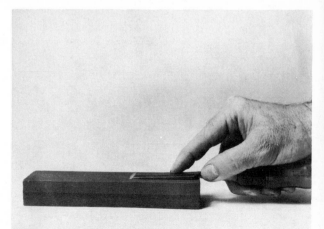

Frequent use of chisel is for pocket cutting, as in mortising for a door lock. Good way to do it is to start by rough-cutting inside the marks (*right*). Then clean up the edges with vertical cuts (*below, left*). Do the final work carefully with hand pressure only, so you can control depth of cut (*below, right*). Note that the chisel is protected from the hammer by the use of a crutch tip slipped over the face of the hammer. Do this when you don't have a regular mallet.

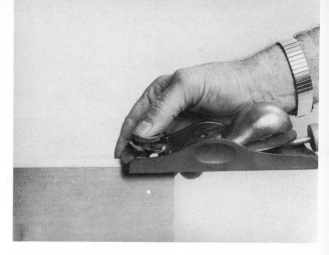

When planing an edge, start with the blade off the wood, all the pressure on the forward end of the plane (*above*). Then transfer the downward pressure directly over the plane for the majority of the stroke (*below*). As plane moves off other end, keep all the pressure on the rear of the tool.

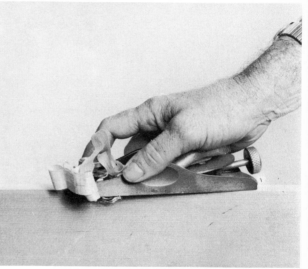

Direction of cut is important to smooth planing. As shown here, the plane is working "with the grain." In the opposite direction, the blade would dig into the fibers, producing a ragged cut.

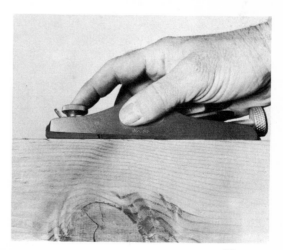

The plane derives its name from the word "plane" in plane surface — meaning flat. One of the purposes of the plane is to give you level surface, usually a new-cut edge or end, since planing the faces of lumber is normally done at the mill. The plane will also follow *outside* curves, making them smooth. However, the tool won't do any of these things unless you control it properly. Keep these planing principles in mind as you work.

First, keep enough downward pressure on the plane to hold it in contact with the work along the entire length of the stroke, without jumping, plus enough forward pressure to keep it cutting.

Second, do not let the plane rock, either to the side or over the ends as you start or finish a stroke. This means you must keep your downward pressure *directly over* the stock, at all times. The position of the pressure on the plane, however, changes. At the beginning of a stroke, the pressure must be on that part of the plane which extends forward of the blade. When the plane is entirely on the wood, the pressure must be even, fore and aft. As you reach the end of the stroke, transfer the pressure to that part of the tool back of the blade. If you do this, the cut you produce will be very close to perfectly plane.

Third, you must keep the plane at right angles to the surface if you want the edge to be square.

Fourth, in planing end grain you must alternate your strokes from one corner in toward the center, to the other corner. If

Trick to help you make an absolutely square edge: Clamp a block of wood to the side of the plane. The top of the block is cut out so the blade hangs over the edge.

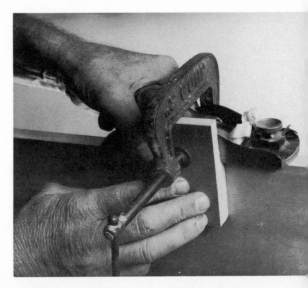

Your accuracy with an electric saw is close to perfect with a guide like this. Held as shown, it cuts square. Flop it to use the angled edge as a guide and you get a perfect 45-degree miter cut. Diagram below shows how to build the guide.

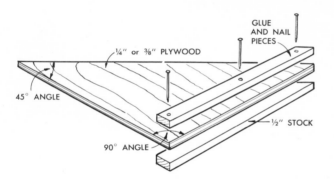

GLUE AND NAIL PIECES

¼" or ⅜" PLYWOOD

45° ANGLE

90° ANGLE

½" STOCK

To make a pocket cut, that is, a cut in the middle of a piece of stock, rest the saw on the front edge of the bed and hold the tool guard up. Then slowly and carefully lower the saw into the wood. Cutting out a square opening, you do this four times, working up to the corners. Use a handsaw for the few strokes needed to finish the corners.

you let the plane run over the corner, it is sure to chip the edge. It is on end-grain work that the low-angle block plane truly proves its worth, particularly if you hold it at a diagonal and give the edge a slicing-planing action.

One of the reasons why a worthwhile amount of home upkeep and repair is easily within the capabilities of many is that the tools you work with — as this chapter has indicated — are simple and easy to master. You may not be an expert the first time you take a tool in your hand, but you're not far from it.

A PLACE TO WORK

JUST AS WE LOOKED in the last chapters at how few tools you can own and still do a good house maintenance job, let's now look at how little space you need. Although not every home has room for a full-scale workshop, pleasant as one might be, it takes only a small amount of ingenuity to come up with working areas that take as little as zero space and work very efficiently.

WHERE TO FIND A PLACE TO WORK

You can do a lot of home repair work right on the kitchen table. Get hold of a piece of ½″ insulation board and cut it to fit the table top. When you need to press the table into service, the insulation board protects its finish. Between jobs, stand the sheet of insulation board against the wall in the garage or someplace. Eventually, it will get worn and dirty, but it costs so little you won't mind replacing it.

A variation of this is a piece of plywood about 2′ x 4′ that you can put on the washer-dryer setup temporarily or on a kitchen countertop. You get handy, convenient-height working space that disappears when you aren't using it.

One step up from such kitchen adaptations is a temporary knockdown type of bench you put together this way: Buy two sets of folding sawhorse brackets at the lumberyard, along with two 12′ and one 8′ 2 x 4s and a piece of ³⁄₄″ plywood 4′ x 4′. Cut the 12-footers into eight 36-inchers and the 8 footer into two 4-footers. These are the components for two sawhorses 36″ high. The 4 x 4 plywood piece is the top. You may want to make the legs longer or shorter, if you are tall or short, to provide a comfortable working height.

Also, since it is easy to change the legs in the sawhorse brackets, some home repairmen like to supply themselves with two sets of legs. The longer set brings close-up work higher and closer to your eyes and elbows and is easier to work on. The shorter legs put things lower down, things you might like to put your weight on a little to hold them while you work on them. And of course, the sawhorses can be used without the plywood top for a lot of work, such as painting storm windows, etc.

You can make this plywood-sawhorse work surface even more useful by covering one side of it with a piece of carpet. Visit a floorcovering store and buy 4′ x 4′ of whatever remnant they have that's cheap. Fasten it on the plywood with a mastic. Now, when you work on rough projects, use the plywood side. When you tackle something delicate, turn the board over.

One of the most convenient features of this bench is that you can set it up right at the job in many cases, cutting down on the running back and forth between job and work area. The entire unit, with the sawhorses folded tight, stores in very little space, against the wall or even on overhead joists, if they are available.

FOLD-DOWN WORKBENCH

When space is at a premium but you want a completely work-able bench, the fold-down style is the answer. It can go at the side of a garage or at the front. It can be mounted on the wall of a utility room, where it may cramp things while it's in use, but not when it's at rest. When a basement is needed for non-shop purposes, the fold-down can share space with a laundry or be fitted into the furnace area. In use, the fold-down bench gives you full-scale utility in an adequate working area when you need it but returns the space to other needs between jobs.

The fold-down bench shown here is easy to build. It utilizes standard lumber sizes. And it has carefully planned operating features that make it just as workable as most permanent-type benches.

Most important, it is designed so that when it is dropped down, you still have a shelf against the wall, on which you can place tools and odds and ends. In other words, you don't have to go find a place for every last item on the bench before you can let it fold down out of the way.

As the drawings and photos show, the bench is formed of a hinged top (the back plank of which is the shelf) and a pair of hinged brackets. The brackets swing in against the wall to let the top fold down. In open position, the brackets meet the cleats which hold the top together. You can build the bench in a couple of hours, following these steps:

Fold-down bench provides plenty of rugged working space against one wall of basement or garage. It is fastened to the wall studs and is supported by heavy brackets.

Between jobs, it folds down, but there a shelf remains where you can store a few things you may need when you go back to work.

1. Cut four 2 x 8s to the length you decide on. As shown the bench is 6' long. You could go longer if you wanted to.

2. Use 2 x 4 stock to cleat three of the four 2 x 8s together, running 2¼" No. 12 screws through the cleats into the 2 x 8s.

3. Spike or lagscrew the 2 x 4 cleat along the wall, horizontally at the height you want the bench to be. Also, fasten up the verticals to which the brackets will hinge. Use masonry fasteners if the bench goes on a brick or block or concrete wall. If it's a stud wall, the verticals will spike into two studs normally 4' apart, assuming 16" or 24" stud spacing. If you are making the bench as long as 8', spread the verticals another stud apart.

4. Nail the two brackets together, using ¼" plywood gussets.

5. Spike or screw the single 2 x 8 along the top edge of the horizontal 2 x 4.

Basic construction is revealed here. Brackets are assembled with plywood gussets, hinged to verticals. The 2 x 6 is permanent, forming the between-jobs storage shelf. The fold-down top is hinged to this.

In-process photo shows how brackets fold to the center to allow top to be lowered.

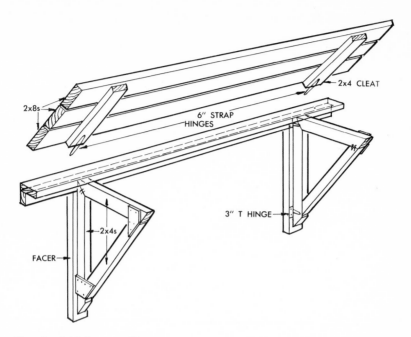

2x4 CLEAT

2x8s

6" STRAP HINGES

3" T HINGE

2x4s

FACER

Plan for fold-down workbench.

6. Hinge the brackets to the vertical 2 x 4s with the top surfaces snug up under the 2 x 8 that's now in place.

7. Hoist the 2 x 8 unit into position, and screw on the hinges underneath.

If you like things neat, give the top of the bench two or three coats of high quality glossy enamel. This finish not only looks good, but allows you to wipe spills off instead of letting them stain an unfinished top into an ugly mess.

Most home upkeepers like to put a tool board up back of the bench, using it as the major tool storage unit. There the tools are handy, and the bench serves as an assembly area when you pack up a complement of tools to lug off somewhere in the house.

You'll want a vise of some sort, and experience will convince you that the *better* it is, the better. The ideal setup is a 10″ woodworking vise, since it has large faces, capable of gripping material without denting or marring it, particularly if you line the faces with pieces of ¼″ plywood held in place with contact cement. Mount the woodworking vise exactly at the corner of the workbench, making whatever modifications may be necessary in the top to adapt the vise you select. Since this type of vise is flush with the working surface, it gives you the greatest possible utility, without acting as an obstruction the way top-mounted vises do.

The typical steel machinist's vise, however, is very useful when you work with metal. You may find your purposes well served with this vise, bolted to a corner of your bench. A good way to meet both requirements, though, is to bolt the machinist's vise to a square piece of 2 x 6. When you need its features, clamp it in the woodworking vise. Other times, stow it away where it won't interfere with work on the bench.

For minimum work around the house, particularly if you do not put together a formal workbench, you may need nothing more complicated than a portable type of vise such as the Stanley 700. It clamps to any work surface, and holds objects on either the vertical or the horizontal in a pair of L-shaped jaws. When it's not in use, you can dump it in one of your tote boxes.

BASIC SUPPLIES

The kinds of supplies and materials you need for individual jobs, such as plumbing and electrical repairs, are covered in their own sections of this book. There is, however, a short shopping list of the kinds of odds and ends you're likely to need in the course of ordinary home repairs. You can wait until you need them, picking them up as you go, or you can lay a few supplies in advance of actual need, ready to use when the problem calls for them.

Paint. You should have about a gallon of the housepaint color current on your home, and about a quart of interior wall colors and trim enamels. Of course there are always paint leftovers, and if you seal the cans up well, you may have all you need. But if your painting comes out pretty near the bottom of the can, buy another can as insurance. Why not buy it later, if you need it? Simply because, if it is a stock color, the makers may discontinue the color. And if it is a custom-blended color, you often find that the pigments involved vary a little a year or so later, and it is awfully hard to get an exact match. It's a good idea, when paint is to be stored for a long time, to put it on the shelf upside down. Then when the pigments settle, they end up on the lid, where you can scrape them off easily and be sure you are stirring all the color back into the paint. Once more: be sure the lids are on tight.

Keep a gallon of paint thinner on hand, or turpentine, which costs a little more than paint thinner, but does most things better. You may need a quart of lacquer thinner and one of denatured alcohol, too, if any of your finishes involves lacquer or shellac.

Wallpaper paste. Keep a small package of the new, quicker and easier cellulose paste on hand, and you'll be able to catch loosening wallpaper before it becomes a major problem.

Filler materials. There are several kinds of filler materials you'll find handy. Plastic Wood is excellent for small holes when quick drying is important. Durham's Rock Hard Putty mixes with water, an excellent material when you have a large hole to fill. DAP spackling compound is intended for plaster cracks. In addition, you should have a can of Thoroseal on hand for masonry repairs, as well as a small sack of Sakrete sand mix. These are trade names of commonly available materials. Your dealer may not have them but will be able to supply comparable products.

Glue. Keep some Elmer's on the shelf for ordinary wood gluing in non-moisture situations. Weldwood plastic glue is more water-resistant. Elmer's Waterproof glue is a two-part adhesive, entirely waterproof, for use outdoors. In addition, there are many new adhesives in tubes now on the market that do special jobs on glass, crockery, bathroom tiles, etc. Having them in the house means a quick repair when the need for it arises.

Lubricants. You'll want a can of 3-in-1, and one of Liquid-Wrench, the first for light oiling, the latter for loosening nuts that have corroded. Also, a can of SAE 30 motor oil, and one of general purpose grease. Today's market is full of spray-on lubricants, excellent for situations which won't tolerate the messiness of oil or grease.

Nails, screws, fasteners. Many hardware and lumber outlets now carry convenient 1-pound put-ups of nails and plastic envelopes of screws. Over a period of time you'll find need for the following: 4d, 6d and 8d in finishing nails, and the same plus 12d and 16d in common nails. In screws you'll find the greatest use for 1¼″ No. 8 flatheads; buy other sizes as you need them.

Now, with tools and supplies and a place to work all set, let's go looking for trouble.

KEEPING UTILITY SYSTEMS IN REPAIR

This section covers the things you should do, and should not do, to repair breakdowns or malfunctioning in the utility systems of your home—electrical, plumbing, and heating.

6

KEEPING THE ELECTRICAL
SYSTEM AT WORK

NOTHING IN ANYBODY'S household is as useful as the electrical
system. Even though it started originally as a means of providing light, its role in the functioning of a house now reaches
into every aspect of homemaking and housekeeping. When
something goes wrong in a house electrically, things stop
dead. For that reason, electrical repairs and upkeep are among
the most important of all fix-it jobs.

Fortunately, they are also the easiest. You need less skill to
make electrical repairs than to fix anything else around the
house. All you work with, for most jobs, is a screwdriver and
a pair of pliers. The most complicated manipulation you can
encounter is twisting some wires together, and maybe a little
soldering now and then. Anybody can do it.

Also, anybody can get killed doing it. Electrical repairs can
be dangerous. They don't *need* to be, and simple methods of
making them safe are covered in this chapter. But it is never
too early to emphasize firmly: electrical repairs can be dangerous.

THE NATURE OF THE SYSTEM

The electricity you use comes to your house from a generating plant somewhere in the area, conducted by heavy cables. Although the wires are huge as they leave the generator, they undergo a series of stepdowns, branching out to serve individual areas and eventually individual homes. They enter your house through a meter which registers the amount of electricity you use. Inside, the cables run to a service panel, "a fuse box" or a group of "circuit breakers." From that panel, individual "circuits" emerge, serving specific functions or single, relatively small areas of the house.

Each of these small units functions as its own system. What happens to one circuit does not affect the other. This is a tremendous convenience, since a breakdown in one circuit won't shut down the entire system; the house goes on functioning while the relatively localized trouble is taken care of. There are other reasons why the multi-circuit idea is used in all residential wiring, and we'll come to them later.

Wiring. Electricity is carried around the house through wires that are, normally, buried in walls and floors where you can't see them, although they do show up sometimes in basement ceilings and attic floors. The wires are encased in several different ways, the most common of which are: conduit, a thinwall metal pipe or tube through which the wires are threaded after the pipe is in place; a unitized cable, called BX, with a flexible spiralform metal cover; insulated wires, covered additionally with *extra heavy insulation,* called Romex.

An electrical "run" is normally composed of three conductors. Two of them are conspicuous insulated wires, one white, one black. These carry the electrical current needed by lighting fixtures, appliances, etc. The third conductor is an inconspicuous little soft metal wire that almost looks as though it got in there by accident. Its function is to tie all of the mechanical components of the system (boxes for outlets, fixtures, switches, and so on) together and to connect them to "ground." This wire safeguards you and your property against the dangers of short circuits or faulty insulation. Potentially dangerous "loose" electricity is carried harmlessly to the ground. Thus, you are protected from serious electrical shock, should you happen to touch a switch plate, outlet cover, or other mechanical components of a system in which there is a short.

All electrical equipment used around the house is fitted with *two contacts,* which connect with the black-white pair of wires. If you've ever looked at the metallic base of a plain, ordinary light bulb, you've noticed that in the center of the "bull's eye" of components is a small lead-colored spot, surrounded by a little ring of copper. Around that is a black ring of insulating material; then there is the metal with the threads that screw into the socket. The lead-and-copper center forms one contact, and the outer threaded metal cup forms the other. The socket into which the bulb screws has mating contact parts, and these are connected to the black and white wires.

On plug-in appliances, of course, the two prongs of the plug function in the same way. When you shove the plug into an outlet, the prongs fit into metal clips which are fastened to the electricity-bearing wires. In addition, there are certain appliances (stoves, dryers, water heaters, for example) which are connected directly to the power, again to both sides.

Two wires simplify things greatly. The black wire carries the current *to the fixture or appliance.* That is why electricians often call it the "plus" side or the "hot" side. The white wire completes the circuit, which goes all the way to that generator plant, and is often called the "minus" or "ground" side.

In view of the presence in the circuit of another wire specifically intended for grounding, one of the oddities of an electrical circuit must now be explained. You can create a functioning electrical contact without using the white wire. Just make contact with the black wire for one side, and for the other side, make contact with a water pipe or any other piece of conductive metal that runs into the ground. This contact may also be made with the little ground wire, with the outlet box, or with the conduit pipe or BX sheathing, since these elements of the system are grounded. What this means is that it is possible, although not workable, to complete the circuit back to the generating plant by sending the current through the earth.

WHAT FUSES OR CIRCUIT BREAKERS DO

To utilize electrical current, it is necessary to make contact with both the plus side and the minus side, thus completing the circuit. When such a connection is made across the two wires, *there must be utilization or absorption of the energy.* The light bulb filaments heating incandescent-hot, for instance, use the energy. A motor running or a stove heating does it, too.

If there is no utilization of the energy, as in a short circuit, the result is overheating of the wires. They would, in fact, get hot enough to burn through their insulation and possibly set the house afire. It is to safeguard against this that fuses or circuit breakers are installed in all houses. This is how they work:

• In a fuse there is a small piece of metal with a low melting point. A short circuit or other electrical malfunction causes this piece of metal to melt, breaking the circuit. You straighten out the reason for the problem, and then replace the fuse.

• In a circuit breaker, the electrical continuity is interrupted by means of an automatic switch which reacts when activated by heat. When the problem is rectified, the switch must be closed again.

Both fuse and circuit breaker do their jobs also if there is *too much load* on the circuit—too many appliances or motors or bulbs or fixtures. The reaction is less violent than that of a short circuit. The short produces an instantaneous failure, but when you overload a line, it may take several seconds or even minutes for the heat to build up sufficiently to cause a reaction.

LEARN HOW YOUR OWN HOUSE IS WIRED

In spite of the fact that the foregoing is much simplified and ignores a great deal of electrical engineering, it is still pretty academic. *All you ever see* of your electrical system is the fixtures, the outlets, and the fuses or the circuit breaker panel.

These are all simple, easy enough to understand and repair if anything goes wrong, and the times are rare when you must go into it any deeper.

You must, however, know *how* your house is wired, if you don't already. Sometimes, if a house is new, you can get a wiring plan from the builder or his electrical subcontractor. If not, make your own.

What you need to know to make the plan is which outlets and fixtures are on which circuit emerging from the fuse box or circuit breaker panel. Common wiring practice usually follows fairly logical "zoning." For instance, one side of the house, one floor of the house, one partition, one end of the house, one wing of the house, and so on. Keep in mind that the electrical contractor had to run wires through walls and partitions, and you'd expect him to be as efficient about it as possible.

To pinpoint a circuit, start at one end of the house, and plug a lamp into every outlet, on all floors and in the basement. Be sure that all wall and ceiling fixtures are turned on. Now, station someone in a position to observe these lights *on the main floor*, with instructions to yell when they go out. Go to the service panel and start unscrewing fuses or deactivating circuit breakers, as the case may be, screwing them back in if your observer *doesn't* yell. When he does yell, you'll know that the fuse you just handled is the one that controls the first floor at the end of the house.

Now, check the basement. Did the lights there go off? If they did, it's the same circuit. Check the second floor. Then the attic. By a process of elimination, you finally learn which of the outlets and fixtures are on that circuit. Make a label to be tacked up at the service panel, listing the walls or areas of the house that are on that circuit. Now, move to another area, repeating the entire process. Eventually, you'll have a label at the service panel which *lists every outlet and fixture in the house and the fuse or circuit breaker it is on.*

This is a very important accumulation of data. It means that if you ever have any work to do on a given outlet or fixture, you can deaden it by breaking the right circuit at the control panel.

HOW TO BE SAFE

Before we go any further into the techniques of electrical repairs, it is important to re-emphasize the precautions necessary to eliminate chances of injury from electrical shock. Keep the following facts in mind:

• If you touch the "hot" side of an electrical circuit while you are standing on a concrete floor or on the ground, you will be part of an electrical circuit. The electricity will pass through your body from the wire to the ground. The resulting shock may be just a vibration-like jolt if you are "poorly grounded." It may be lethal if you happen to be standing on damp or wet ground, if you happen to be wearing wet shoes, or (!) if you should happen to be barefoot.

• If you touch the "hot" side of the wire and the grounding system (boxes, conduit, BX, etc.), you are subjecting yourself to shock even if you are wearing dry rubber soles and standing on a wooden floor.

• If you touch both the "hot" side of the system and the "minus" side, you are plugging yourself in.

You do not want any of these things to happen. So, you never work on an electrical outlet or switch or faulty fixture without first making sure that the circuit is dead. It is a common practice among home upkeep experts to place a rubber door mat on the floor in front of the service panel as an insulated place to stand when they handle fuses, switches, etc. An adequate substitute for the rubber mat is a small platform of dry boards.

Many an experienced electrician, working in a house with a circuit breaker, will deliberately short the outlet he wants to work on. This of course breaks the circuit. This same electrician, if he is any good at all, will admit that this is a bad practice. It makes more sense and is safer to go to the service panel, locate the outlet on the chart you made, and deliberately break the circuit. If you have a fuse box, of course you'll always unscrew the fuse, because it makes little sense to burn out a fuse and have to put in a new one. *Important:* When you remove the fuse, be careful not to touch any part of it except the knurled glass rim, and don't touch any of the other parts inside the box. In fact, some experts prefer to throw the main switch, if there is one, before touching a fuse. However, since this turns off all electrical elements in the house, including clocks that will need resetting, it is just as well to leave the juice on and be careful manipulating fuses. Remember, even though the circuit is dead when you unscrew the fuse, the *fuse socket is still very much alive*. Do not touch it.

With the circuit broken, you are now safe working on any of its outlets or fixtures. To be doubly sure, test the circuit by plugging in a lamp you know to be working, or use a little pigtail electrical tester available at electrical supply outlets. Just for security's sake, it's a good idea to mention to the rest of the household that you're at work on the electrical system, so someone doesn't discover that "the lights are out" and restore the circuit while you have hold of one white and one black wire.

There is a shortcut to all this in some situations. If the outlet or fixture that needs attention happens to be on a switch, you can kill the electricity merely by flicking the switch off. Test the point you'll be working on with the pigtail or by plugging in a lamp.

Incidentally, if you happen to find it necessary to do all this at night, you'll discover another advantage of the multi-circuit system. You can plug a lamp into an extension cord and get the light to see by from another circuit that's still functioning.

THINGS THAT GO WRONG AND HOW TO FIX THEM

The most frequent problem with electrical systems is, of course, that much-mentioned service panel, the blown fuse or circuit breaker. As was discussed above, a circuit blows for one of two reasons: a short or an overload. It is usually possible to tell which condition causes the trouble by analyzing the nature of the "break." Here are the situations.

• If you plug in an appliance—anthing from a bridge lamp to a hair dryer—and the rest of the lights in the vicinity go dead instantly, almost with an audible click, the problem is almost sure to be a fault of the appliance. In other words, a short in any piece of equipment you plug into a circuit is the same as a short in the circuit. The fuse or circuit breaker then goes instantly. If it happens that no other lights are on to signal the circuit break, *but if the equipment you* plug in fails to function, switch on a light. If it doesn't go on, chances are pretty good that the circuit has blown.

• If you plug in something and everything goes fine for a few seconds or longer and then the lights in the area go out, the indications are that the line is overloaded. It just took a little while for the circuit to heat up enough to blow the fuse.

In either case, the first thing to do is to unplug the thing you just added to the circuit. If the circumstances indicate that the appliance or other equipment is faulty, you of course take it to be checked out and fixed. If the slight delay indicates an overload, you simply do not add any additional equipment on that circuit. It is already carrying as much as it should, perhaps too much if it is that close to blowing.

It is good to remember that the typical household circuit should not handle more than about 1300 to 1500 watts. That is the reason why your house is zoned, electrically, in the first place. It spreads the load around, so that there is less chance that any individual set of wires will be asked to handle too much at one time. If any of the circuits should show a tendency to break time and again, on account of overload, there is one thing you must *not* do. *You absolutely must not under any circumstances install a heavier fuse with the idea that you are strengthening the circuit.* What that could do is increase the breakdown level to a point where the load might cause serious damage in the actual wiring, or even fire.

The 1300- to 1500-watt figure mentioned above is arrived at by rough mathematics applied to simplified electrical engineering. Multiply the amp rating of the fuse by 100. Thus the 1300 figure is fairly conservative for a 15-amp fuse. For a 20-amp fuse, you'd be in the conservative range with 1700 watts and, pressing the circuit a bit, at 2000. You can use this figure to reduce the chances of overload this way:

• Check the rating in watts of the items you might logically be using on the circuit. Light bulbs, of course, are clearly labeled as to wattage. You can usually find the rating of small appliances if you look at the labeling on the back or bottom. Or you can use the round-figure table below.

• Add up the wattage of lights and appliances you might use at any one time. For instance, you might use a blender to mix canned orange juice at the time you use the toaster. But chances are you wouldn't have an electric iron on at the same time.

• If the total wattage comes close to 100 times the amps labeled on the fuse, you should either rearrange your way of using the circuits or call in an electrician to go about *professionally* increasing the capacity of the circuit if possible.

Slow-blow fuses. Some of the appliances common in every household present the special problem of a high initial load, as the machine starts. A refrigerator or a washing machine may need a great deal more current when it turns on than when it gets going. Very often, the spin cycle of a washer-dryer puts a lot of start-up strain on the motor when that wet, heavy load starts to spin. With ordinary fuses, the circuit would go instantly. However, there are special "slow-blow" fuses intended specifically for such conditions. They will take a bit of overload for short periods, long enough for the machinery to get going. Pick up some fuses of the slow-burn kind *in the same amp rating as those now in use,* if your heavier equipment does tend to blow fuses when it starts up. (Many modern circuit breakers are slow-blow engineered.)

In ordinary house wiring, there are usually some circuits with 15-amp fuses, some with 20. The 15-amp capacity is generally used when ordinary lighting is all that the circuit will carry. If there are appliances, the fuses are more commonly 20 amps. In a workshop where there is relatively heavy power equipment, fuses may go to 25 or 30. *The fuses are not interchangeable, because the original electrical engineering did not assign the same type and degree of work to all the circuits.*

TABLE OF APPROXIMATE WATTAGES
TYPICAL HOUSEHOLD EQUIPMENT

15–100	*150–300*
Light bulbs	Three-way lamps
Table lamps	Electric blanket
Bottle warmer	Blender
Clock	Hair dryer
Electric fan	Mixer
Heating pad	Refrigerator
Knife sharpener	Ventilating fan
Can opener	
Radio	
Record player	
Sewing machine	
Shaver	
Vacuum cleaner	

350–800	*1000 and up*
Sun lamp	Countertop oven
Coffee maker	Broiler
TV set	Electric skillet
Waxer-polisher	Corn popper
	Deep fat fryer
	Electric iron
	Ironer
	Portable heater
	Toaster
	Waffle iron

NOTE: Appliances with motors take many times the normal wattage during the start-up. A notable example is the refrigerator.

It is usually simple to determine which fuse has blown. As you look through the tiny glass window in the front of the fuse, you see a small ribbon of metal which is notably narrower in the middle than at the ends. The narrow place is where the fuse gives way. If you can see that the metal ribbon is intact, the fuse is most likely good, although there is a faint chance that the fuse may blow without giving this visual clue. On the other hand, if the ribbon looks melted away in the middle, this is exactly what has happened. It *has* melted away, breaking the circuit. Unscrew the broken fuse and replace it with another of the same rating.

It is convenient and very sensible to lay in a stock of two or three fuses in each of the sizes you see in your fuse box. Then you'll have them as you need them. When the stock of any size gets down to one, put fuses on the shopping list for your next trip to a hardware or electrical store.

Circuit breakers, unlike fuses, do not have to be replaced. The short or overload breaks the circuit by automatically throwing a switch. When the problem that caused the break has been taken care of, you merely reset the switch. Some circuit breakers have push button switches. One push turns them on, another push turns them off, and it goes on, in rotation. Others are toggle switches. Usually, to reset these, you press the toggle beyond the "on" position, then release it. In both cases, the labeling is plain. To find out which one blew, just run your eye down the row of "on" labels until you find one that says "off." The reset position is usually also labeled on the toggle-style breakers.

Electrical shops sell circuit breakers that you can screw into the socket of an ordinary fuse. If the breaker is rated the same, it will function the same as the fuse. The difference is that you can reset it instead of replacing it, as you would an ordinary fuse. Many home owners replace fuses as they go, with the screw-in breakers. Others make a wholesale sweep of the matter, buy a complement of circuit breakers, and screw them into the old fuse box.

Electric ranges, water heaters, and other high-capacity electrical equipment usually have special fuses or breakers, and individual circuits. On the panel of the circuit breaker you'll see some outsize buttons or toggles, frequently labeled with the name of the equipment. They operate the same as other breakers. Fuses for heavy appliances may be in a separate box, and in some cases they may be "cartridge" style. The cartridge fuse is a high-capacity type, in the form of a cylinder with metal contact points capping each end. These ends fit into a pair of clips. Otherwise, they function the same as screw-in fuses.

HOW TO APPRAISE YOUR SERVICE PANEL AND CIRCUITRY

Except for the problem of fuses blown because of faulty equipment and short circuits. you probably should call in a competent electrician or an expert from the power company if you are frequently bothered with fuse trouble. Particularly in older homes, the extent of wiring inadequacy is fantastic. Many electrical systems just do not have the capacity to handle an ever-growing houseful of appliances and gadgets that need electricity. The result is lowered operating efficiency and the possibility of fire. If you don't think the threat of fire due to electrical shortcomings is worth worrying about, it may jar you to learn that in many cases your fire insurance is not effective if it can be shown that your house was not properly wired to safeguard against fire.

There are a few methods of checking superficially to see what the probable worthiness of your system is. If your fuse box only has two fuses in it, or if the circuit breaker shows only four or five switches, you are probably flirting with trouble, with an obsolete system capable only of handling lights and a few small plug-in appliances. If you find four fuses in the box or eight or so switches on the breaker panel, you are in the minimum range and can handle major appliances. In either case, you are below what the electricians call adequate wiring: "100-amp service."

With 100-amp service you'll find a dozen or more fuses or switches. You can expect that a fuse will virtually never blow due to overload, unless you do something as remarkable as try to iron clothes while the waffle iron and the broiler-rotisserie are both going, all on the same circuit as the toaster. But you'll have enough power to run just about any normal combination of appliances and lighting, probably even central air conditioning.

If you are living with adequate wiring or even with just about break-even wiring, it should be among your top-priority improvement plans to do something about it.

7

ELECTRICAL REPAIRS
ANYONE CAN DO

BEYOND THE ULTRASIMPLE matter of changing fuses or resetting circuit breakers, there are many items of electrical
repair that the nonprofessional home owner can handle. Most
of these involve the points where electricity comes to the
surface around the house, namely at outlets, switches, and
fixtures. In addition, some improvements, rather than pure
repairs, you can make give you more service from your
system.

WHAT TO DO ABOUT OUTLET TROUBLES

There are several reasons why you might want to replace an
outlet:

• Because it is old and worn with broken plastic parts and
worn or loosened parts that fail to hold the prongs of the cord
when you plug it in.

• Because you want to replace it with a better style. For
example, with children in the house you might want to replace some outlets with the special variety which "closes"
when a cord is removed. Then youngsters can't normally
figure out how to manipulate them.

• Because you may want to introduce three-hole outlets to accept three-prong plugs found on many portable electric tools. Although this is not always possible, it very often is, as noted below.

• Because you may want to replace it with an outlet that accepts three or four plug-ins, instead of the standard two. This is a better idea than the common practice of plugging in an adapter with provision for additional cords. However, even with the extra-outlet fitting wired in, you must *continue to operate the circuit with regard to the wattage it will accommodate.*

• Because you find it would be convenient to have a switch and an outlet at a single location. Combinations are available.

• Because the outlet seems to be faulty. In this case, be sure it's the outlet that's to blame. If you plug something into it and nothing happens, plug the same thing into another outlet *on the same circuit.* Again, if nothing happens, check the fuse. If the fuse is okay, and the rest of the circuit is okay, make one more test. Try another lamp or appliance in the outlet; sometimes a certain plug and a certain outlet will develop a lack of function, and if this is the case it may be easier to change the plug on the cord, instead of replacing the outlet.

When you've finally checked it out in all directions and the outlet seems at fault, kill the circuit and get out the tools.

First, remove the screw between the two outlets that holds the cover plate on. If the plate does not drop off easily, do not pry it off or you may cause unsightly chipping of the paint at the edges. It is recommended painting practice to remove all switch and outlet plates when you paint and replace them only when the paint is dry, even when the plates are to be painted the same color as the wall. However, painters sometimes ignore this bit of painting wisdom and brush over a plate. The paint seeps under the edges, dries, and cements the plate in place. When this is the case, and the plate is stuck on, carefully cut around the four edges with a sharp knife, making sure the knife goes through the paint. Then, when you pry the plate loose, the result will be neat and clean.

With the plate off, you'll find the metal box, to which the outlet is fastened with two screws. Remove them. Now you can pull the outlet out of the box, still attached to its wires. Enough slack is left in the wires to allow this. There may be only two wires, one black and one white. This is the situation when the box is at the end of a run. If the run continues past this box to others, there will be four wires, two black and two white.

Outlet at the end of a run is mounted on a box with only two wires coming into it—one white, one black. The black wire goes to the "brass" side of the outlet; the white wire goes to the "silver" side.

When an outlet is in the middle of a run, two wires come into the box and two go out. The blacks go to the brass side, the whites to the silver side. The electricity serves that outlet and passes on to additional outlets.

(Since it is our first look inside a box, this is a good time to mention that there may be *a red wire* in there. If there is, it means that the electrical contractor utilized the extra convenience of a three-wire cable, making his job faster and easier. If that is the case, consider that the red wire is black, because it is, in function, a "hot" wire.)

To remove the faulty and outmoded outlet, loosen the screws that hold the wires. But first, notice exactly how the wires were connected. You'll find that the *black wires are connected to the brass-colored screws;* the white wires are connected to the silver-colored screws on the opposite side. This is the right way—the only way—to make the connection. When you put in the new outlet you must connect the black to brass, white to silver and a good way to remember this is the phrase, "black to brass."

The best way to fasten the wires to the terminals is with a hook bent at the end, to slip around the screw. If you put this hook on so that it bends in the direction the screw turns as you tighten it, the head of the screw will tend to draw the wire tighter and tighter.

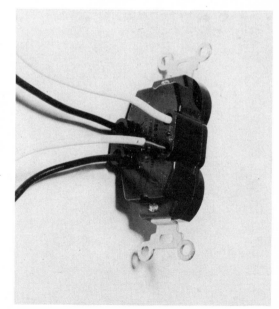

Some outlets have "shove-in" connectors. You merely force the wires into holes where toothed clips hold them. It is important to remove the right amount of insulation: just ½", as shown on the near wire. If you use outlets like this you'll find one side labeled "white," the other "black."

Example of safety outlet. A slotted cover is automatically held over the outlet so that nothing can be inserted into it without deliberately turning the cover 90 degrees. This is usually too complicated for experimenting children.

When the wires are snugged up on both terminals, gently bend and loop them so that they fit back inside the box as you position the outlet and replace the screws that hold it in place. Put the plate back on, and the job is finished.

What if you are putting in a three-holer? The purpose of the third hole, as you know, is to accept the third or "grounding" prong of the plug. This prong slips into a metal clip that is connected to the flange which fastens to the box. It is connected, also, to a third type of screw, neither brass nor silver, but green. When you install a three-hole outlet, you should connect the little stray uninsulated wire to this green screw if there is such a wire. In a system without the grounding wire, effective connection is automatically made to the box and the BX or conduit when you screw the outlet into place. It is to be assumed that the metal sheathing of the wires has been connected to ground somewhere in the system, so that the third prong of the plug will be grounded. You can check this with your electrical tester. Contact one point with the black wire, and the other with the wall of the box. If the light goes on, the ground is complete, and any three-prong tool you plug into the outlet is grounded.

If the outlet you are working on happens to be controlled by a wall switch, you may find a slight difference in the wiring inside the box, in what is called a "switch leg." The white wire will go directly to the silver side of the outlet, but the black wire may take a detour. It will enter the box along with its white wire teammate. Then it may be spliced to one of another pair of wires leading out of the box. The other of this pair of wires would then be fastened to the black side. At the far end of this pair is a switch. Thus, the electricity in the black wire must make a detour through the switch leg before it can reach the outlet. If the switch is closed, the electricity reaches the outlet via the detour, but if the switch is open, the outlet is dead.

HOW TO INSTALL A NEW SWITCH

There are as many reasons for replacing a switch as there are for changing an outlet:

• The switch may be worn out, as often happens in an active area of a house.

• You may want to replace the noisy click of ordinary switches with the silence of mercury or other quiet versions, particularly in bedroom areas and most particularly in the nursery. The mercury switch makes contact when a drop of mercury flows between the connection points, as you activate the toggle. Other silent types use terminals of some high-conductivity metal, such as silver, so that the contact can be made gently.

• You may want the convenience of switches with toggles that light up when they are in "off" position. You can find them in the dark.

• Or you may want one of the dimmer switches available to adjust the brightness of the illumination in a room from bright enough to read by to dim enough to watch TV by.

There are many versions of the dimmer switch, carried by electrical supply houses. Some have just two or three positions such as high, low, medium. Others provide a continuous range of brightness. Ask your dealer about them.

Before you start to work on a switch, be sure that you deactivate the circuit it is on by removing a fuse or hitting a circuit breaker. Even though there is ordinarily no electrical action that you can see at a switch, the hot wire is there and you could get a shock.

Switches are housed in metal boxes identical with those used for outlets. The switch plate is held on by two screws. Remove them (use the techniques covered under outlets, above, to avoid damaging the paint job) and inside you'll find the switch, fastened by means of two flanges and screws. Loosen those screws and the switch comes free, fastened now only by its wires.

When a switch is on a "switch leg," you'll find two wires in the box. One goes to each of the two terminals on the switch. The color of the wires is not significant in this situation.

When a line goes through the switch box on its way to an outlet or fixture, you'll find four wires. The white wires are spliced as shown here. The black wires are attached to the switch terminals. Thus, the black side (the "hot" side) can be interrupted by flicking the switch to the "off" position, activated by flicking it to the "on" position.

Inside you'll find one of two situations:

• Two wires come into the box. One of them is fastened to each of the two terminals on the switch. There is no "brass" and "silver," since there is no "hot" and "ground" in the switch operation. This is the "switch leg" method of wiring. It is used when the electrical run doesn't happen to go past the point where you want the switch to be. So, the electrician wires in the detour mentioned in the discussion of outlets, above.

• A black and white pair of wires comes into the box, and a black and white pair goes out. The two white wires are spliced together. The two black wires are connected to the terminals of the switch. This line switch technique is used when the electrical run does happen to go past the point where the switch is needed.

To replace a switch, simply remove the wires from the old one and reconnect them to the new one in the same way. There is no "hot" side, no "ground" side, both terminals are brass colored.

If you are using a mercury switch you must make sure to put it in right side up. Otherwise it will not work, since gravity is the force used to move the mercury into position when the switch is flicked. Mercury switches are usually clearly marked with "top" on one of the flanges. If you can't find the mark, remember that in standard installations the toggle is up when the switch is on. That way you can tell top from bottom by the on-off designations on the toggle.

Some specialist switches, such as the dimmer types, may have other wiring requirements. If they do, ask the electrical dealer what the tricks may be. If the type of switch you select presents problems you can't readily handle, have the change made by a professional. For the most part, however, a switch is a simple matter of interrupting the black wire, and only two terminals are involved.

One more type of switch is the two-way installation with which you can turn a light on or off from two different locations. This involves fairly complicated wiring, including insulation of three different colors, switches with three terminals, etc. The best way for you to handle the two-way switch replacement is to note carefully which wires go to which terminals. An easy way to do this is to make a simple sketch with numbered terminals and matching numbers on wires, before you disconnect the switch. Then take it to the electrical shop and buy one that matches it, so you can make the reconnections the same as the originals.

WORKING ON WALL AND CEILING FIXTURES

Wall and ceiling fixtures are, basically, nothing more than stationary lamps. There is a base, a globe, a socket or two or more, and some mechanical means of holding all these parts together. The whole thing, in turn, is mounted on a metal box in the wall or ceiling, connected to ground through the grounding wire or the continuity of BX or conduit systems, if properly done. The box is normally square, not rectangular.

There is a great variety in the design of wall and ceiling fixtures, and that makes it difficult to pinpoint the method of dismounting them. Usually, however, you can see what goes on by examining the fixture. If there is a globe, remove it and you'll probably see screws that hold the fixture to the box. If it has a central column, chances are there is a knurled nut at the end of the column. Unscrew it and the entire thing comes apart. Sometimes there is a yoke across the box, diagonally, held in place with two screws. In the center of the yoke is a

Typifying wall and ceiling fixtures, this light base shows its black and white wires, fastened to the black and white wires of the circuit. The base covers the connections, held in place by a simple flange-and-screw setup attached to the box.

threaded hole into which the central support of the fixture screws. However the specific unit may be designed, it is sure to be simple enough to come apart easily.

Inside the box you'll find the standard pair of wires, one white, one black. These connect to the short wires of the fixture. If there are two bulbs or more, you'll find that all the wires for each side of the circuit come together, usually where they are spliced to the main wires.

What goes wrong? Most fixtures with globes that enclose the bulbs are fitted with minimum sockets, often of plastic. The amount of heat generated by the bulb, confined by the globe, tends to cause relatively early deterioration of the socket and of the insulation leading to the sockets as well. This may cause the contact at the bottom of the socket to lose its spring, so that it does not connect solidly with the bulb. It may cause the plastic to chip and loosen around the socket. It may cause insulation to dry out and fall away.

When this happens, you may be able to replace the socket in some fixtures; in others, you may find it riveted in place. If you are handy enough to improvise with sheet-metal screws, perhaps you can replace even those sockets that are riveted. Otherwise, a new fixture may be the only answer.

If the problem is merely a bad contact in the bottom of the socket, you can most likely fix things by reaching into the socket with a small screwdriver and gently lifting the contact.

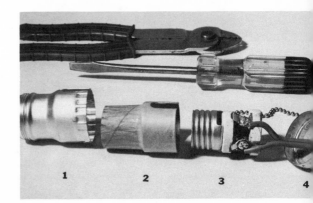

Anatomy of a light socket: Left to right are **(1)** the metal casing, **(2)** the paper insulative liner, **(3)** the actual socket with screw connectors, and **(4)** the cap. Replacement is a simple plier-and-screwdriver job.

1   2   3   4

By all means be sure the socket is "dead" before you do this.

You can go a long way toward avoiding troubles of this kind by heeding the labeling of the fixture which tells you: "Caution—use so-many-watt lamps or less."

When you replace a fixture, you'll find that the electrical connections are simple. Just remove the insulation or wire nut and untwist the wires. If they are soldered, you may have to cut them, but you'll find soldered joints rare in wall and ceiling fixtures. Then, reconnect the new fixture the same way the old one was hooked up. No matter what the design of the new fixture, it will mount on the existing box, although you may have to pick up some parts, for instance, the diagonal yoke, a short length of threaded tube, or other items all carried in stock by electrical and hardware stores.

Almost always, you'll find that the wires coming into the box are single strand, heavy copper, while the wires of the fixture are multiple-strand, many small wires. It is often difficult to twist the two together, since the solid wire is much stiffer than the multiple wire. A good way to simplify this job is to tape the two wires together *where the insulation starts,* just above the bare wire. This holds them together, in spite of the fact that the actual twist may come apart easily. Then, after you've twisted the wires, add more insulation or preferably a wire nut.

HOW TO ADD TO A CIRCUIT

If you find that it takes a tangle of extension cords to put lamps where you want them in any room in the house, but *there is capacity in the line* to handle more lamps, you might want to extend a line rather than put up with extension cords. This is easier than you might think. Here are the steps you take adding on from an existing box.

Get enough BX to reach the distance you want the new line to go, plus about 3′. Also, an outlet box (*without* mounting flanges) and two BX connectors, if you need them. (Some boxes have built-in connectors, but be sure to check the existing box, because you may need at least one.) Buy the outlet, possibly a three-holer, and a cover plate.

Remove the baseboard and shoe mold along the wall where the extension will go. Directly below the existing outlet, right at the floor, knock a hole in the plaster within the area covered by the baseboard. Do the same thing at the point where the new outlet is to go. *Important:* This must be adjacent to a wall stud, and a stud is easy to locate since one of the baseboard nails came out of it. These two holes have to be only a couple of inches in diameter, and since they will be covered, they needn't be neat.

For the new outlet, move up the wall the proper distance and cut a hole into which the box will fit, with one vertical edge right against the stud. The easy way to do this is to punch through close to the stud, to locate it precisely. Then position the box on the plaster and trace around it with a pencil. Make the cutout with a keyhole saw in plaster, or simply by cutting and breaking in plasterborad. Insert the box in the hole and fasten it to the stud with a couple of screws. It may be necessary to drill holes in the side of the box, depending on its exact style and on the thickness of the plaster.

The final step in preparation for the line is to chip and cut away a channel in the plaster right at the floor, large enough to accept the BX. In the case of plasterboard construction, the channel may not be deep enough. That is, the diameter of the BX may be greater than the thickness of the plasterboard. In that case, you can saw or plane a little off the lower back edge of the baseboard, leaving a space which is later covered by shoe mold. If you do this, take pains when you re-nail the shoe mold not to nail into the wiring.

Prepare the ends of the BX to go into the boxes by removing about 8″ of the armor. The photographs help show how this is done. Strip about ¾″ of insulation off the ends of the white wire and the black wire. If you are using BX fasteners — that is, if the boxes do not have built-in methods of clamping the cable — remove the nuts and set them aside. Then slip the little fiber sections into the ends of BX and put the connectors on, tightening the screw firmly. If the outlet is a regular three-holer, you'll connect the little ground wire to it later on. If it does not have the ground screw, wrap the grounding

Test a circuit with one of these devices. The professional tester has two pointer terminals that you can use to puncture insulation to check wires between outlets. The pronged socket and small light bulb give you a check on any ordinary outlet.

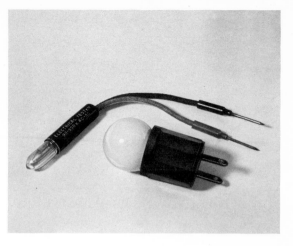

Basic components of the BX system are the spiral wound cable, housing a black and a white wire, plus the uninsulated ground wire. The cable slips into a fitting, held there by a screw. The fitting then goes into an electrical box, where a flat washer holds it tight. The ground wire is shown here wound back over the cable, to insure contact. In some situations you may find a special screw on the outlet, usually green, to which the ground wire can be fastened.

To cut BX cable, first hacksaw through the spiral, easy to do if you hold a loop as shown here. Then, bend it back and forth to break the remainder of the spiral wound metal. This exposes the wires. Cut them with regular wire cutters. When you make a connection to a box, you cut away about 8" of the BX casing, as is being done in this photo. Then, merely pull it off, leaving 8" of wire ready to use.

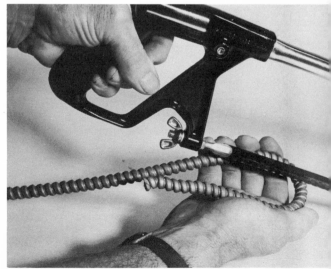

wire around the BX cable so that it will make perfect contact, metal to metal, and remain held there when the assembly is complete.

To install the BX, untwist a wire coat hanger and form it into a long-stemmed hook. Knock out one of the plugs in the existing outlet box, slip the coat hanger hook through the hole and wiggle it around until the hook shows up down at the floor, where you chipped the opening. Fasten the wires of the BX to the hook, and pull them up through the hole. Screw on the fastener nut. Do the same at the other end.

Finish the connection by bending small hooks in the ends of the wire and placing them around the proper screws, black to brass and white to silver, on the new outlet. On the original outlet only one of the terminal screws on each side may be in use. When that is the case, fasten the new wires to the other terminal screw. If both screws are in use on both sides, you must make one of them on each side do double duty, holding two wires. Carefully bend the wires so that they go inside the boxes, screw the outlets in place, and put on the cover plate.

Important: In some communities, it may not be permissable for you to do even such a simple wiring job as this yourself. You may be required to hire a licensed electrician. The electrical dealer from whom you buy your materials will be able to tell you what the situation is, as well as any aspects of the local building codes which may be involved.

HOW TO JOIN TWO WIRES TOGETHER

All joints in a modern electrical system are made inside outlet boxes, or in "utility" boxes when a splice must be made at some point other than an outlet. Two kinds of splices take care of just about all kinds of situations. One is the "pigtail" and the other is a line splice, most usefully a clever version called the "Western Union."

Most pigtail splices involve two wires that are identical or almost so. (See page 85 on wall and ceiling fixtures for an exception.) If you are working with solid wire, strip at least 1″ of insulation. Hold the wires *crossed* at the point where the insulation ends, and twist them clockwise using a pair of pliers. (Linemen's pliers, with a square nose, are best for this kind of work.) You must twist the wires enough—at least four or five turns—to make a joint that is mechanically sound. Do not depend on insulation to hold the wires together. Finish off the splice with wire nuts, or with plastic electrical tape. You need at least two thicknesses of tape but three are better.

Making a pigtail with multiple-strand wires, you can usually twist the wires tight with your fingers. The mechanical

Most wire-to-wire joints in electrical systems are "pigtails," made by twisting the ends of two wires together for a distance of about ½". Be sure the twist is clockwise. Square-nose electrician's pliers are excellent for this job.

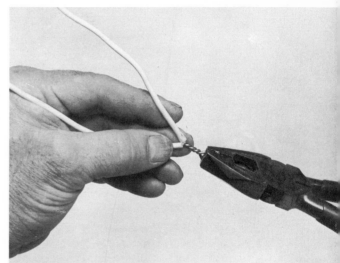

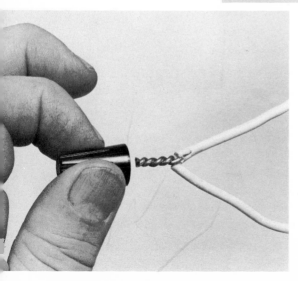

After cutting the twist off square and true, twist on a "wire nut." This plastic gadget insulates, but also holds the joint tight because of the grip of a metal liner.

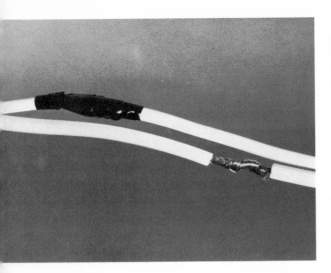

Most acceptable of the in-line splices is the so-called "Western Union." To make it, cut the ends so that one is longer than the other on each wire. That way, when the joint is made, the splice on one wire is next to untouched insulation on the other. As shown here, one splice has been wrapped with electrician's tape. Next, the other splice will be wrapped, and finally the entire job will be covered with tape.

Handy electric working tool is pliers that combines cutting with stripping, plus crimping teeth (at end) for connectors that clamp on the wire. Tool provides for different sizes of wire.

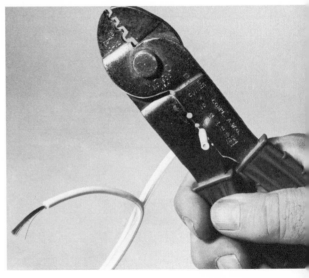

strength of the joint will depend on how much wire you strip, and it should never be much less than an inch. For the best splice with multiple-strand, use solder after the wires are twisted. Then put on the wire nut or plastic insulation.

The clever thing about the Western Union splice used on pairs of wires is the way the two joints are staggered, so that both are opposite undisturbed insulation on the other wire.

To make the splice, you cut 2″ or 3″ off the white wire of one pair and off the black wire of the other pair. Next strip the insulation and twist one splice together. Wrap it with electrical tape. Then twist the other splice and wrap it. Finally, wrap the entire thing with tape.

In-line splices are, of course, not pigtails. They are made by winding one of the wires around the other for five or six turns, then winding the loose end in the opposite direction.

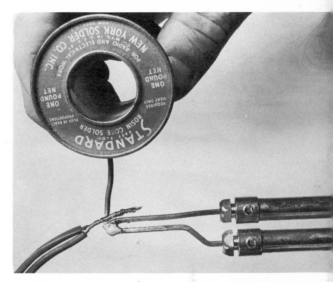

When you work with multiple-strand wire, which means just about everything but actual wiring circuits, you get the best joint with solder. Use rosin core — not acid core — solder. Proper technique is to apply the iron to one side of the twist and the solder to the other side, so that the wire itself is hot enough to melt the solder.

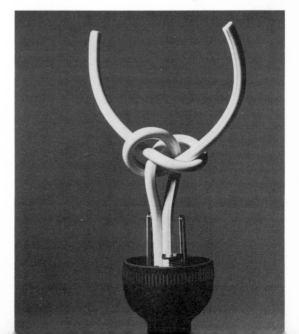

Underwriter's knot in the cord when you put on a new plug forms a "glob" of wire too big to pull out of the plug, and thus insures somewhat against damage when someone jerks on the wire.

You get a job that stays put, also, by bringing the wires around the prongs before you fasten them to the screws. Then, fill the entire cavity with silicone calk.

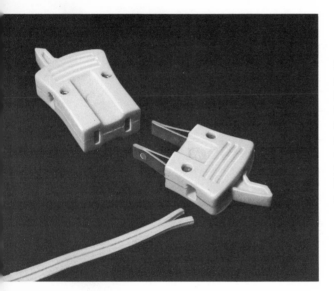

Fastest and easiest plugs merely require insertion of the cord into a hole, after the two wires have been separated for about ½". Inside, the plug turns one wire up, the other down. When you depress the lever, teeth bite through the insulation, making the connection.

8

SIMPLE REPAIRS KEEP
A PLUMBING SYSTEM WORKING

WATER COMES TO YOUR home, whether from the water company or from your own well, under pressure. It leaves through drains, moving toward a sewer system or to your septic tank under gravity feed. The fact that the pressure is a relatively strong force causes about a third of plumbing system troubles, such things as dripping faucets, leaking joints, noisy pipes, etc. The fact that gravity is a relatively weak force in the sewer system just about accounts for another third, clogged and flooded drains. The remaining third can be blamed on such natural phenomena as excessive chemical content in the water, excessive rusting of iron pipes and fittings, deterioration of rubber or plastic parts, and the inevitabilities of wear and tear.

THE NATURE OF THE SYSTEM

The water main runs past your house, a huge pipe big enough to carry all the water that you and your neighbors up and down the street are likely to use. That water is under considerable pressure, so that you and four or five people in the neighborhood can all flush a toilet or turn on the dishwasher at the same time without having things slow down to a trickle.

In front of your house, a smaller pipe branches off. It is still big enough, however, to supply all the water that you and your family are likely to use, and there is pressure enough so that you can use water for two or three or more functions at the same time. This pipe makes its way underground, passing through a meter at some point along the way, and comes through the foundation into your basement, crawlspace, or utility room. There it breaks down further into smaller runs, each headed for a water-use area such as kitchen, bathroom, laundry etc. At these points, the water comes to the surface for use when you open the faucet or flush the toilet or turn on some mechanical device such as the lawn sprinkler or dishwasher.

(If you have a well and your own pump, it works the same way—except that there isn't any meter.)

Once it is used, water funnels into the drain system which is composed of large pipes, all either vertical or pitched downhill so that wastes run off. (In some cases, a house may be so designed and situated that a pump is necessary to lift the sewer drain over a hump.) Eventually the drain system connects with sewers and the water is back out in the street again, headed for your community's sewage disposal system.

There is one more element in the water system: the vent. In order for the gravity system of sewage draining to function without "air locks," each vertical drop has pipe running downward and upward. This pipe comes through the roof and is open to the air, so that there can *never be a vacuum* in the drain system under normal operating conditions.

Starting with a main shutoff valve just this side of the meter (or just inside the basement wall, if the meter happens to be located outside the house), there are a series of shutoff valves. Their frequency and location may vary, depending on the philosophy of the original plumber, but they should appear:

• Wherever a run branches off from the major feed line coming in from the street main.

• Wherever a sub-run branches off, as for instance, where a run headed for a bathroom splits off to service a powder room.

• Wherever the water enters, and often where it leaves, the water heater.

• Just before the water reaches any fixture or appliance.

Naturally, these shutoff valves are located in hot water as well as cold water runs.

The purpose of these shutoffs will become apparent to you the first time you have to work on a plumbing problem. You've got to shut the water off or you cannot do the dismantling required to make the repairs. When the system is well engineered, the shut-off valves will be numerous enough and well enough located so you can shut off the minimum amount of service. For instance, you could tackle a dripping faucet in the kitchen by first turning off the main valve, but that would shut the entire system down. So, you shut off the valve *closest to the trouble*. In most cases of today's plumbing, this will be a faucet directly under the fixture involved.

Over on the sewer drain side of the system, although there are no valves, there are one or more clean-out plugs. These are big, up to 3″ across, with provision for a good-size wrench. They provide access to the lines when there is serious stoppage of the sewers.

THE DRIPPING FAUCET

The day will come when faucets drip no longer. Modern types manufactured by nearly every producer in the plumbing fixture industry have licked the problem. New faucets no longer make use of the primitive design that sooner or later had to start leaking.

For that reason, if you have a chronically dripping faucet in a kitchen, bath, or other frequently used location, why not replace it? It is almost as easy to do this as it is to fix the dripper (how-to details later in this chapter), and although it does cost a few dollars, many homeowners consider the saving in nuisance worth the price.

What causes faucets to drip? Inside the housing there is a valve seat. Attached to the bottom end of the spindle which turns when you turn the faucet handle, there is a rubber or plastic washer. As the faucet handle turns, this washer twists

down against the valve seat. Over a period of time, the washer
wears out. It no longer screws tight against the seat. If there
happen to be a few grains of sand or some rust flakes in the
water, they provide abrasion that speeds this wearing out
process. It is the twisting-tightening action that destroys the
washer. Those modern faucets are designed so that the
washer—if there is one—simply presses straight-on against
the valve seat, without twisting, and that is why they just
about never wear out.

A faucet may also leak around the stem. This happens when
the packing wears out or packs too hard. The packing material
is fibrous, much like a soft, yarn-like cord and often lubricated with graphite, which is wound around the stem below
the packing nut, a dome-like cap which screws down on the
top of the faucet housing. As this nut tightens down, it compacts the packing material around the stem, making a watertight joint but permitting the stem to turn. Whenever you replace a faucet washer, you should check the packing.

Step by step, taking a typical faucet that's dripping, these
are the steps to follow:

1. Turn off the water at the shutoff valve closest to the
faucet. As mentioned above, this valve may be right under
the sink or lavatory involved. Or it may be back along the line,
where it branches off from the pipe entering the house. In the
most obscure cases, you may have to shut off the entire system, back just this side of the meter.

2. Remove the handle. It is held on by a screw into the end
of the spindle. In some cases, this screw may be hidden beneath a chromium cap. If so, dig the cap out carefully with the
tip of a kitchen knife or other sharp tool. After you take out
the screw, you may have to pry gently, since handles often
fit over a knurled taper on the step and may be frozen fairly
tight. Some purely functional faucets do not require removal
of the handle, if it doesn't form a cap over the packing nut.

3. Put a wrench on the packing nut. It's best to use a regular monkey wrench or a Crescent, instead of a pipe wrench,
because the sharp teeth of the pipe wrench might mar the
fitting. If the pipe wrench is the only tool you have that will
open wide enough to fit on the nut, you must use it, of course.

 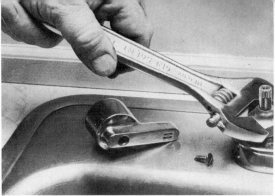

1. To replace the drip-causing faucet washer, first remove the screw that holds the handle on, and lift off the handle. This may take a little leverage with the screwdriver.

2. Use a wrench to loosen the hex nut under the handle. Once it's loosened, you can twist it free and unscrew the faucet core completely.

HOW TO FIX A DRIPPING FAUCET

3. With core removed, the worn-out washer on the end of the spindle is revealed.

4. Remove the screw, throw away the old washer, and replace with a new one.

But, to safeguard the nut, cushion it with a dishrag or a couple of thicknesses of masking tape. Then remove the nut completely.

4. With the packing nut off, twist the handle in the "on" direction until the entire handle, stem, and spindle come out. On the bottom of the spindle you'll find the offender: a black rubber-like washer held in place by a round-head brass screw. The washer will be badly impressed and flattened, and in some cases it will show signs of ragged wear.

5. Remove the screw, throw away the washer, and replace it with a new one of the same size and general shape. At any

hardware store or plumbing outlet you can buy a packet of washers in various sizes. Usually the packet includes two or three replacement screws, to be used if the old screw is damaged by repeated washer changes. Sometimes the screw is badly corroded and refuses to come out. When this happens, when the screw slot finally becomes useless with many slips of the screwdriver, you may have to drill the old screw out, then tap new threads for a new screw. At that point, it is always easier to buy a new faucet.

6. With the new washer in place, twist the spindle back into the housing.

7. Tighten the packing nut *just enough to prevent leakage* around the stem. If you tighten it too much you may make the faucet hard to open and close, and you hasten the day when the packing will have to be replaced.

Slip the handle on the spindle and turn the faucet off. If the handle is not in the proper position, that is, doesn't point in the direction you want it to, lift it off and reposition it without turning the stem. Then replace the screw that holds the handle in place.

Replacing the packing. If the faucet leaks around the stem, but doesn't drip, your first step is to tighten the packing *gently*. This makes the packing material fit more snugly around the stem and it should stop the leak. However, the time comes when tightening the nut won't do the job any longer, and you must replace the packing. Pick up some packing material at a hardware or plumbing store, the genuine item. Don't be deluded by claims that you can do the job with ordinary string. You can, but you'll have to do it again in a short time.

Turn off the water and follow the steps given above for taking the faucet apart. Use a screwdriver, an awl, or a nail to dig out the impacted material inside the hollow packing nut. Then wind the new packing around the stem, making enough turns to fill the hollow. Push it in with your fingers. Then put the faucet back together. Tighten the packing nut *only enough to prevent leaking.* If you feel that the nut has screwed on too far—that you may find yourself working on it again before long—take the time right now to disassemble the faucet and put a few more turns of packing around the stem.

Damaged valve seat. A more difficult problem than replacing a faucet washer or renewing the packing arises when the valve seat is damaged. The slightest roughness will, of course, cut the faucet washer to pieces. Some faucets have removable seats, which can be replaced. Quite often, however, you must "dress" the seat with a special tool that fits into the housing and grinds the roughness away. Plumbing supply outlets carry valve seat dressing tools, if you need them.

Servicing new-style faucets. Although it is uncommon for one of the newly engineered faucets to give trouble, it can happen. For instance, a faucet washer may last for years and years, but if a particle of dirt happens to stick between it and the seat, it cannot close, and the faucet will drip. It is easy to take such fittings apart and examine them when you suspect this to be the case. Just keep track of the way you unscrew things, and

Some newer variations on the old standard include: a unit that slides up and down in a sleeve, with a washer at the bottom (*above left*); a washer that squeeze-fits over a knob on the end of the spindle (*above right*); an eccentric type used on mixing faucets (*right*). These newer devices give far less trouble than standard twist-on-twist-off washer, and no repair trouble beyond the need to find the exact replacement at your plumbing shop, not, as a rule, at hardware stores.

make sure that you screw them back in the same order and facing the same way.

Many of these faucets depend on a small dab of grease to keep them running smoothly, since they are not lubricated by the water, as a standard old model is. If, while working on them, you wipe off the grease in the interest of easier and cleaner handling, be sure to relubricate the slides and threads as you reassemble. A small amount of general purpose grease does it.

If it should happen that any of the plastic or rubber parts of a modern faucet should become damaged, your best bet is to take it to a plumbing supply house and ask for a replacement. Chances are the typical hardware store's plumbing department will not have what you need.

One-handle faucets. There are several different styles of faucets that operate with a single handle or knob, instead of one for hot and one for cold. Moving the handle laterally (or turning the knob) controls the temperature, while raising it up or down (or sliding the knob in or out) controls the rate of flow, and there are variations on the theme. The insides of these faucets are just as complex as an ordinary faucet is simple. There may be an encapsulation of steel balls and eccentrics and cams, activated by the handle to blend hot and cold. There may be interfitting tubes and oddly positioned "O-rings" with holes that match or mismatch.

It is easy enough to dismantle one of these faucets and remove its operating core. Sometimes an O-ring can be replaced; now and then its function can be restored simply by turning it over. But most of the time the best thing to do is to show the core to the man at the plumbing shop and ask him to sell you a new one just like it.

Clogged aerator. All but the most primitive of faucets, such as sillcocks and the like, have aerators these days. Their purpose is to break up the stream of water with bubbles so that there is less splashing, and to filter out solids. The aerator is composed of several fine screen disks enclosed in a screw-on attachment. The water, passing through the aerator, creates

Modern shower faucets are often the one-handle type. Fixing them may mean replacement of the entire spindle, which is full of neoprene O-rings.

This is what's behind the wall in the shower. When you unfasten the faucet handle, you find a keeper ring, removable with any sharp-pointed object.

Out comes the spindle. Take it to the plumbing shop, where the O-rings may be replaced, or where you can buy a new spindle.

a vacuum (Venturi effect) which draws air in through tiny holes arranged around the fitting.

When the screens accumulate dirt, the flow of water is cut down. To remedy this, simply unscrew the rounded "nose" at the discharge end of the faucet. Clean the components with an old toothbrush, then put the aerator back together again.

Important: Note carefully how all parts of the aerator are assembled. If you do not put them back the same way, the device may spray water out of the holes that it is supposed to draw air through.

Malfunctioning sink spray. If your kitchen sink setup includes a spray hose, it is likely to slow down over a period of time, due to accumulation of dirt at the nozzle, particularly if it has an aerator like the one on the sink faucet. Nozzle and aerator are simple to take apart and clean by the methods covered for aerators (above) and shower heads (below). Spray hoses that are quite old are probably made of materials that deteriorate and become brittle. If your hose is in this category and is giving you trouble, you'll be ahead of the game to pick up a new one at a plumbing supply outlet. The dealer will have to know the brand name of your kitchen fittings; better still, disconnect the hose, and take it down to the store, and ask for one like it.

Clogged shower head. If your shower has the "sieve" type of head, the holes eventually become clogged both by particles of dirt and by slow rust deposits. When this happens, the number of solid streams of water gradually cuts down, and the size of the spray pattern becomes smaller and smaller.

It is a simple matter to remove the shower head. Cushion the fitting to prevent damage from the wrench. Use a paper clip or a darning needle to punch the accumulated rust out of the holes. Working *inside* the head, use a stiff brush or steel wool and a cleanser such as Ajax to scour away as much of the rust accumulation as possible. Be sure to rinse out the particles you loosen, or they'll go back to work immediately clogging the head again.

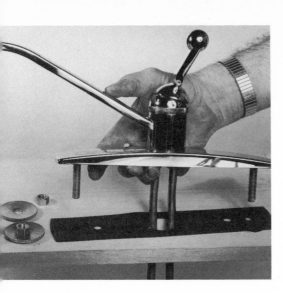

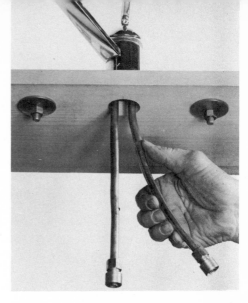

Modern faucets, engineered to fit most old fixtures, are easy to install. For instance, this one (shown in a prototype setting) replaces the old two-faucet nuisance with a single handle, using the same holes in the sink top, over a rubber gasket. The whole unit bolts in place.

Beneath the sink, the soft brass tubes of the faucet bend to the proper spacing for the plumbing already in place.

HOW TO INSTALL A NEW FAUCET

Connection of faucets like this is usually by means of squeeze fittings. The lower part of the fitting screws (or solders) to the plumbing. The hookup is a simple wrench job.

The single-lever principle is the same in faucets for bathroom lavatory use, as shown in this prototype setup, illustrating the way flanges and bolts fasten it to the standard lavatory. Spikelike rod in the middle is for hookup to sink stopper.

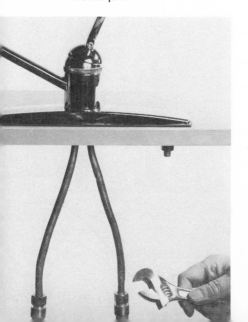

THE TOILET THAT RUNS AND RUNS AND RUNS

One reason why the slowly trickling toilet may be worse than the slowly dripping faucet is that it can go on for months without anybody knowing it. It is normal to assume that a toilet is working; you flip the handle and go away. The leaky toilet doesn't make any noise, except for a tiny watery hiss you can hear is you put your ear against the tank. It doesn't make any visible fuss, either, except for a gentle rippling of the water. Unless there is a fairly major leakage, which will make itself noisily apparent.

These subtleties in toilet malfunction are your clue to detecting problems. Every month or so glance at the water in a toilet that was flushed some time ago. If there is motion in the water, you know that there is a trickling leak. Listen for that whispery noise, too.

And, take a look inside the tank. In some cases there may be an obvious indication of trouble: water overflowing into an overflow tube.

Basic mechanics of a toilet. All of the working parts of a toilet are located inside the tank, excepting of course the handle and the shutoff valve which you'll find below the tank, on the lefthand side. Here's what happens when you flush a toilet. (The numbers refer to the accompanying drawing.)

When you activate the handle (1) it lifts on the upper lift wire (2) which is connected by means of the guide wire (3) to the stopper ball (4). This raises the ball from the seat (5) and the water immediately starts to rush out. The ball floats in the water until has all drained out; then it reseats.

Meanwhile, the float (6) drops with the water level, and the float arm (7) causes the ball cock valve (8) to open. Water starts coming in, although at a much slower rate than it is rushing out of the tank and into the toilet.

When the water is all gone and the stopper ball has dropped, closing off the seat once more, water continues to fill the tank. As the level rises, the float rises until finally the action of its lever shuts off the valve. The tank is full, ready for use again. If for some reason, the valve should not close, the water continues to rise until it spills over into the overflow tube (9).

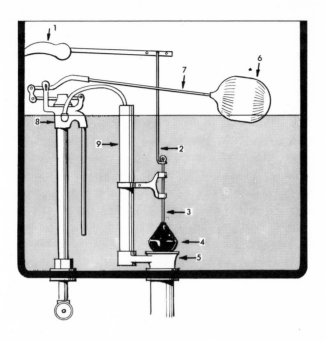

The foregoing step-by-step covers standard toilets of the design found in most homes. If your toilet is of a more modern design it may not look like the drawing. It may look much simpler. But all the functions mentioned are there, and you'll be able to translate easily.

There are four reasons why a toilet may trickle.

• The ball may be deteriorating to a point where it no longer functions as a "cork" in the valve seat.

• The ball may have accumulated a coating of slime and water and dirt that makes it impossible for it to seat properly.

• The ball linkage to the handle lever, through the guide, may not be sliding smoothly.

• The supply valve may not close when the float has reached the proper level, owing to wear, dirt, or other impediment.

HOW TO MAKE REPAIRS INSIDE THE TANK

Like most other plumbing repairs, work at toilet maintenance involves the simplest of tools: wrench, pliers, screwdriver. The first step is to turn off the valve beneath the tank. Next flush the toilet. It will drain to the level of the valve seat.

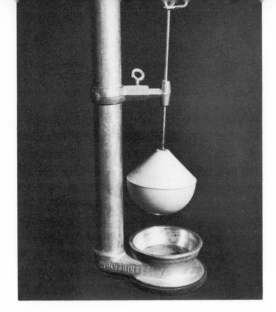

Most toilets have a stopper-ball like this, with a rubber ball that drops into a brass or bronze seat to stop the flow of water once the toilet has been flushed. Replacing it is a simple job.

Replacing the ball. In the standard tank, the ball unscrews from the lower lift wire. You may need a pair of pliers on the top loop of the wire. A handhold on the ball should be enough. If the ball is old, chances are you'll wreck it in the process of removing it. Okay. You need a new one, anyway. If it comes off in good shape, wipe it clean. Check the ball seat, to be sure it is clean. If it is encrusted with water-borne deposits, use steel wool to clean it smooth and bright. Screw the ball back on.

There are new stopper-ball gadgets that eliminate much of the chronic trouble with the old standard. One in a cage and another on a hinge get rid of the hang-up caused by the wire, and insure perfect alignment at all times. Installing them is a screwdriver or even a simple slip-on job.

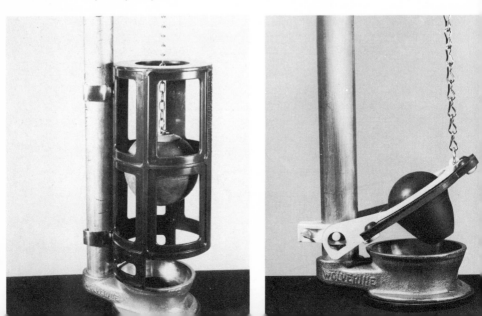

When your decision is to replace the ball, you can buy a new one for very little money. For a little more, you can buy a modern version of the ball-and-linkage that works better and lasts longer than the old-fashioned kind. These new gadgets ordinarily clamp around the overflow pipe, the same as the guide on the old one.

If the wire sticks. When the lift wire sticks in the guide, the ball cannot, of course, drop to the valve seat when the tank has drained. The water just runs. This problem arises most often when someone has been monkeying with the flush system and has bent the wire. It can happen, also, when the arm extending from the handle is bent, so that the linkage is out of line. Try bending things back in line. Make sure the lower wire is straight and that the guide is centered over the valve seat. After years of service, the upper wire in the linkage may become worn, both where it loops into the arm and where it loops around the lower wire. You can replace its function, and eliminate a lot of problems, by replacing the upper wire with a length of nylon twine tied to the arm and to the lower wire, above the guide.

This is an entire ballcock unit. Plumbing shops sell them. If continued problems convince you that your old one is worn out, buy a new one, drain the tank, and put the replacement in. It threads into the old system, and only needs minor adjustments to maintain proper water level.

Some modern variations. In some makes of modern toilets, the ball-valve arrangement may not be a ball at all. Instead, it may be a form of flange that rests in the valve seat, hinged so that it will rock up and away when the handle is activated, freeing the tankful of water to flush the toilet. Attached to the stem of the flange is a little cylinder, open at the top and with a small hole in the bottom. This cylinder is full of water when you first flush the toilet. As the water rushes out, the cylinder gradually drains through the hole in the bottom. When it is empty, the weight of its water gone, the center of gravity moves out over the flange, and it flops down in position on the valve seat where it stays until you flush the toilet again. There is little to wear out and nothing to get stuck with this sort of flush valve. If the flange should go bad, it unscrews to be replaced. The entire unit lifts out when you remove a couple of screws.

A leaking supply valve. As the tank fills, the float rises on the end of the lever, exerting the pressure needed to close the supply valve. Over a period of time, the bushings and valve seats involved become worn or compressed. More "throw" is needed to close them. This means the water level has to be higher, so that the float can rise higher, to provide the necessary pressure on the valve closing mechanism. Eventually the water reaches the overflow level, but the supply valve still hasn't closed.

In most cases, the lever is made of soft copper or brass, easy to bend. All you need to do is gently bend the float end of the lever downward. When you do this, the rising float again exerts the pressure necessary to close the valve.

Some toilet mechanisms have adjustment screws near the valve end of the lever. By tightening or loosening these screws, you can raise or lower the water level at which the float shuts the water off.

Important: In some toilet designs, bending the rod may cause the float to interfere with the functioning of the flush valve. Flush the toilet after adjustment and watch the happenings inside the tank. If everything works, you re all set. If the float does interfere, loosen the set screw holding the lever at the valve end and remove the entire float and lever. (In some cases, the lever may be threaded and screw into the valve mechanism.) Straighten the lever to restore it to its maximum length. Replace it, and then do the bending necessary *very close to the valve end*, making the bend as sharp, i.e., not rounded, as possible. This will provide the float pressure when it is needed while shortening the lever by the least possible amount.

If you don't stop the leak in a supply valve by adjusting the float and its lever, the problem may be dirt in the valve or terminal bushings, etc. Check this by lifting on the lever, applying more force than the float would provide rising normally. If this additional force doesn't check the flow, take the valve apart and clean all the metal and plastic parts that form the closure. If inspection should reveal serious wear on plastic parts, replace them.

Should your toilet be quite old, parts may not be available to repair the supply valve. You can, however, buy an entire unit which will fit in any toilet, regardless of age. Replacing the flush valve unit is simple. It is fastened to the bottom of the tank by means of a flange, a gasket and a collar which unscrews. When you buy the replacement, a new gasket and collar comes with it. You have no trouble making the replacement watertight, and you let yourself in for the extra years of more reliable service the newer designs provide.

OTHER TOILET REPAIRS

What else can happen to a toilet? Not much, but there are a few things that bother.

Loose seat. A toilet seat and lid and its hinges and bolts are a unit; you can buy them in a package at most good hardware stores. They fasten in place by means of a pair of bolts running through holes in the toilet with washers and nuts beneath. Sometimes the nuts loosen. Sometimes the washers rust away. The seat becomes wobbly. Fix it by tightening the nuts and replacing the washers if necessary. Be sure to buy brass washers so, this time, they won't rust away.

Some units have hinge barrels formed as part of the seat and the lid. The hinge pin passes through them. In other cases, the barrels or their equivalents are fastened to seat and lid by means of screws. They can work loose and become a source of annoyance. When they do, tighten them. In extreme cases, it may be necessary to replace the screws with the next size larger. Or, fill holes that are worn too large with wood plastic, let it dry, predrill, and run the old screws back into the new holes.

Broken tank cover. Sometimes in the processes of repair, or in the rough-and-tumble routine of a house full of active kids, a toilet tank cover gets knocked off on a tile floor and breaks. Epoxy glue, the two-tube kind, glues the pieces back together. Follow mixing instructions carefully. Support the broken lid on an end or an edge. so that gravity holds the cemented joint together. If you pick the "quick dry" epoxy, the lid will be ready to go back on the tank in two or three hours. Or—more safely—the next morning.

Scattered porcelain domes. The toilet is fastened to the floor and to the disposal system with bolts. For the sake of appearances, the plumber puts decorative porcelain domes or caps over these nuts. After a few years of floor moppings, these domes come loose. Put them back over the nuts with a dab of wood plastic to hold them. If it ever becomes necessary to lift the toilet, it is simple to pry the domes off with a screwdriver and scrape away the wood plastic.

Miscellaneous leaks. The toilet gives mighty little trouble in spite of the fact that it is formed of two open tanks that might leak. Why don't they? Lack of pressure. Aside from the pressure from water mains on the supply valve, all you ever have to worry about is the weight of the water. That makes it possible for the toilet to be assembled and installed in a very simple manner. But, now and then there may be a leak between tank and toilet, or at the floor. There are only two joints in the toilet. One is between the tank and the toilet. (This joint is eliminated in contemporary one-piece units.) The other is between the toilet and the waste line. In both cases the joint is a gasket. Between the tank and the toilet, the gasket is rubber or plastic. A pair of bolts draw the tank down snugly, compressing the gasket into a non-leak joint.

A leak at this point would make itself apparent by a presence of water on the flat part of the toilet, back of the place where the seat and lid hinge. It would be a waste of time to try to correct this leak by tightening the nuts underneath the back overhang of the toilet. The right way to fix it is to replace the gasket. Turn off the valve under the tank. Flush the toilet and bail and mop it dry. Unscrew the water connection. Remove the two nuts holding the tank to the seat. Now the tank will lift off. Remove the worn gasket and buy another one like it. With the new gasket in place, reassemble the unit, reconnect the water, and open the shutoff. Look closely to see if there is any leakage. If there is, tighten the nuts slightly, until it stops leaking. *Important:* Try to snug up the nuts an

The tank of your toilet fits on the seat like this. There is a gasket which seals it leak-tight. The two bolts tighten up from the bottom, holding the tank in place and keeping the gasket snug.

equal amount on both sides, in order to keep the tank seated squarely on the gasket.

A leak at floor level may reveal itself as moisture on the floor. Or, the leak may be visible only if you happen to inspect the waste line in the basement. Or, it may come to light eventually in the form of loosened plaster on the ceiling of the room below the toilet.

To fix it, turn off the water, flush the toilet, bail and sponge the tank dry, and use a plunger to force as much water as possible from the toilet. Disconnect the water line. Now loosen the nuts which hold the toilet to the floor. Gently rock the unit until it loosens, then lift it up off the stud bolts and out into the middle of the room.

Underneath where the toilet was, you'll find a flange and the remains of a "wax ring." This ring is a "donut" of waxy substance about the consistency of soft caramel. Its purpose is to form a perfectly fitting gasket between the toilet and the waste line. Since it is soft and fits into circular grooves in both of the parts, it does not have to be squeezed in the manner of most forms of gaskets. The weight of the seat slipping into the proper position squishes out a little surplus wax, but the majority of it stays in the joint, making it quite watertight.

To replace this gasket, merely scrape and clean away the vestiges of the old one, position a new one (from a hardware or plumbing store), and carefully settle the toilet back over the bolts. Run the nuts back on, replace the porcelain domes, and that's it. There is no worry about the nuts drawing the toilet down to snug up the gasket. It fits purely because of its soft, gooey nature. All the nuts do is hold the fixture from tipping.

PROBLEMS WITH
SEWERS AND DRAINS

MOST OF THE TROUBLES on the incoming side of the plumbing system are due to the pressure which causes water to run even when you don't want it to. The reverse is true on the outgoing side, where the problems all arise from the fact that there is no pressure, other than the pull of gravity and that convenient law of physics which makes water run downhill. Very often the downhill flow is so slow that sediment builds up, like sandbars in a slow-running river. With no pressure to force things along the drains and sewers, it doesn't take much to clog the system.

HOW TO PREVENT TROUBLE

Fortunately the soaps and detergents we use today help keep the sewers clean. A well-engineered system utilizes large pipes, as smooth as possible on the inside, to offer a minimum of resistance to flow. And, there are preventive measures many homeowners have found effective.

• Don't ask the drain-away system to carry out the garbage for you, unless you have a regular garbage disposer in the system. Keep the sink strainer in place, and don't let bits and hunks of waste go down the drain. Eventually they may combine with grease and with each other to produce serious blockage. Unfortunately, sewer stoppage caused by accumulations of this kind are usually pretty well along in the system, where they are hardest to get at.

• Take advantage of the worthwhile drain chemicals sold everywhere, as a means of forestalling trouble. Their highly caustic nature cuts grease and speeds the breakdown of solids. It really is a good idea to use these chemicals preventively, routinely, not merely when trouble arises.

• Now and then let the hot water run for several minutes, or dump successive teakettles full of boiling water down the drains. This softens congealed grease and solids, and gets them moving again.

• Never toss large objects into a toilet. Even if they do flush away, they are likely to get hung up on down the drain. Never, never put plastic wrappings, cellophane, vinyl bags, etc., in the toilet. Not even small scraps. These materials are slow to disintegrate in water (some of them may be non-biodegradable and will remain in solid form practically forever) and cause a great deal of drain and sewer trouble.

WHAT TO DO WHEN A DRAIN STOPS UP

To begin with, don't wait for it to stop up. At the first sign of a slowdown of any drain, do something about it while it is still a simple problem.

The first step, however, is to make sure you are working on the problem in the right place. It may be that you will first notice a slowdown in, for instance, a bathroom lavatory. There is a chance that the problem is somewhere farther down the line. Check the drains in other sinks and lavatories. If no other outlet is running slow, you can be fairly sure that the original offender is the one. However, if other drains are slow too, you can expect the trouble to be below the one that is *lowest on the system.*

There are various methods of attacking drain problems, and you can tell which is likely to work best by analyzing the trouble:

• If the slowdown builds up slowly, it is usually a sign that grease, soap solids, small particles of garbage, or in bathrooms, hair, are gradually building up inside the discharge pipes. These accumulations give way readily to drain chemicals or to flushing with boiling water.

• If the stoppage is sudden, it is often a sign that some single object has entered the system and blocked it. A plunger can usually be counted on to take care of impediments.

Important: Some drain chemicals carry a warning against use in drains that are completely stopped, because the chemical action doesn't have a chance to work through the stop-up. Break through a stubborn and complete stoppage with plunger or snake, before cleaning things up finally with the chemical. Since caustics are extremely strong, be careful when you use them. Wear rubber gloves if you think there is any chance that you might splash caustic-filled water on your hands. Try not to expose enameled fixtures to the action of the powder (particularly full strength), or it may eat away the porcelain. Work cautiously, to avoid splashing your skin or your clothing with caustic.

HOW TO WORK WITH A PLUNGER

Always remove the plug or stopper in a sink or lavatory when you work with the plunger. And, always work with the fixture at least half full of water. If the stoppage is not complete, i.e., if water runs out slowly, turn on a faucet to keep the water level up. This helps seal the edges of the bell-like end of the plunger and gives it more efficiency.

A plunger can be made to create pressure or vacuum, depending on how you work with it. To open a drain by forcing the foreign matter on through, place the plunger over the drain, positioning it carefully, and then jab it quickly down.

To lift the clogging material in the drain, in the hope that it can be loosened and brought up and out into the sink or lavatory, you must handle the plunger in a way that makes it produce a vacuum. To to this, gently push the bell down over the drain until it is completely compressed. Then jerk it sharply upward. Do this several times.

It is generally wiser to loosen a stoppage by lifting it loose in a vacuum than to force it on through under pressure. The reason is that the pressure may impact whatever it is that is clogging the drain, making its removal harder than before.

There is one additional factor in making a plunger work properly in a lavatory or bathtub. It involves the overflow opening which is always present in these fixtures and may also be found in some sinks. Since the opening is connected to the drain, it allows the pressure or the vacuum to escape, unless it is plugged while the plunger is in use. An easy way to plug an overflow is with a wet towel or washcloth wadded over the opening. Sometimes you can handle the wet towel with one hand and the plunger with the other, but it is better to enlist some help to handle the towel.

A little patience helps a lot when you work with a plunger. Keep at it until you get results before you become convinced that the plunger can't produce enough vacuum or pressure to work things loose. Even if it takes a while, curing a clogged drain with a plunger is easier than dismantling the trap or working with a plumber's snake or both.

When it's a toilet that's plugged up, the plunger is less effective than it is on sinks and lavatories. But it's worth a try. Rather than attempting to control pressure versus vacuum, simply fit the plunger into the toilet and jack it up and down rapidly a dozen or more times. If you get no results, you'll have to turn to the snake.

DISMANTLING A SINK TRAP

Many of the foul-ups in sinks, lavatories, laundry tubs, and other basin-type fixtures occur right in the trap, the "S-curve" in the system located directly beneath the bowl. Its basic purpose is to seal off the fixture from possible foul odors and gases that might come from the drainage and sewer system. The seal is formed by a pool of water which always stands in the bottom loop of the trap. The curves in the trap often collect hair, bits of paper, lint, and other debris. When the plunger won't blow the accumulation through or suck it out, you may have to take the trap apart.

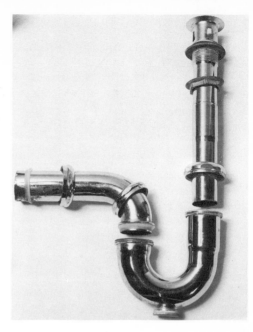

Most traps are composed of several pieces, to make installation easier and to facilitate clean-out. The top clamps into the sink opening, with a gasket. The straight tube slips into the U-curve and the nut tightens its gasket over the top of the U. The same type of joint occurs at the other end of the curve, and finally the trap gaskets into the discharge pipe. To unblock the drain, first try removing the small drain plug at the bottom. If that doesn't do it, loosen the nuts and remove the U. Finally, run a plumber's snake through the drain.

If the trap has a bottom plug, and you remove it, you can usually fish the clogging material out with a bent wire, until the drain runs free.

If the drain doesn't have a removable plug, you may have to dismantle it completely. The picture shows how a typical trap goes together—a series of slip joints, gaskets, and ring nuts. Nothing complicated about it. Use a pipe wrench to loosen the nuts. Cushion the chromium tubes with masking tape if you have to counter-wrench and might mar the finish and if the trap is in a conspicuous place. You'll spill a little water, a trapful, during this operation. Put a basin beneath the fixture to catch it.

Before you put a trap back together, check all the washers and gaskets to make sure they are worth putting back to work. If they are badly deteriorated, pick up replacements, as a means of forestalling the trouble that might come later as a result of their failure.

HOW A PLUMBER'S SNAKE WORKS

The typical plumber's snake you might buy at a hardware or plumbing supply store is about 6' long, plenty of length for the kind of probing the typical home repairman undertakes on his own. There are several different styles, operating on the same principle. A flexible shaft twists and threads its way through the fixtures and pipes, as you push on it while turning a crank-like handle to rotate the shaft.

One of the most useful styles has a tube at the business end, and there is a rounded right-angle bend in this tube. You can insert the bent end in a toilet or a disassembled trap and thus give the snake a good start in the right direction. One of the special advantages is that the bent tube protects the fixture from damage which might result from the contact of the rotating shaft.

A snake will follow any gentle bend in a plumbing system, and will make some pretty sharp turns in drainpipes that are 3″ or 4″ in diameter. However, if they come up against the dead end of a T, that's as far as they go. It is for this reason that well-engineered sewer systems take their turns gently, and are often provided with special cleanout openings in the vicinity of Ts.

Professional plumbers have longer versions of the snake, some of them driven with an electrical motor. With these models they can take over when the drain clog is beyond your reach.

In a stopped up toilet. A plumber's snake will follow the curves of a toilet without much trouble and ordinarily reach at least as far as the vertical drop, usually in the wall behind the fixture. All you must do is apply pressure on the flexible shaft and turn the handle. But first, pour enough water into the toilet to bring it well above the normal water level. Then, when your action breaks through the stoppage, the water will run out signalling your success.

If the water doesn't drain when you've snaked as far as the tool will reach, it means either that you have not reached and cut through the trouble, or that the snake is acting as a plug in the hole it has burrowed through. Seesaw the snake in and out for a foot or so, as a means of breaking up the deposits.

In the case of stoppage due to the accidental flushing of a diaper or other fabric, the hook will twist into the obstruction, sometimes without releasing the flow of water. But, when you pull the snake out, dragging the diaper with it, the water will run free.

In a lavatory or sink. It is ordinarily impossible to run a snake down through the drain hole in a sink or lavatory, because it reaches the trap and is stopped by the relatively sharp curves. Therefore, when a plunger fails to break loose the stoppage in a sink, and when you dismantle the trap without discovering the problem, you can run the snake in through the openings where the trap connects. This will dig loose any obstructions at least as far along the system as the point where the drain meets the vertical drop.

In a bathtub. Bathtub drains are usually designed so that the snake will work its way into the system through the regular drain, after you remove the stopper.

WHEN YOU CAN'T REACH THE PROBLEM

Most of the troubles with plugged drains occur within a few feet of the fixture, before it reaches the vertical lines. Once debris of most kinds gets that far, the force of gravity is much stronger than it is along gently sloping lines. It will usually carry problem-makers down with enough force to swing them around and along the next horizontal run.

Therefore, the next place to suspect when you can't get things draining is the basement where the drop levels off.

If you'll follow along the sewer drain line, you'll discover that every time it turns a corner and every time a new line joins it, there is a Y with a removable plug, or a T used as an

When drains block up farther down the line, look for cleanout plugs at angles in the system, and now and then along straight runs, as shown here. Unscrew the plugs so you can reach the trouble with a plumber's snake.

angle, with a plug screwed in the other end. You can chase down a serious lower-system foul-up by working from one plug to the next, driving a snake in, downstream. The length of the snake you use will depend on the length of the straight-away (which can be an entire side of the house in some cases), but it will undoubtedly be longer than the snake homeowners normally have.

For this, if for no other reason, it is not recommended that the typical home repairman involve himself with trouble-shooting in the big-pipe plumbing of sewer lines. The work is harder, the equipment is bulkier, the mess created is greater. Rent the equipment if you want to, but most of the time you'll be better off hiring a professional whenever you can't get yourself out of drain trouble with chemicals, the plunger, or the typical snake operated from the convenient vantage point of the fixture that won't drain.

10

WORKING WITH STANDARD
PLUMBING MATERIALS

IN ORDER TO CARRY plumbing maintenance beyond the relatively simple problems of faucets that won't shut off and drains
that won't drain, it is necessary to go into the methods of
working with pipes and fittings. The techniques used by
regular plumbers are not particularly difficult; the appropriate tools are not hard to handle. With a little practice and
an understanding of the possibilities and shortcomings of
plumbing materials, you can probably take care of most
small jobs of repair in your own plumbing system.

BASIC MATERIALS

There are three kinds of pipes and tubes commonly used in
standard residential plumbing. Galvanized iron pipe has been
pretty much the standard for many years, and you find it in
most older homes. It is the cheapest to buy but the most complicated to use, requiring several special tools.

Copper tubing costs more than iron pipe, but not so much
that price should be a deterrent in typical home maintenance
work. Copper is much easier to work with, completely within
the abilities of anyone who is at all handy. Because of ease

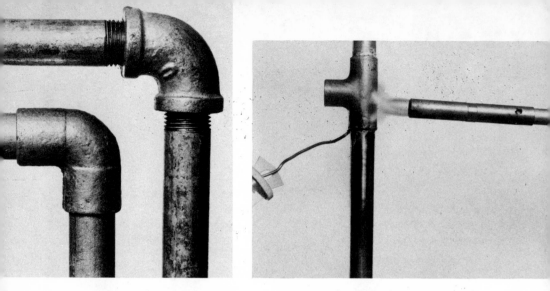

Galvanized iron pipe now comes in two forms. The old standard threaded variety continues. In addition, there is a specially engineered type of iron pipe that you can joint with solder, using a common household propane torch.

Copper tubing, much easier to work with than threaded iron pipe, can be soldered somewhat more easily than solderable iron pipe. Generally, application of heat to one side of a fitting will draw solder around and up into the joint.

Simplest of all to use is plastic tubing, which goes together with slip-joints, held tight with hose clamps. Basic tools are a handsaw and a screwdriver. Plastic is limited to cold-water runs.

and speed of handling, copper appears more and more often in recently built homes.

Plastic tubing is the third plumbing material. It is even easier to work with than copper, but it is restricted in use to cold water runs, and in some localities may even be restricted by building codes. Research continues on plastic, and the development of new materials will undoubtedly broaden the application of these handy, easy-to-use tubes.

122

WORKING WITH IRON PIPE

The basic iron pipe system involves threaded ends on pipes, and a variety of fittings into which the pipes are screwed. Pipe comes in a variety of standard lengths, including short "nipples" already threaded. However, when you need a non-standard length, you must cut the pipe and run threads on it. The job is simple enough, but the cutter, reamer, and thread-cutting dies are expensive. They can be rented, of course, and it is the policy of some retail outlets to loan tools to homeowners when they buy materials.

There is, also, a variation of iron pipe that can be joined with solder. The difference is that the pipe and fittings are made to more exacting tolerances, so that solder will work properly into the joints. Also the fittings are somewhat lighter. They will heat to solder-melting temperatures with reasonable torch time. Sizes are limited to $^{1}/_{2}''$, $^{3}/_{4}''$, and $1''$.

Since iron pipe is entirely inflexible, it must be carefully fitted into a series of straight runs, with corners limited to 90 and 45 degrees. Wherever two lengths of pipe come together, you use the fitting that meets the requirements of the situation: coupling, angle, T, cross, street L, reducer, etc. The pipes must be tightened with two pipe wrenches, one to grip the pipe, the other the fitting.

There is one additional and essential fitting required for threaded pipe: the union. It's a special method of joining two

It is possible to switch from iron to copper—or to plastic—for add-on plumbing. Shown here, typically, an iron pipe run from the right connects with a coupling. The other side of the coupling accepts a conversion fitting which screws into the coupling, but has "sweat joint" design at the other end, to accept a soldered copper tube. Conversion fittings come in straight, T, and other styles.

pipes together *without twisting the pipes*. This is necessary because of the fact that screwing a pipe into a fitting at one end would mean unscrewing it out of a fitting at its other end. The union overcomes this by providing a sort of "slip joint" in the pipe. You screw everything tight on both sides of the union, then tighten the union. (See photo.)

Although it is possible to make a continuing series of iron pipe joints without a union, it is sound plumbing practice — and it is easiest — to insert a union in every straight run, looking forward to the day when it may be necessary to take the line apart for repairs or additions.

Generally speaking, a homeowner is wise to have any iron pipe he needs for a repair job cut to length and threaded by a plumbing supply shop. This leaves only the matter of screwing the elements together. If the circumstance requires it, as it surely would fitting a single piece of pipe into the middle of a system, the length must include a union.

A joint in iron pipe should always be put together with pipe joint compound. This paste-like dope, available in tubes, lubricates the threads as you tighten them and also makes it somewhat easier to break a joint loose, if you ever have to take it apart later. Most important, however, the solids in the dope fill any voids in the joints and guard against leaks.

A key to working with threaded iron pipe is the "union." At top is a regular coupling. A pipe can be screwed into it from either end. However, when you start to screw one of those pipes into another fitting, you unscrew it at this end. The union (*bottom*) is a sort of slip-joint. Its two halves are screwed on the two pieces of pipe. Then, when the pipes have been twisted into their respective fittings, the collar nut of the union can be tightened.

When you make a joint in a threaded iron pipe, always tighten it completely, but don't put too much pressure on the wrenches or you may strip threads, especially when you're working with small pipe sizes. It is usually easy to tell when a pipe joint is tight. It seems to turn fairly easily, then suddenly comes up snug. This is due to a certain amount of "taper" in the threads as they are cut by a standard die, matching the taper in the threads of the fitting. When you feel the pipe and fitting come up snug, give the wrenches a good firm pull, wipe off the excess pipe dope, and that's it.

Measuring pipe. It is a little tricky to determine the length of pipe you need to reach between two fittings, because of the distance the pipe screws into the fitting. When you are replacing a pipe, it is fairly simple to remove it and measure it. When this is impossible, make the measurement from the *inside face* of one fitting to the inside face of the other. Then add on the screw distance. This is given in the following table.

Size of Pipe	Distance into Fitting
$1/8''$	$1/4''$
$1/4$	$3/8$
$3/8$	$3/8$
$1/2$	$1/2$
$3/4$	$1/2$
1	$9/16$
$1 1/4$	$5/8$
$1 1/2$	$5/8$

Remember, if you buy a piece of iron pipe that is to go between fittings, it must include a union, and the union must be included in the total length, not added afterwards.

Soldering iron pipe. A great many of the problems involved in threaded pipe and fittings disappear when you use iron pipe intended for assembly with soldered joints. All of the

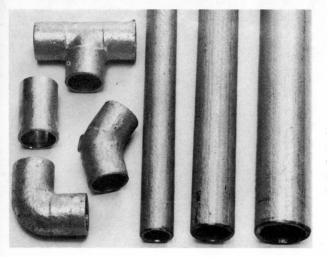

Solderable iron pipe comes in sizes up to 1", with typical couplings, T's, etc. Tolerances are narrowed and some gauges made slightly smaller, to facilitate soldered joints.

standard fittings are available, and as a consequence you can do any normal repair or replacement or addition with solder instead of pipe wrenches.

The soldering process with steel pipe is basically the same as for copper tubing (covered below), with a few modifications.

• Always use 50-50 solder with iron pipe, for maximum strength combined with meltability and technical performance.

• Brush-on type of liquid flux flows deep into the joints.

• You can speed up the job by using a larger blow-torch nozzle for the propane torch. It burns more gas than the smaller nozzle, but there is some saving in an on-off lever which cuts the flame down to pilot size when it isn't in active use.

• The mass of the fittings in solder type iron pipe has been reduced so much that they heat more readily than the pipe itself. For that reason, most of the heat must be directed at the pipe, rather than at the fittings.

With the 1" pipe size, it is not enough to apply the heat to one point only, counting on conductivity of the metal to carry it all around the joint. You must, instead, work slowly around the joint, heating and flowing in solder as you go. In cases where you cannot reach all sides, leave both ends of a run free, so you can rotate the entire assembly as you work joint by joint. Finally, finish off the end joints.

As with copper tubing, the solder "follows the heat," and you must always heat the iron hot enough to melt the solder, never letting the heat from the torch do the melting.

When the pipe and fittings are both clean, apply a brushful of professional tinner's fluid as a flux. Clean metal and proper fluxing are the two most critical phases in soldering iron pipes.

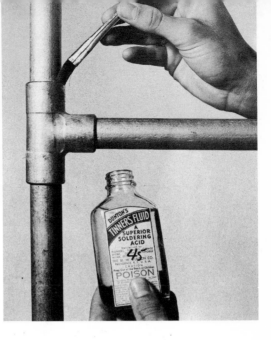

It is important to direct the heat from the torch toward both the pipe and the fitting until melting temperature is reached. Keep the torch on the fitting, so that the "solder follows heat" principle will bleed solder into the joint. Be sure the metal is hot enough to melt the solder; don't let the torch melt it.

Although the new Bernz tip can handle iron pipe, you'll find the job a little faster with the professional torch tip (left). It has the advantage of an on-off lever. Depress it for full heat. Save gas by letting it drop back to pilot flame between actual applications.

WORKING WITH COPPER TUBING

Copper tubing comes in two weights, a heavy (type K) which you should use underground, and a light (type L) which is plenty rugged enough for use in residential plumbing. There are two basic alloys, a stiff metal, and one that is quite soft and easy to bend. Copper is simple to work with, for several reasons.

• It's flexible. Even the rigid alloys can be made to undulate through somewhat irregular passages. Of course, the soft, flexible tubing will wind through a maze of openings.

• Copper tubing has no threads. In regular, routine runs, the tube slips snugly into its fittings and is sealed tight by means of solder. Although soldering may be less familiar to many home handymen than threads, it is an easy process to master.

• There is no need for unions, since the tubes do not have to be twisted to thread them together. Even when circumstances require the use of threaded fittings (see below), the job can be handled with a "flare" fitting, which involves turning a collar, not the tube.

• Copper tubing is lighter, easier to work with, taking up less space, requiring smaller holes through studs and joists.

Which tube to use. It is the best practice to use the rigid tubing whenever possible. For horizontal runs it is just about imperative, since the more flexible alloy will sag, making it impossible to drain the system when necessary, and making it difficult to maintain definite drain pitches. The flexible tubing, however, is a worksaver on vertical runs, for it can often be "snaked" up through walls in a way that would be impossible with a more rigid material.

Cutting and handling. Copper tube is easy to cut and to join. For a few dollars you can buy a cutter which includes a reamer. The torch you use is the common little propane model every hardware store sells, although you might want a blow torch head for the small tank or even a professional size outfit if you have to work with the heavy tube (type M) used for waste lines.

These are the steps involved in copper tube joinery:

1. Cut the length required, using the regular cutter or a hacksaw. With the saw, you may want to improvise a "bench hook" such as the one shown in the photo, to make square cuts simpler. Be sure to include the space taken up by fittings when you compute lengths. It is simple to do this, because you can slip a fitting on for measurement, a trick that is difficult with threaded iron pipe.

2. Ream the "burr" from the inside of the pipe. The cutter has a sharp-edged V for the job. If you saw the tube, you can remove the burr with a rat-tail file. It is important to do this, because the jagged edge cuts down on the flow of water and may impede normal movement through the tube of any chance solids.

Cut copper tubing either of two ways. A special cutting tool with a hardened steel wheel (*left*) cuts as you swing the tool around and around the tube, gradually tightening the handle. Just as easy is a hacksaw (*right*), used with the benchhook shown here. Just nail a scrap of wood on top and bottom of a piece of 1 x 6 or plywood. Precut a slot in the piece of wood, lined up carefully with a square, as a guide when you saw.

3. Burnish the metal shiny bright with steel wool, both on the *outside* of the tube and the *inside* of the fitting involved.

4. Rub a coating of paste-type solder flux on the tube. Insert it in the fitting and twist it, to distribute flux over both surfaces.

5. Apply the torch slightly more to the fitting than to the tube. Heat the assembly *hot enough to melt the solder.* Do not let the flame from the torch melt it. But be careful not to heat the joint too much, or you may burn the flux and you'll have to start all over again with steel wool.

6. If the joint is properly heated, the solder will flow instantly around the joint and be drawn inside the fitting by capillary action. Remember that the solder will "follow the heat." Be sure to keep the copper hot enough to melt solder *ahead* of the point where you are applying the solder.

7. When the joint is complete but before it cools, wipe it smooth and neat with a rag — if you are interested in appearances.

If you don't want to bother with a torch, or if you are working in a location where the flame might present a fire hazard,

In either case, you should ream the inside of the pipe smooth, so the water can run free. Otherwise, snaggles stimulate deposits that effectively reduce the diameter of the pipe.

Use steel wool to burnish the tube bright before you slip it into the fitting. Also burnish the inside of the fitting. Then, flux and solder will flow into the joint, for a strong, tight job.

You'll find two types of fittings. The cast style (*left*) takes a little more heat to joint. The stamped style is easier for most home handymen to handle.

a good many of the joining operations in *soft* copper tubing are possible with "flare fittings." The joint involves flaring out the end of the tube, forming a flange. A nut slipped over the tube seats around the flange, then threads on the other half of the fitting, drawing the flange tight against a conical seat. This type of a fitting is often used to connect copper tubing to a plumbing fixture.

Another type of connection you may encounter is the "squeeze fitting" used on hard tube. This also involves threads, but instead of a flange, there is a double-tapered collar that slides on the tube. When you make the connection, the collar is forced by a nut into a seat, making a tight seal. This sort of connection is quite commonly used to connect tube lines to modern faucets.

A "flare" connection with soft copper tube (it won't work on hard tube) is made with a flare tool (*left*) which puts a little "mushroom" on the end of the tube. The flared end fits over the beveled end of a flare fitting, held tight by means of a collar nut. This type of fitting is often used where copper joints faucets or fixtures, because it is easy to disconnect.

A third type of fitting found on copper systems and quite often at fixture connections in iron pipe systems is the "squeeze fitting." It involves a small double-cone collar which is wedged into the opening under pressure from the hex nut. Squeezing against the tube and the fitting, it provides a leak-tight joint that is easy to dis-assemble.

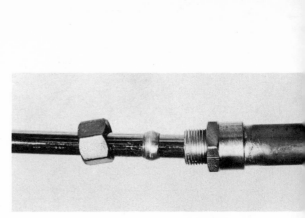

Tube fittings involving threads, in a copper system, always have hex nuts. You can work them with a Crescent wrench, and there is no need for a pipe wrench.

Bending copper tube. When the situation permits, you can often save time and work if you make corners in copper tubing by bending it, using the soft tube, of course. Although you can gently work a bend into the tube with your hands, or by pulling it around your knee, the best way to do it is with a short length of coil spring that slips inside and prevents the tube from collapsing. Plumbing outlets sell coils for this purpose, and they are a worthwhile investment if you do much bending.

WORKING WITH PLASTIC TUBING

Plastic tubing, like copper, comes in a relatively stiff form as well as one that is relatively flexible. Soft plastic comes in coils. It is made of a plastic such as polyethylene or poly-propylene, extremely resistant to chemicals, very elastic. A more recent plastic tube, more accurately called pipe, is of polyvinyl chloride. It is quite rigid and is sold in lengths, rather than coils. The PVC variety is stiff enough for hori-zontal runs, with reasonable support. It cannot be used in freezing situations, whereas the flexible material withstands freezing without any damage.

The biggest difference between the two is in methods of joinery. The PVC pipe is the easiest of all plumbing mate-rials to join—metal or plastic. The pipe slips snugly into PVC fittings. You flood the joint with a solvent which softens and partially dissolves the plastic. Then it hardens and the resulting joint is a "plastic weld," as strong as the original material and entirely leakproof.

The major advantages of soft plastic tubing are lightness and flexibility, plus an ease of handling that is barely more complicated than woodworking. The tube is easy to cut with a handsaw. Just remove the burr with a sharp knife. You make joints by slipping tubing over fittings and locking them tight with a hose clamp that tightens with a screwdriver.

Plastic tube shares with soft copper the disadvantage of sagging on horizontal runs. You can overcome this, however, by laying the tube along a "shelf" of 1 x 4 boards. Or, support it at close intervals with hangers.

All of the common fittings are available for use with both kinds of plastic, including conversion pieces that screw into iron pipe fittings, with provision for standard hose-clamp or solvent-weld attachment to the other end. This makes it easy to use plastic for replacements in an iron pipe system.

Despite the natural flexibility of plastic tubing, you cannot bend it into as tight an angle as is possible with soft copper. Heating the tubing helps, but the safest and best way to turn sharp corners is with an L or T.

11

HOW TO HANDLE TROUBLES
IN PLUMBING LINES

PROBLEMS DIRECTLY RELATED to the plumbing, not the fixtures, range from damaging flooding to bothersome noises. Many of them can be handled with routine tools and methods, covered in preceding chapters. Some require new techniques.

HOW TO THAW FROZEN PIPES

Plumbing that freezes presents two problems: first, thawing the pipes; second, keeping the freeze-up from happening again. A pipe that freezes is always one that is isolated in some way from the heated part of the house. It may be in a basement. It may be in an outside wall. Very often it is at floor level, where a plumbing run makes its turn upward toward a bath. *Almost always it is a pipe that is not protected by insulation.* Correcting the problem is not difficult, although it may involve some time-consuming carpentry. But first, thaw the pipe.

The simplest, quickest, safest way to thaw a pipe is with a heating cable. You can buy one at most hardware stores, a length of insulated resistance wire—sometimes a loop—that heats electrically, for the same reason that a hot plate gets

135

hot. You wrap the cable around the frozen pipe and plug it in. It doesn't take long for the ice to melt.

There are other methods. An electric iron works. So does a heating pad. You can wrap a pipe with heavy cloth and pour boiling water on the cloth. If—and only if—the pipe is entirely in the clear, well away from potentially flammable materials, you can use a propane torch. Don't let it get too hot. If the pipe feels warm to your hand, that's good enough. You can count on the heat traveling along the pipe for a considerable distance, particularly if it's copper plumbing.

The first thing to do when you turn on a faucet and nothing happens—and the weather is such that freezing seems likely—is to try to find the place where the pipe is frozen. Start at the end of the run and open faucets one by one, working back toward the beginning of the run. If you open a faucet and it works, you know the freeze-up is somewhere between that faucet and the last one you checked that didn't work.

Close the functioning faucet, but open the one that doesn't work. You do this so that water can move through the line when the ice starts to melt. Moving water will, of course, help the melting operation. Meanwhile, the faucet starts to run and you know you've done the job.

Start the melting operation at or near the faucet and gradually work back along the line. You can tell when you reach the frozen section of pipe, because it takes longer to turn warm on account of the ice. It is particularly important to start at the faucet, and it is vitally important to *leave the faucet open* if you are thawing with a torch. Otherwise, you could easily create enough steam pressure to damage the system.

What if the frozen pipe is behind a wall? Try a heat lamp, or a photoflood in a reflector, aimed at the wall, far enough away to avoid scorching the paint or paper. Usually the heat will penetrate the plaster or paneling and raise temperatures inside the wall to thawing level. Sometimes the heat lamp can be positioned in a crawlspace or basement so that its heat is carried up the stud space by convection, gradually melting a considerable length of frozen pipe.

To avoid future freezing. If that pipe had not been isolated from the heated part of the house, it would not have frozen. The trick, then, is to put insulation between it and the cold, or to devise a means of conserving the heat in the pipe, to keep it from freezing.

When pipes run in the open, it is simple to encase them with insulating material. The insulation comes in different forms. Some is in strips that you wrap spirally around the pipe. Some is molded in two halves to fit around the pipe, held there by means of metal strips. One molded plastic type is full-form, with a slit to let it slip over the pipe.

In some situations, however, it is easier to insulate the space through which the pipe runs than to insulate the pipe itself. It isn't usually necessary to do a complete job of insulation, as long as you provide a blanket *between the pipe and the outside cold.* For example, a strip of glass or mineral wool bat between the pipe and the outside wall sheathing may be enough to prevent freezing. If the pipe happens to ride close to that outside wall, try to devise a means of springing and holding it away, to make room for insulation.

Again the problem arises: What if the pipe is inside a wall? The most certain solution is to open the wall, examine the situation to find out what causes the freezing, and remedy it. You may find that the insulation in the wall, if any, is actually between the pipes and the heat. You may find a vertical run that has bowed outward, putting some of its length in actual contact with freezing-cold exterior sheathing. Whatever you find, there is work involved cutting open the wall and repairing it. You may be able to get by with less work.

• Try opening a small hole in the wall and pouring it full of expanded-mica insulation. You can't be sure this will help, but if the pipe happens to be well away from the outside of the wall, the mica will sift in behind it and cut down the heat loss. On the other hand, if the pipe happens to be close to the outside of the wall the small amount of insulation between it and the cold may not be enough. If it freezes again, open the wall.

• How about a little preventive maintenance? Assume, for

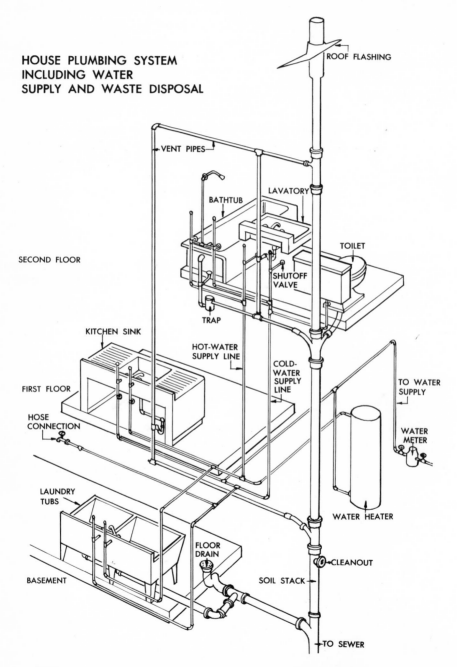

HOUSE PLUMBING SYSTEM
INCLUDING WATER
SUPPLY AND WASTE DISPOSAL

ROOF FLASHING

VENT PIPES

BATHTUB

LAVATORY

TOILET

SECOND FLOOR

SHUTOFF
VALVE

TRAP

KITCHEN SINK

HOT-WATER
SUPPLY LINE

COLD-
WATER
SUPPLY
LINE

TO WATER
SUPPLY

FIRST FLOOR

HOSE
CONNECTION

WATER
METER

LAUNDRY
TUBS

WATER HEATER

FLOOR
DRAIN

CLEANOUT

BASEMENT

SOIL STACK

TO SEWER

138

example, that the pipe in a powder room wall freezes. On a very, very cold night, the same heat lamp that would thaw a frozen pipe would also keep the pipe from freezing. In some cases, nothing more complex or expensive than a 100-watt light bulb fairly close to the wall will hold temperatures above freezing. In countless homes, merely leaving the door of that powder room open at night will allow enough extra heat to circulate so that nothing freezes.

You may be able to save yourself a lot of trouble if you take some precautions on those winter nights when your thermometer promises trouble.

Freezing sillcocks. One place where freezing is an ever-present wintertime danger is in sillcocks, where you hook on a garden hose. Normally, these cocks are installed with a shutoff valve inside the wall. Come winter, shut off the valve and untwist a little knurled knob, letting the water drain. Okay until spring. But, if you want to use the water during those not-so-cold days in winter (for instance, to hose highway snow-control salt off your car) it's a nuisance to go through the routine of opening the sillcock and closing it again. You can replace sillcocks with a special "long-shank" variety which goes through the wall. It has the knob and the nozzle outside, but shuts off the water at a point safely inside.

WHAT IF A PIPE SPRINGS A LEAK?

A pipe may freeze and crack open. Or, for such reasons as corrosion, physical damage, the house settling, etc., a pipe starts to leak. Investigate these possibilities:

• If *iron* pipe leaks at a joint, and if there is a union, loosen the union and tighten the pipe into the leaking joint. To be even more certain of results, turn off the water and take the leaking joint apart. Dry the threads. Apply a good smear of pipe dope and put it back together.

• If there is no union, get out the hacksaw and cut the pipe in two. Now you can unscrew it. Make the cut near the leak, and it may be that you can put things back together again with a *union* and a short, inexpensive nipple.

• If the leak is not at a joint, but rather in the pipe itself, take it apart and appraise the situation. Is the entire length of pipe likely to be going bad? Should it be replaced entirely? Is the leak due to local damage? Would it be a worthwhile saving to cut out the damaged part and replace it only? Is the situation such that you could replace the pipe with a length of plastic pipe or tube?

• If a joint in *copper tubing* springs a leak, drain the line, then put the torch to the joint, with some flux and solder. You may be able to flow things back together. However, in some cases the solder may refuse to fill in the rupture, the opening through which the joint is leaking. If that happens, heat the joint, take it apart, clean it the way you would any copper connection, and resolder it. (It is usually possible to spring copper tube enough to take joints apart, unless the run is short, in which case you may have to cut the tube in two.)

• If a leak is in the run of tubing, cut out the damaged length and replace it with a short piece and two couplings, unless the total length is so short that this would be a waste of time.

• In some cases a defective length of copper may be so short or situated in such a manner that you can't remove it in one piece. You therefore can't replace it in one piece, either. When you run into this problem, hacksaw the tube out. Replace it with a length which includes a flare fitting. Solder the ends into their fittings. Then tighten the flare nut.

Patching plumbing. Although it is usually wisest to replace a defective plumbing component entirely, there are times when it may be quicker, easier, more economical, and technically okay to use patching methods.

Plumbing shops and some hardware stores sell a variety of clamp-on devices in sizes to fit standard piping. In combination with rubber gasket material, they cover small cracks or rust-throughs. Also, there are epoxy-and-fiberglass systems. Many homeowners consider such repairs to be temporary, although they may never get around to making permanent repairs, once the leak dries up.

Leaks on the discharge side of plumbing do not have to resist the pressure of the water mains. You can usually take care of them with epoxy patching compounds. If a serious break occurs in the heavy plumbing at the lower end of drains, put in an emergency call to the plumber, whose heavier equipment and specialized materials are needed for such work.

Owing to the nuisance-plus-damage of leaking plumbing systems, it is a good idea to invest in a few sizes of clamp-ons and gaskets. They go on quickly, before the place gets too badly deluged. And they ordinarily do not require that you drain the system. Just shut off the water while you clamp the gadget on the pipe.

PIPES THAT DRIP

On the other side of the calendar from pipes that freeze are pipes that drip during the humid summer months. The reason is condensation of moisture on the cold surfaces of the pipes; you never get the problem with hot water lines.

To prevent the dripping, simply keep the air away from the pipes. An easy way to do it is with an insulating, self-sticking tape sold for the purpose. Pick a time when the pipes are dry (any fairly cool day when humidity is low) and spiral-wrap the pipes with the tape. If the condensation is severe, work the tape as well as possible around valves and other fittings to cover exposed metal.

In some cases, the pipe that sweats is the same one that is exposed to possible freezing. In such cases, you can do two jobs at once by encasing the pipes in the insulating material intended for protection from freeze-ups. It will double most efficiently as an anti-drip covering.

PIPES THAT SQUEAK, RATTLE, AND BANG

The water moving through a houseful of tubes and pipes under pressure is an active force. When the force is blocked, shunted in a different direction, squeezed into smaller space, and otherwise frustrated, it complains. Noisily. There are different kinds of noises, and they are silenced in different ways.

Water hammer is the name given to the crashing bang you sometimes hear when you turn off a faucet quickly. It is caused by the fact that the water, coursing through the pipes, is suddenly brought up short. Since water is just about incompressible (it's a mighty solid liquid), it crashes to a stop.

In modern plumbing, this is prevented almost completely by means of one or more air cushions in the system. The cushions are formed by inserting vertical "dead end" pipes in the system. These pipes are full of air, and they are sealed airtight. When you turn off a faucet suddenly, the water expends its energy *compressing* those cushions of air. When the momentum of the water has been overcome, the compressed air pushes everything quietly back into place.

If you are equipped to handle minor plumbing projects, you can install air suctions in your system. All it requires is a T in the line. Install a riser in the side of the T, pointing straight up. Cap off the riser. Ideally, it should be about 3′ long. It's a good idea to make the cushion of a pipe or tube larger than the line, by inserting a reducer, used as an "expander," in the T. The best place for air cushions is at the *high point* of a plumbing run, if possible. Located there, it will drain when you drain the run — if it should by chance leak air and gradually fill with water. (Air cushions are available commercially, too.)

Squeaking pipes are always on hot water runs, most especially in hot water heating systems. They are caused by expansion and contraction of the pipe or tube being heated by water coming from the heater. As it expands, the pipe thrusts through hangers or slings, and the friction makes the noise.

Don't try to lick this noise simply by tightening the hangers. Instead, loosen them slightly, insert a little fiberglass or rock wool insulation in the opening, then tighten them again. This material forms a sort of slippery cushion for the pipes to ride through, and the squeaking disappears.

Angle bang is usually not as loud as water hammer, and may not be consistent. It is caused by water making a sharp (90 degree) turn when a faucet is opened suddenly. Many modern automatic appliances have solenoid-operated valves that go from closed to wide open almost instantly. The water moves instantly, and the impact at a corner may cause the plumbing to vibrate and bang against its mounting. Chase down the noise to find where it is happening, and either cushion the hangers to absorb the shock, or deliberately block any motion by nailing up short lengths of 2 x 4 pressed hard and tight against elbows to oppose the action of the water. This prevents the pipe from banging by eliminating its chance to travel.

The sudden forward movement or sudden stopping of water when valves open or close quickly may also cause slightly sagging pipes to slap against the joists they hang from. Correct this by installing more hangers. Make sure existing hangers are not loose. This will eliminate the vibration that makes pipe chatter.

Faucet stutter occurs sometimes when you open a faucet only part way, and it vibrates noisily. The reason is a faucet washer loose on the spindle. Remove the spindle (see faucet maintenance in Chapter 8) and tighten the screw which fastens the washer in place. If the washer is worn or seriously compressed out of shape, replace it. The problem of faucet stutter comes up most often in sillcocks and other utility outlets.

ADDING A NEW PLUMBING RUN

It is not always necessary to dismantle a section of plumbing in order to branch off or add on a new run, even if it must originate right in the middle of a pipe. At a plumbing shop, buy an adapter that clamps around an existing pipe. To install it, clamp the adapter in place with the gasketing material that comes with it. At this point, turn off the water, and drill a hole through the pipe, inserting the drill bit into the opening in the adapter. Fasten on the new pipe, and the new run is functioning.

If the new line can be extended from an existing elbow, and if there is a properly located union to enable you to unscrew the fitting (or if you are working with soldered joints), you can replace the elbow with a T, a very simple job that gives you a connecting point. In fact, thoughtful plumbing contractors often foresee the chance of an addition at certain points and deliberately use a T with a plug instead of an elbow. When this is the case, you merely remove the plug and hook on the new line.

HEATING SYSTEMS
AND FIREPLACES

DESPITE THE EXTREME IMPORTANCE of the heating plant in the home, its operation is actually quite simple. There are few things that can go wrong, and they fall into two sharply divided categories: the things you can and should take care of yourself and the things you shouldn't touch, but rather put on a warm sweater and call the service man. Fireplace troubles are rarely urgent, since the fireplace is rarely a vital source of heat, but it can cause dangerous situations.

TODAY'S HEATING SYSTEMS

Heating systems are categorized by the fuels they use and the methods by which the heat is delivered from its source to parts of the house where it is needed. Many types of controls and mechanisms, such as the thermostat, are common to all of the systems.

Fuels for heating. The fuels most used for residential heating today are oil, gas, and electricity, with coal still burned in some older houses.

Electricity is the simplest of the three, since the power company delivers energy to the house, ready to be converted into heat. In some cases, when the heat load is not great, the electricity merely utilizes resistance heating elements located in radiant heat units. In other systems, electrical heat is used in furnaces, much the same as gas or oil.

Gas and oil must be converted into energy through combustion in a furnace. Gas, in vapor form, is flammable as it arrives through its copper tubes ready to burn. Oil arrives in liquid form, relatively unflammable until it is forced through a nozzle, converting it to a mist which is sprayed over an electrical igniter.

Delivery systems for heat. Except for the direct use of electricity in resistance coils in radiant units (and the occasional use of baseboard, in-the-wall, and other units burning gas), the heat must be piped to the rooms of the house from a furnace. The vehicle for this heat transmission is usually water or air, although steam is still used in some older dwellings.

Water is heated as it passes through coils exposed to the heat in the furnace, and is then pumped through pipes to radiators in the rooms, where it transfers its heat to the air and returns to the furnace. The circulation is continuous as long as there is need for heat. The most common type of heat transfer is through baseboard radiators usually located along outside walls. When the heating plant is properly engineered, there are enough lineal feet of radiator to provide a curtain of warm air between the cold outside and the rooms inside. In a few modern versions, there may be motor-driven fans to speed the movement of air through the radiators.

Air, when it is the heat transporter, is warmed passing over fins in the furnace, and blown through ducts to outlets throughout the house. It returns to the furnace through another set of ducts. Thus, most of the air in the house moves continuously through the duct system when it is in operation. This makes it possible and sensible to filter the air and control its humidity, and more and more heating plants these days include filters and humidity control units. And cooling units.

Steam systems work much the same as hot water, except that the extra heat of steam is transferred into the room air via smaller, more concentrated radiators.

HOW TO AVOID HEATING PLANT TROUBLES

Because the failure of a heating plant can result in such disasters as frozen pipes, the thing to do is to avoid trouble in the first place. Although this is close to impossible, it is fairly easy to make sure that any troubles you have will be easy and quick to fix before the consequences of failure become anything greater than a little temporary discomfort.

The secret of dependable, trouble-free functioning, regardless of fuel, is a reliable annual checkup. Normally, you'll get a communication from your oil dealer sometime during the off-season, suggesting that he come in to clean, adjust, and check out the furnance before the wintertime need for heat arrives. If you burn gas, the gas company may make the same suggestion. Failing a contact from him, call him yourself. In any case, set a time when you'll be home and make friends with the service man. Watch him as he works. Ask him what he is doing and why. Find out those things *in your individual heating system* that may need attention. Find out where switches and controls and oil holes are. Listen to the noises the furnace makes when he has it working to his satisfaction, so you'll be alerted by any strange sounds that you may hear during the winter.

Most important of all, ask him to help you make a checklist of the things you should do during the winter, to keep the system in working order. Again, this list will pertain to *your own heating plant,* and this is important, because while furnaces themselves may be identical in many houses, the rest of the system may have a personality of its own, varying from house to house.

HOW TO CHECK HEATING EFFICIENCY

Not all furnace failure is in the catastrophic category. The furnace doesn't have to go dead to indicate that repairs and adjustments may be necessary. Heating experts have devised a series of simple tests through which you can ferret out sub-par performance. The following circumstances should be investigated and remedied.

Uniformity of heat. The difference between high and low as the heating system cycles on and off is easy to check by placing a good thermometer on a card table or equivalent in the middle of the room. Observe the coldest temperature registered by the thermometer, and the highest. An excellent system will show a difference of two degrees or less. If the difference is four or five degrees, you suffer not only lack of comfort but higher than necessary operating costs, since the furnace must work hard, repeatedly, to bring that temperature back up.

The fault may lie with the thermostat, or it may lie with the on-off phasing switches at the furnace. Begin by checking the thermostats. Be sure the contacts are clean, free of any particles of dust that may interfere with the on-off function. (Modern thermostats with enclosed mercury switches cannot be thrown out of kilter by dirt.)

Location of the thermostat is important, and if you do not get the heating performance you deserve, you may have to move it. Basically, the thermostat should be on an inside wall in the living room or another center-of-living area. *The room on the other side of the wall should not be an unheated space.* The thermostat should not be sheltered from normal air movement by such things as draperies, wall hangings, books, pictures, large pieces of furniture, etc. Be sure heat-producing objects such as lamps, television sets, etc., are not located closely enough to the thermostat to influence its opinion as to whether the room is warm or cold. It should not be located on a wall through which heating pipes or ducts — or a chimney — pass. The sun should not shine on it, nor should the rays of the sun be reflected on it from a bright white wall, a mirror, a window, or other highly reflective surface.

If you consider it necessary to move a thermostat, the job is simple enough. Except for electrical heating systems which usually operate thermostats on full voltage, the electricity used for communication between the thermostat and the furnace is 24-volt or lower, representing no danger in handling. It comes from the transformer. To prevent possible damage to the mechanism, however, be sure to disconnect the wires from the transformer before you work on the system.

Dismount the thermostat and cut a same size hole in the wall where the new location is to be. Thread wires from this location to a point where they can connect with original wiring. The light gauge wire is simple to conceal, back of moldings along the floor, if you find it difficult to "snake" them through the wall.

It is easy to figure an ideal spot for a thermostat if you realize that it should be in the middle of an entirely typical situation, in a place where you would expect the temperature of the air to typify that of the whole place, and in a place where that air can circulate freely by.

It might be a good idea to consider installing *a new thermostat* if the one you have is very old. And it might be a good idea to enlist the advice of your heating fuel supplier about this. Some of the best modern thermostats are far quicker in their reaction to temperature changes than the older models, utilizing the extra stimulus of tiny heating elements within the mechanism.

Another feature that will put your heating system on a more even rotation is an outdoor thermostat, which anticipates changes in the outdoor temperature and forewarns the heating system that it has a hard job ahead, or maybe a breathing spell. Thus alerted, the furnace and its controls avoid overheating in the face of rising temperatures, or slacking off without realizing that the outdoor thermometer is falling. The actual step-by-step of installing such a device depends on the exact situation in your house, but it involves nothing more than running wires and fastening the thermostat under the eaves, as recommended by the manufacturer.

Variation room to room. To check whether the heating plant is delivering heat uniformly (or with *desired* variations) to the various rooms of the house, you need two thermometers.

And, they must read identically or you must allow for differences. Place one thermometer in the "base" room and leave it there. Take the other to the other rooms, one by one, and note the variation from the "base" room.

You can use this procedure to standardize heat, as you might want to do between living, dining, and family rooms. Or, you can use it to produce deliberate non-uniformity, as you might want between living room and game room, or between the nursery and master bedroom.

In order to get the desired variations or eliminate those you don't want, you may only have to adjust radiators or registers. Sometimes cutting down the heat delivered to a too-warm room will apportion more to a too-cool room. Closing down dampers or valves in lines delivering heat to a room that is too warm will, of course, reduce its temperature.

Sometimes you may find that a room is colder than you want it to be because it is at the end of a relatively long run. You can usually correct this by insulating or double-insulating the extra long run, so that it doesn't waste its heat along the way. This is particularly important if the run passes through unheated crawlspace or along an outside wall.

When differences in temperature from one room to another are great, and when adjustments in the delivery system won't solve the problem, you may need a two-zone, two-thermostat setup. This will enable you to use one thermostat setting for one "zone" and another for a different "zone." It may be best for you to hand this problem over to a heating contractor, since some major ductwork or tubework will quite likely be involved.

Floor-to-ceiling differences. The heating industry has set up some arbitrary but functional figures for this factor in heat comfort. The standard is that there should be no more than *one degree* for each ten degrees difference in temperature between the temperature outdoors and the temperature in your house.

The reason why a greater difference in floor-to-ceiling temperature may exist is that warm air rises. If there is no circulation of the air, it will eventually stabilize with the warm air at the ceiling and the cold air at the floor, and the difference may be extreme. If the air is "stirred up," however, it mixes hot with cold and evens out at a uniform average.

That is why an improvement in convection (normal circulation of air as warm air rises, then falls as it cools or is driven down by warmer air) will correct the ceiling-floor discrepancy. If you have hot water heat, ordinarily not provided with a mechanical means of moving the air, you can usually improve air circulation by vacuuming or blowing any accumulated dust from the radiators, clearing them for air movement. Also, be sure that movement of air up from baseboard radiators is not blocked by draperies, furniture, etc.

When floor-ceiling variations are too great in a house with warm air heat, the reason is usually too long an "off" period in an on-off cycling. The ideal solution to this is, of course, continuous air circulation; CAC is, in fact, the ideal warm air setup for many reasons. Lacking CAC facilities, you can shorten the on-off cycle at the furnace by adjusting controls that turn the fan on and off, unless they are already set as "close" as possible.

Improvement of air circulation helps solve a related problem: floors that are too cold. If your thermometer reads 65 degrees or colder when it is lying on the floor or carpet, you need some correction. This is particularly true if children play on the floor. Cold floors are, naturally, always those floors over an unheated basement, crawlspaces, etc. In the interest of comfort and fuel savings, you may want to insulate the floors. This is easy to do, using foam "planks" that fit up between floor joists, held by mastic or wooden strips nailed to the joists below the insulation. The job can be done, too, with rock wool or fiberglass bats stapled up between the floor joists.

A GENERAL FALL-OFF IN PERFORMANCE

Sometimes you may notice that the furnace seems to be working harder, more continuously, but the house or some rooms in the house aren't warm enough. This is most often caused by interference with heat delivery in the pipe system (hot water) or duct system (warm air), and the interference most always means this:

Warm air. The filters need cleaning or replacing. Some furnaces have filters you can rinse clean; others must be replaced. When they are dirt-clogged, they block the passage of air and no matter how hot and how long the furnace burns, it cannot deliver enough heat. Check your filters often, more often than the furnace manual suggests.

Hot water. The radiators need bleeding. Air often accumulates in the hot water system, reducing the effective size of the passages the water goes through and lowering the amount of hot water working through the system. In some cases a circuit may be blocked entirely, leaving radiators in some rooms cold.

The remedy is simple. At the end of each radiator, near the top, opposite the shutoff valve you'll find a small bleeder valve. It looks like some form of a screw-in plug with a slot for a screwdriver or a hex-head for a tiny wrench or key. Sometimes it has the appearance of a miniature faucet. If you unscrew this valve, you'll hear air hissing as it escapes. Eventually the air will all be discharged and water will come out, so be prepared with a cup or pan to catch it. Move from one radiator to another along the run, letting the air escape. This should be done regularly to all radiators at the beginning of each heating season and during the season whenever you find a radiator standing cold, or a room that is notably less warm than it should be.

Malfunctioning pump. The water in a hot water system is moved through the pipes and radiators by means of a centrifugal pump, driven noiselessly by an electric motor. Sometimes, at the end of an off period, most particularly at the end of the summer, the system may ask for heat, but the pump doesn't function. The reason, 99 times out of 100, is a piece of dirt or rust in the pump. It isn't much of an impediment, but it keeps the pump from starting. The motor, equipped with an overload disconnect, clicks off. You would hardly know that all this happened except that the radiators don't warm up.

Check it out by having someone turn the thermostat to the heat-requesting position *while you observe the pump.* You'll hear the "on" click. You'll see the pump motor give a little futile heave. Then you'll hear the overload click things off.

Turn the thermostat back down. Study the construction of the pump and motor to find out how the motor dismounts from the rest of the mechanism, through some sort of flange or collar held by two or four nuts or bolts. Unfasten the motor and you'll find that there is a coil spring in the drive mechanism put there to absorb shocks and cut down noise. The spring will give enough slack so you can put a pair of pliers on the shaft and give it a few jiggles and turns, to break loose the dirt that is keeping the pump from turning. Put things back together again, and from now on the pump should be okay.

Is it a good idea to drain the system, to get rid of such dirt particles? *No, it is not.* You won't get rid of many, if any. Meanwhile, the new water will introduce still more elements of corrosion and oxidation, and you'll end up with added dirt and more chance that trouble will recur.

Steam heat maintenance. The functioning of a steam heat system is much like that of hot water. There are similar pipes and valves and clean-out problems. There is the necessity of keeping the water circulating, part of the way in the form of vapor, much of the way in the form of water. There is no pump.

Because of this, it is essential that the pipes through which the vapor and water pass must slant downhill from the radiators to the boiler. Ordinarily this is taken care of in the original installation, but settling of the house can destroy the downhill pitch. It is relatively simple to check this by putting a carpenter's level on the pipe runs. Use one of the smaller "torpedo" levels for cramped spaces.

The remedy, when you find pipes that slant the wrong way,

is to raise the radiator and put wooden blocks under all four legs. The system usually lets you know when there is water pooled in the pipes, by the banging noise it makes, but since the same noise can be caused by other things, check these:

• Be sure that the radiator valve is wide open. Valves should never be partly closed as a means of "controlling" heat, because the competition of the condensed water and the steam for the valve opening may result in no heat at all.

• Be sure that the vent valves are functioning. These valves are designed to open under vary slight pressure, and for that reason tend to fail readily. Some of them have adjustment screws; if yours don't and they do give you trouble, replace them with the adjustable kind. They give you a more efficient system, anyway, since you can use them to adjust the amount of heat in one room compared to another.

• Clean the boiler. Ordinarily, you can't clean a boiler yourself, but it does help to drain it, flush it out, and refill it at time intervals recommended by the manufacturer. The tank should be filled only three-quarters fill to allow for steam expansion. You can buy boiler-cleaning compounds which you pour into the boiler through the hole into which the safety valve is screwed. It is recommended, however, that these be used only about once a year. Be sure, when you remove the valve for this job, that there is no steam pressure in the boiler.

Other than these checks on performance, steam heat requires little more than proper water level in the boiler. Since the water is reused, converting to steam then back to liquid in the heating process, additon of new water is not often necessary. However, it is sound practice to look at the water-level gauge at least once a week.

WHAT TO DO IF THE FURNACE GOES DEAD

Unless your sense of timing is good and your ear is attuned to the sounds your heating system makes, you may not notice that the furnace has gone dead until you feel chilly. You take a trip to the furnace room — and find out that it's off.

First, attribute the blame to human failure or mistake. Check the thermostat, to be sure that someone has not acci-

In addition to the master switch (usually with red cover plate, located at the entrance to the furnace area), most systems have switches at other points. An example is the box housing the "high-low" settings for hydronic (the industry's term for hot-water heat) systems. Warm-air heating plants have similar controls in the air-circulating system. Be sure that the settings and switches are set properly.

dentally set it too low. If the thermostat setting is at least three degrees above the thermometer reading (it shouldn't be that much, but here we're trouble-shooting), you can go on the assumption that the thermostat is okay.

Second, check the on-off switch that controls the furnace. This switch may have been accidentally flipped, even though it has a bright red cover plate marked "Furnace" and is unnaturally located outside the entrance to the furnace room.

If it's on, make the next assumption: The electricity is getting to the furnace, unless there is a blown fuse or circuit breaker. Usually, the breaker that safeguards the furnace is labeled as such. Check it or examine the fuse that does the job. Reactivate the breaker or put in a new fuse. *If the new fuse blows,* or the breaker refuses to function, call the service man, for this means something has shorted out somewhere in the furnace. If the fuse situation is okay, move on the "stack control" box.

Stack control box guards against the damage which could result if an oil burner clicks on but does not ignite. Failing to sense heat in the flue, the control turns everything off. Otherwise, you might find a pool of oil on the floor of the furnace room. To reactivate the system, you click the switch on this box. If it again turns things off, call the repair man.

On the stack back of the furnace you'll find this "stack control" box. It is a significant and important mechanism in the team of relays and controls that monitor your furnace. The stack control functions through its ability to detect heat in the stack; if the furnace is called into duty and the stack doesn't heat up, the stack control indicates that something is wrong. Thus, if the thermostat should call for heat, activating the ignition system, *but the furnace doesn't turn on,* the stack control shuts things off before the place fills with nonburning fuel.

Flick the switch on the stack control just once. If the furnace doesn't come on, turn to the reset button on the motor, usually red. Depress it, holding it for a few seconds, and then release it. If the motor doesn't start, call the service man. (Some motors now reactivate automatically; read your manual.)

If you burn gas, there are a few steps not involved in oil heat. In this system, the pilot light is often an indicator. To begin with, it should burn with a notably bright blue flame. This indicates the proper balance of oxygen and gas. If the pilot is burning yellow, it means there is not enough oxygen. To fix it, make sure the oxygen intake opening is not plugged. This opening is just in front of the pilot light, usually on top, sometimes at one side. A fine wire, such as one of the filaments of a multi-filament copper wire, can be used to clean the oxygen intake.

If the pilot light should go out, *immediately turn off all fuel-feed valves and get out of the area.* Don't return for half an hour, because there may be a dangerous amount of gas accumulation.

Also there may be even more gas concentration inside the furnace, making it risky to attempt to relight the pilot. Using a heavy cardboard as a fan, or an electric fan, or the blower from the vacuum cleaner, blow the gas out. This step may not be necessary unless you can smell the gas, but it is a safety measure well worth the nuisance.

Now open the valves again, and follow the directions, in the instruction manual or on a metal plate fastened to the furnace, for relighting the pilot. If the pilot doesn't light, turn off all the valves again and call the service man.

PHYSICAL REPAIRS AND TROUBLE BUSTING

Except for failure to heat the place, many of the things that can go wrong with a heating plant are difficult to detect because they don't graphically draw attention to themselves. For that reason, you may have to prod the system a little to make it reveal malfunctions, or give it a careful, analytical examination now and then. Some things you'll find:

Flue and chimney. The joint between the galvanized metal flue and the masonry chimney must be airtight, not only to prevent smoking or possible fire danger, but also to provide the right draft. Ordinarily, the flue-chimney joint is sealed with asbestos cement. If it becomes loose, if you can wiggle the flue, if you can see cracks or voids in the cement, the joint must be repaired. With a chisel or awl, dig out the loose plaster. Trowel in enough asbestos cement (from hardware or lumber yard) to fill the spaces. Be careful not to push the flue into the chimney any farther than it was, or you might cut down on the effective flue size.

At some point along the stretch of galvanized duct leading from the furnace to the chimney is a draft control mechanism.

In the flue is a draft regulator which controls the amount of "draw" created by the heat in the stack or chimney. A small counterweight can be adjusted to affect the required draft. When it is out of balance, the furnace burns noisily. When it shows an accumulation of soot, as shown here, the indications are that serious imbalances are causing poor combustion and poor discharge of combustion fumes. The furnace repairman should be called, since adjustments are necessary both at the flue (discharge) side of the system and at the motor (air intake) side.

It looks like a T in the system, with a pivoted "gate" in the opening. Its purpose is to "leak" a little air into the flue as the draft increases and to close entirely when the draft is too light. The adjustment is simple, nothing more than a weight you can move closer to or farther from the pivot, thus increasing or decreasing the effective leverage of gravity on the "gate."

In operation, the resistance of this gate to the intake of air above the furnace must be in balance with the intake of air at the combustion chamber. Tue adjustment of this balance is one of the functions taken care of by the serviceman during his off-season checkup on your plant, but it can go out of kilter during the season, nevertheless. The signal to you of trouble is not always obvious, but it ordinarily takes one of two forms: a rattling noise, as the gate vibrates on its pivots, usually accompanied by a soft booming noise in the furnace; or a visible accumulation of soot around the gate.

When you discover either of these indications of draft control trouble, it may be best to call the serviceman, and it is almost surely a sign that you need help if the soot accumulates around the opening. You can correct the rattling noise, usually, by adjusting the position of the weight so that the gate opens a little more freely. However, if this doesn't take care of the problem, call the man, since the malfunction may be actually a case of bad combustion.

In addition to action you may take due to audible or visible signals, it is a good idea to examine the entire chimney at least once a year, in search of flaws, usually in the form of deteriorating mortar. Dig out loose mortar and replace it with the sand-mix mortar that building supply dealers sell in small bags.

HOW TO KEEP A FIREPLACE IN WORKING ORDER

A fireplace is always separate from the rest of the heating plant, not only as it burns different fuel in an open hearth, but also because it has a completely different flue. That flue may be part of the masonry of the entire chimney, but it is a separate "tube." The reason for this is the need for *controlled* draft as part of the combustion processes of a furnace versus the need for a free draft for the fireplace.

You can check out the condition of the fireplace flue by building a good fire, then loading it with a smoke-producing fuel such as wet newspapers. Cover the top of the chimney, then as quickly as thoroughness permits, examine the chimney for evidences of smoke escaping. Plug any holes you find. If you find many, have a mason come in and do a thorough reconditioning job, for you may have a chimney that is a fire hazard.

To clean a chimney, rarely necessary in the flues that discharge fumes from oil or gas in furnaces, climb up on the roof with a burlap bag partly filled with old rags and weighted with a grapefruit-size stone. Tie a piece of clothesline or similar rope to the bag and lower it into the chimney. Raise it and lower it several times. If the rag content of the bag is enough to make it a fairly snug fit in the chimney, you'll dislodge the soot clinging to the flue liner.

The soot will fall into the fireplace, so be sure to cover the opening downstairs with a tarpaulin dampened with water, or an old blanket or some other screen, to keep the dirt out of the house.

Smoking fireplace. Just about every fireplace smokes once in a while, because of shifty winds causing downdrafts, or because the chimney is just plain cold and doesn't provide the updraft required. The remedy is simple: Wad up some newspapers, light a match to them, and hold them well up in the throat of the fireplace. The heat, too high to be forced downward by overpowering, cold-caused downdrafts, puts a stream of hot air into the flue and gets the air going up the chimney, as it should.

If the smoking is chronic, check the following points.

• A tree may have sent a branch close enough to the chimney to cause draft problems. Cut it back.

• Remember of course, that any chimney should rise at least two feet above the highest point of the roof, or downdraft eddies in the winds will cause smoking. Normally, the chimney will be high enough, for few masonry-carpenter teams would build one wrong. But there may have been additions or alterations in the roof shape. If you are in doubt about this, chip off the concrete plaster crown of the chimney, put in a new piece of flue liner, and lay bricks up to the proper level. Trowel on a new crown.

• Your house may be too tightly built for the fireplace to function properly. It always needs enough air to form an updraft, and when there isn't enough, the result is smoking and poor burning. You may have to open a window or door slightly when you burn the fireplace.

• Sometimes a cold hearth will cause down-and-out currents, in contrast to the up-and-back currents a proper draft creates. That is why good fireplace management calls for a bed of ashes under the andirons, to insulate the hearth.

• Are you building your fires too far forward? Although the forward position does produce the most heat, it often smokes obviously because of the position, but also because it fails to warm the back wall of the fireplace. That firewall must be warm for proper updraft. You'll find that, after a fire has built up well far back in the opening, and the draft is well established, you can add logs toward the front. The strong draft will pull the smoke back and up the chimney.

• The smokeshelf may be loaded with soot. This is most certain to be the case after you clean the chimney, for loosened soot falls to the shelf. (See the drawing of the chimney, to see why this must be true.) The shelf may be loaded even if you haven't just cleaned the chimney, if you have been burning such woods as pine, spruce, hemlock and other heavy soot makers. Or if you have built a succession of small fires that have not of themselves created enough draft and heat to keep the walls of fireplace and chimney clean.

There is no pleasant way to clean the smokeshelf. If you can remove the damper, the job is easier. With a spatula or a trowel of some kind and a container, like a big grocery bag, reach in and shovel the soot away by the bagful. A flashlight and a mirror help you see what you are doing.

• An improper opening, mainly one that is *too high,* causes a fireplace to smoke. There are two ways to correct this shortcoming: lower the lintel or raise the hearth. Which is easier depends on circumstances.

When a fireplace smokes chronically, the reason usually is a design failure: the fireplace opening is too high. Check this by slowly lowering a sheet of aluminum or other fire-safe material from the top of the opening, until the smoke stops. This is the proper level for the fireplace lintel.

Start off by holding a piece of plywood or sheet metal over the fireplace opening, at the top, while a fire is burning — and smoking. Gradually lower the shield until the smoking stops. Note the position of the shield by marking its edge on both sides of the opening. Measure the distance down from the lintel to these marks. This represents the distance the lintel must be lowered or the hearth raised to control the smoking.

To lower the lintel, you must install a new one at the proper height. This may not be difficult, if you use a carbide-tip bit in an electric drill to make holes at either side, into which you can run screws and lead anchors to hold the new lintel in place. Then, you lay bricks on it, to fill the space. The type of brick and the exact procedures, of course, depend on the style and materials in your fireplace.

To raise the hearth, you merely lay bricks across the opening up to the proper height, fill partially in back of them with gravel, then lay in another firebed of firebrick. One of the advantages of raising the hearth versus lowering the mantel is that you can sometimes create a hearth high enough to sit on, in which case it should be made to stretch across the entire face of the fireplace.

MECHANICAL AND PHYSICAL FAILURES

The only thing about a fireplace that is mechanical, ordinarily, is the damper. In any fireplace except the one you find in an authentic colonial house, the damper is part of the hood, a steel unit which forms the throat of the fireplace and includes the damper. In some cases, the entire fireplace lining may be prefabricated of steel, part of an air movement system which improves its heat-producing capacity. Usually, the damper itself is held in place merely by two pivots, one at each end, resting in slots. Thus, it can be removed, either for replacement or to facilitate the cleaning of the smokeshelf. And it can be replaced if it is destroyed by rust over a period of years. When this is necessary, check masonry supply houses for a new damper that will fit your fireplace. If you can't find one, take the original to a welding shop and have a new damper made that matches its shape.

The damper opens and closes by means of a lever, often a compound lever and often with a counterbalance. This mechanism, made of cast iron, rarely goes bad, even though the damper itself may deteriorate. Replacement of the lever, when necessary, involves the same procedure as that for replacing the damper. Find matching parts, or have them fabricated at a welding shop.

In some cases, the damper may be regulated by means of a crank or knob located on the breast of the fireplace. This crank activates a shaft with heavy threads on the end, and a lever mating with those threads raises and lowers the damper. It is not common for the crank or knob and the shaft to go bad. However, the damper and the lever attached to it may suffer the same damage as the simpler type and are subject to the same replacement methods.

Deteriorating masonry. Firebrick is extremely resistant to the ravages of heat in a fireplace, and if it is properly laid with fire clay, you needn't expect any trouble from it. If, by chance, mortar (fire clay) should soften and fall away, you can make repairs the same as you would with any masonry. Be sure to use the special mortar-like materials intended for fireplaces and chimney liners.

A very old fireplace may have been made with ordinary bricks on the bed and for the sides and back. Such bricks will eventually fall apart under the stresses of heat, particularly at the back. *When this starts to happen don't use the fireplace until the defective masonry has been replaced with new bricks.* If you are striving for extreme authenticity in a traditional fireplace, you may want to make the repairs with a double wall of ordinary bricks. However, there are reasons for switching to firebrick. One is durability. Another is safety.

The back wall of a fireplace is sure to deteriorate because of the heat, unless it is made of special firebrick. Such brick is always used in contemporary construction, but in an old house common brick may have been used. If any brick shows crumbling such as you see here, you must tear out the old bricks and replace them with firebrick, using fire clay or special cement mortar.

A third is the authenticity, too, of firebrick in a colonial fire-place, since a great many built 100 or more years ago have already been repaired with firebrick. In fact, the use of more modern brick in the more modern herringbone pattern is coming to be almost as classic as the genuine early American. (See the chapter on masonry repairs for specific instructions for fireplace work.)

III

REPAIRS TO THE
STRUCTURE OF YOUR HOME

From roof to foundation, a home starts to fall apart the day it is finished. This section helps you detect hidden and imminent troubles, and tells how to fix things while they are still easy to fix.

13

DOORS AND LOCKS

SINCE DOORS AND WINDOWS *operate*—open, close, lock, switch from wintertime to summertime function, etc.—they present more frequent repair problems than any other component of the house structure. They are the only elements of a house with moving parts that can go bad. They are always subject to traffic and manipulation. Add to that the fact that most of the time a fragile material, glass, is involved.

Fortunately, everything about doors is simple, with the exception of "locksmithing," and can be taken care of with tools around the house. The only requirement is an understanding of the troubles that may arise and of the principles that make doors and windows work smoothly.

THE STICKING DOOR

A door is a fairly big piece of wood, subject to a great deal of swelling and shrinking with changes in humidity. That is the reason why many doors are made in panel form; the individual panels shrink and swell in their own frames without changing greatly the overall size of the door. Shrinkage is also low with most modern flush doors that are of laminated, plywood-like construction over special "cores" that don't react much, if at all, to moisture changes.

With either type of door, however, there is almost always enough dimensional change with weather changes to cause binding at least once. That is, the carpenter hung the door and it worked. However, when the maximum humidity season came along, the door swelled enough to make trouble. Normally, you fix it once, and that's it.

Naturally, it's best to work on the door at a time when it is at its biggest. Your objective should be the closest tolerable fit when the door is at its largest. Do not commit the error of overdoing it, making the door too loose when it is swollen to full dimension, or it may be entirely too small at the other end of the cycle.

Fitting a door without planing. In the majority of cases you can cure the problem instead by manipulating the hinges. It is a little known fact that you can move the "strike edge" of a door toward or away from the frame, and you can tilt that edge up or down through the use of cardboard shims or spaces inserted back of the hinges. To do this, you loosen the hinge screws two or three turns. They are still gripping the wood, so the door doesn't fall, but the hinge flange comes free from the wood. Ordinarily, you will not use enough shimming back of the flange to affect the grip of the screws. However, if you feel they might not be doing their job when you retighten them, remove one screw at a time, stick a couple of pieces of toothpick in the hole, and redrive the screw.

The kind of shim and the specific place where you insert it determine which direction the door takes. The possibilities, illustrated in the accompanying photographs and drawing, are based on shifting the position of the hinge barrel, where the pin is, and thus shifting the position of the entire door.

If a door sticks *at the strike edge,* it must be moved away from the jamb toward the hinge edge. Do this by inserting a strip of cardboard between the hinge flange and the jamb, at the edge of the hinge opposite the barrel, position A on the drawing. This pivots the hinge around the edge of the jamb, moving the barrel slightly away from the edge where it is sticking.

HINGE MANIPULATION SOLVES
MANY STICKING DOOR PROBLEMS

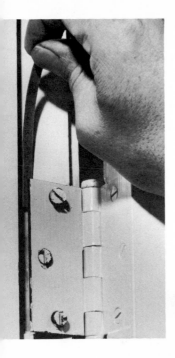

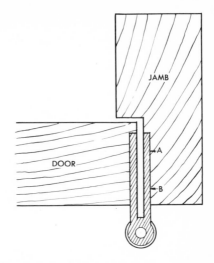

With the screws loosened, slip a piece of cardboard in back of the hinges on the edge away from the barrel (at A in drawing), to move a door away from the strike side.

Conversely, put the piece of cardboard back of the hinge on the side toward the barrel (at B in drawings), to move the door closer to the strike.

To tilt a door, releasing binding at an upper or lower corner, cut shims to fit back of the hinges. Mark the positions of the screws first.

Slip the shims back of the hinges, using two at the top, one in the middle if there are three hinges, and none on the bottom. Or reverse this to tilt the door up. Use shims back of all hinges equally to move the door toward the strike.

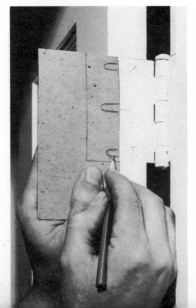

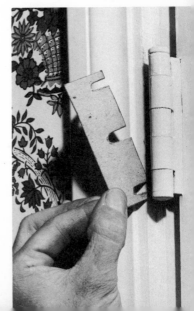

If a door binds *at the hinge edge,* that is, comes up snug against the jamb before it is fully closed, you can loosen that snugness by putting the strip of cardboard between the hinge and the jamb at the side of the hinge toward the barrel position B on the drawing. When you do this, you move the barrel away from the jamb, carrying the door with it.

If a door sticks *at the top corner,* you can tilt the entire door by putting *two thicknesses* of cardboard back of the entire hinge at the top, *one thickness* at the middle hinge if there is one, and none at the bottom hinge.

If the door sticks *at the sill,* reverse the procedure, putting two shims at the bottom and none at the top.

All of these corrections assume that there is, indeed, room for the door to move in the direction it must go to eliminate the problem. If there is no room, if the door is simply too big for the opening, there is no choice except to plane it down. However, try the hinge manipulation technique first; it has the tremendous advantage of producing no raw wood that must be given a finish to make it match the rest of the door.

Planing a door to make it fit. It is usually best to do the planing on the hinge edge. You can take off a few shavings on the strike side if only a small amount of planing is necessary, and you may be able to do it without demounting the door. However, if a considerable amount of wood must be removed, *take the door down.* And do all the planing on the hinge edge.

To move a door away from the strike side, cut the hinge mortises deeper on the jamb or the door, or both.

The reasons for this are important. First, that is the least conspicuous edge, in case you find it difficult to finish the planed areas to match. More important, however, is the problem of planing in the area of the door lock. It must be removed. In severe cases it may even be necessary to modify the holes, actually to *move* the hardware.

It is much simpler to remove the hinges, plane away the required amount of wood, then if necessary cut the hinge mortises a little deeper.

Taking a door down. Remove the hinge pins first (see photo). Take out the pin of the bottom hinge first and the top pin last. That way, the door won't fall over, possibly tearing a lower hinge loose doing other damage. Some hinges have a decorative ball on the bottom of the barrel, to match the knob on the pin. When that is the case, check to see if there is a small hole in the bottom, into which you can insert a nail to drive the pin up. If not, you may have to work a screwdriver into the crack beneath the shoulder of the pin to raise it.

Then with the door down, take out the screws that hold the hinges on. (In rare cases, there may be no hinge pin and you'll have to remove the hinges screws to take the door down.)

If the weather stripping system used in your home has metal parts fastened to the door itself, you will have to remove them in order to do any essential planing. However, the weather-

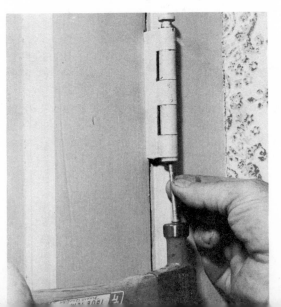

When you must take a door down, to plane it for example, the easy way is to remove the pin. In some cases you may have to drive it up with a nail through a hole in the bottom.

stripped door does not often stick, since the stripping is flexible and occupies enough space to allow for a considerable expansion.

Lubrication. This may lick a sticking door, without any need for planing or hinge manipulation. If the problem is slight, try a little candle wax or "lube stick" at the point where the door sticks. Or, pick up a can of spray lubricant, usually a silicone formula, and treat both the jamb and the door edge. These spray materials usually dry invisibly, and they may cut down friction enough to get you through the high humidity season, until the door starts to shrink again, and the problem disappears.

If a door is too small. It takes tremendous humidity extremes plus some poor handymanship to turn up a door that is too small, that was planed too much when it was installed, or too much at the point of its widest dimension. But it can happen. To rectify the situation, you must add size to the door.

The best place to do it is on the hinge edge. Cut a piece of wood the right thickness to provide the required width and glue it to the edge. Cut pieces to fit the hinge mortises and glue them in place. You will probably find it necessary to put matchstick-size pieces of wood in the screw holes, since the screws will not go as far into the holes as they did originally.

In some cases, on access doors, it may be possible to increase the effective size of a door by installing a type of weather stripping that fills the space more completely.

WHAT TO DO WHEN A DOOR RATTLES

When a door is properly hung and fitted, it closes against the stop and the door catch springs into the strike, and there is no free space. When this rather critical fit is too loose, the door can rattle back and forth between stop and catch. There are several ways to stop the rattling, some of them more suited to inside doors, some to outside doors.

Felt cushion. Once or more thickness of felt, cemented to the stop in the upper corner, will often "squeeze" the door tightly enough between stop and strike to end rattle. This is most likely to work successfully on bedroom and other inside doors.

Weather stripping. If weather stripping deteriorates or compacts over a period of time, it no longer exerts its gentle pressure against the door. You may be able to move the stripping closer, or you may find it necessary to replace it with new material.

Mechanical changes. For the best job, and the only one, in severe cases, you must move the strike on the door jamb, remounting it closer to the strike. Begin by observing the *amount of adjustment* necessary. With the door pushed hard against the strike, scribe a knife-blade mark on the jamb at the edge of the door. Now pull the door hard against the strike and make another mark. The distance between these marks is the distance the strike must be moved. Actually, you'll want to move it a hair more than that—see below.

Remove the strike and fill its mortises with a close-fitting patch of wood, glued in place. When the patch is dry, cut the new mortise in the proper new position and screw the strike on. If your measurements and your mechanics were accurate, the door should now latch when it is closed firmly against the stop. However, if the door is closed gently, it may not catch.

Try this trick. File a gentle bevel on the flat side of the bolt, so that it will catch even if the door is closed slowly. Then, the spring will hold the latch in and any of the sort of vibration that would have caused door rattling will merely result in deeper seating of the catch.

The door doesn't latch. Although it doesn't happen often, there are times when swelling and shrinking of the wooden parts of a door and jamb, settling of the house, or warping may cause a situation in which the spring-driven latch doesn't snap into the strike plate opening when the door is closed. Not even when it is banged shut. It is usually easiest to fix this by removing the strike plate and filing a little metal off the square bolt in the strike, to let the latch pop into place. However, you must first determine where to file. It may be that the latch is catching on the front, or the top, or the bottom. You may be able to determine which by careful examination; you can usually see if it is catching above or below by squinting into the crack when the door is closed. If it seems to be neither, then you can figure that it is the front edge. (It can be both the front *and* the top or bottom, of course.) Put the strike in a vise and do the required amount of filing. Combine this, perhaps, with the latch-bevel filing mentioned above. The two operations should make it unnecessary to move the strike, a much more difficult job.

The door doesn't bolt. If your lock has a "dead bolt," that is, a square, rugged bolt that you must throw by turning a knob or key, it is possible for it to go out of alignment and miss the hole intended for it in the strike plate. Use the filing technique covered above to correct this problem. Do not, however, file the bolt itself.

PROBLEMS WITH THE DOOR LOCK MECHANISM

If the locks on your doors are typical they are likely to have bright and shiny knobs on the outside, but they may have fairly unreliable mechanisms on the inside. Not only does this make them subject to breakdown, but to breakin. In many cases, at the first sign of mechanical deficiency, your best move is to replace the entire lock with one that is equal to its responsibilities, in home security.

The most common problems with locks are these.

Loose handle or knob. Sometimes they're even so loose that they come off. On most locks, the handle or knob slips on a square shaft or screws on a square shaft with threads. It is held in place by a set screw, usually located at the slimmest part of the knob. Because of the constant open-close action, this set screw loosens and so does the knob. To fix it, loosen the screw. Slip or twist the knob up snug, then tighten the screw. With the threaded square rod, you may tighten things a half-turn or so too much. This will keep the knob from snapping back into "neutral," when you let go of it. If this happens, untwist the knob a quarter turn, then set the screw.

You may discover—it happens often—that this problem recurs, because the situation that causes it, traffic, continues. If so, get hold of a small tube of material that locks threads, sold by hardware stores. Or use a dab of silicone calk over the end of the set screw, to keep it from loosening with repeated movement.

This is a typical simple lock. To remove it, loosen a screw on one of the knobs and slip it off. Then, remove two screws through the flange into the door. This lets the two halves of the lock come free. The latch then comes out of its hole in the edge of the door. Some locks may be designed so the knob doesn't have to be removed; you can loosen screws by working around it.

Handles that stick. Gradual infection of the mechanism by moisture-laden air that eventually gums up the operation usually causes sticking handles. If the problem is mild, you can take care of it with "graphite lube" injectors hardware stores sell, or with spray lubricants. Turn the handle to retract the catch. Spray through the opening. Let the handle return to its normal position. Open it again, and again spray or inject.

If a few rotations of this procedure do not free the stickiness, you may have to remove the lock from the door and give it a thorough cleaning and oiling. This is not difficult with the average lock, and the following steps can be adapted to handle most circumstances:

Unscrew the set screw and remove the inside knob. Now the "twisting mechanism" of the entire lock should pull out, on the inside. Next remove the screws in the edge of the door holding the lock in place. You should be able to pull the latch mechanism out. The accompanying photograph is typical of the most common type of locks. If you will put it together in the open, as shown, it will help you to understand the mechanism from now on.

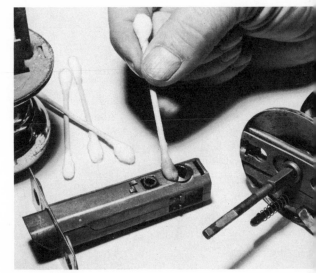

Although a lock can usually be lubricated by spray graphite or other lubricants, it is sometimes necessary to dismantle the entire setup and swab the working parts with light oil.

To restore this lock to excellent working condition, you should dunk it in a solvent (kerosene, gasoline, paint thinner) to clean away old, thickened lubricants and any accumulation of dirt and grease. Then daub it with three-in-one oil, or equivalent, to make all springs, slides and turns free acting.

Catches that stick. Usually victims of the same situations as stuck handles, they are, fortunately, more easily licked by spray or injected lubrication. Spray in the opening, then jab the catch in repeatedly with repeated spraying, until the mechanism works smoothly.

REPLACING A LOCK

Even if the locks on your access doors are not giving you any trouble, it may be that you should replace them, as a means of giving trouble to other, unwelcome people. It is a fact that the typical lock on the typical door is not much of a barrier to the typical breaker-and-enterer. There are locks, however, that make breaking in such a nuisance that he'll go somewhere else. And such locks are not difficult to install in place of present hardware.

If you feel a replacement lock is necessary, visit a locksmith or a *building* hardware dealer and get some professional help selecting the new hardware. (Most ordinary hardware stores don't handle the better-than-typical locks.) You'll find that the lock comes with a "templet" which you use to position all the holes and mortises.

In some cases, one or more of the holes or mortises required by the new lock may coincide with those of the old ones, particularly if they are by the same manufacturer. Holes and mortises that do not coincide must be filled with cut-to-fit plugs. It is worth the bother to cut the fillers so that the grain runs the same way as the surrounding wood, for greatest

When you change a lock on a door, try to find one that matches the holes and mortises already there. If you can't, or if you want a bigger, tougher lock, fill the openings with cut-to-fit wooden plugs.

Much more secure than typical house locks is one that has a deadlatch (pencil points to it here) that locks the latch in its extended position, so it cannot be slipped open by burglars. Look for this feature when you buy a new lock.

permanence. Fasten them in with glue, but without metal fasteners which might interfere with cutting the new holes and mortises. It may be necessary to fill the cutouts in the jamb, also, to accommodate the new strike.

With the fillers in place, follow the instructions that come with the lock. You may want to take care of any finishing problems to make the wood patches match before you finally install the new lock.

Even more secure is a deadlock, shown protruding from door above the regular deadlatch. This bolt must be activated by a knob on the inside, and a key on the outside. Still better than this is a deadbolt which must be key-operated on either side.

WHEN WEATHER STRIPPING DOESN'T STOP THE WEATHER

There is enough space around a properly hung access door to throw a snowball through, if you multiply an eighth of an inch or so by the distance around the door. This space is ordinarily filled with weather stripping of one form or another that through cushion-fit or spring-fit closes the gap. The most common types are foam plastic, plastic-sheathed jute or other soft cord, and metal. They can lose their springiness, all of them, and no longer do the job.

Fortunately, hardware and building supply stores now carry, almost universally, weather strip kits of sizes for both doors and windows, complete with instructions, all very easy to install either with adhesives or brads.

How do you tell when your weather stripping is no longer stopping the weather? By feel. On a day when the wind is blowing more or less right at the door, hold the palm of your hand along the edge of the door, across the top and the bottom. If you can feel coolness, your stripping isn't doing the job.

Some houses are equipped with weather stripping that can be adjusted, to snug it up against the door. Usually, you loosen some screws, push the material up, and tighten the screws. In other cases, you can accomplish the same thing by lifting brads, most often brass, and redriving them.

However, if the weather stripping itself is deteriorated, if the foam-plastic type or the plastic-sheathed jute type is compacted, it might be best to replace it. Modern varieties are made of better materials, including plastics that resist most stubbornly any tendency to go out of shape.

Many doors are installed without any weather stripping at the sill, which is a serious mistake. You can buy, at building supply outlets, a special type of stripping intended for the bottom edge of doors. There are several individual types, but most of them involve a mechanism which, when the door closes, pushes the sealing material down against the sill. Therefore, *it doesn't scrape on the sill and wear out.* Nor does it require any installation on the sill itself, which might cause someone to stumble and fall. Installation of such stripping is simple, as you'll notice when you read the instructions packaged with it.

STORM AND COMBINATION DOORS

If you have aluminum or other metal storm doors, you are being spared the trouble which often comes up with wooden doors. Because combination doors must be designed to allow interchange of screens and storm sash, because they are always fitted with closers often causing severe rack and twist strain, and because they must be of relatively light construction to stay within cost limitations, wooden doors tend to come loose at the joints after a few seasons.

The quick and easy way to handle this problem is to take the door down, clamp it tight together, and fasten strips of hardboard from edge to edge, holding it back just far enough to miss the doorstop on each side. If you put this reinforcement on the inside of the door, fastening it with small flathead screws and painting it to match the rest of the door, you'll never see it. But the door will be stronger than ever, with one strip across the top and a wider one across the bottom. Do the job in the spring or fall, halfway between the cold season and the insect season, and you can take your time at it.

(For repairs to the glass and screen inserts, see the following chapter on windows.)

14

WINDOWS AND SCREENS

EXCEPT FOR THE INSTANT problem of broken glass, most of the things that go wrong with windows and screens come along so gradually that you can anticipate trouble before it actually occurs. The best example is deteriorating putty. Although modern "glazing compounds" are relatively permanent and flexible, the putty of a few years ago tends to get brittle. With dimensional changes of the glass and the window sash, it gradually chips away. Eventually, it is all gone. If you spot this sort of deterioration in time, you can fix it at your leisure, before it becomes critical. The same is true of slowly deteriorating old window screens, now easy to improve with screening that lasts much, much longer.

TECHNIQUES OF GLAZING AND REGLAZING

Although installing new glass in a window has the look of daub-and-glob, there are some methods that make the job better and longer lasting.

• Have the glass cut about ⅛" or ³/₁₆" smaller than the actual dimensions of the sash it goes into. This allows a little space on all sides for expansion and contraction. Naturally, the need for this space is greater with bigger sheets of glass, less for smaller sheets.

• When you clean out the remains of the glass and putty being replaced (wear gloves handling the glass and be careful), be sure to clean it *all* out. In some cases, this may entail removing a few slivers of wood, but it is important. Otherwise, you will not be taking full advantage of the adhesion and flexibility of the glazing compound.

• Brush on a wood preservative such as "Woodlife" before you do anything else. This tends to stabilize the wood and forestall both rot and paint deterioration.

Seating the glass in the frame. It is a mistake merely to put the glass in place, drive glazier's points, and then putty. Properly done, you line the frame with glazing compound *first*. Then when you put the glass in, the compound will ooze up around the edges, so that the glass is *not in contact with the frame itself at any point*. When you finish the glazing, you'll have the glass "floating" in the glazing compound, sealing the opening completely against air and moisture, yet free to come and go with the elasticity of the compound.

As you handle glazing compound, you'll discover that it softens and becomes more plastic with manipulation and from the warmth of your hands. In a few seconds, a wad of the fairly stiff material scooped from the can is quite soft. You can roll it into a "snake" between the palms of your hands. And this is the key to compound application, both under the glass and in the troweled bevel on top. These are the steps:

1. Roll out snakes of compound and run them all around the opening, roughing them into place with thumb or finger. You don't need a lot of material in this operation, just enough to fill beneath the glass. Move as rapidly as is convenient, because the compound tends to reharden rather quickly once you stop manipulating it.

2. Position the glass in this bed of compound and carefully press down on it, so that it sinks into the material. If the glass is small, you can usually do this in a single operation, with your fingers spread to distribute the pressure. With larger glass work carefully along one side, then the next, and on around the pane. When this job is done properly, compound

1. Apply glazing compound to the sash all around before you put the glass in place, so that it rests in a complete bed of compound. This is easiest to do if you roll compound into snakes between palms.

2. Position glass in the bed of compound; then gently press it into place. The material should ooze out beneath the glass and up around its edges. The excess below is easy to clean away.

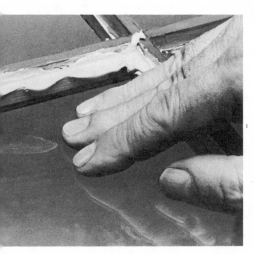

3. Glazier's points come in many different new shapes, including varieties you can push into the sash with the end of your glazing chisel. Apply them after glass is pressed into compound.

4. Regular triangular points may come packaged with a driving tool like this. If not, improvise with something like a ½" steel washer.

183

5. When the points are in, roll out more snakes of compound and glob them into place. Then use chisel or putty knife to smooth the bevel. As the photo shows, the knife should ridge the glass and the corner of the sash, at an angle of about 45 degrees. Excess compound peels off clean and easy.

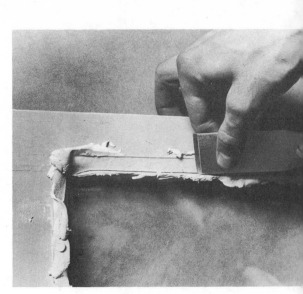

6. Paint over glazing compound should extend just barely on the glass, to seal it entirely. Easiest way to make this edge neat is with masking tape applied carefully to leave about $1/16''$ of glass exposed. Or, use special scraper with a shoulder that rides sill and leaves proper amount of paint on glass and a neat edge.

will ooze up around the glass, and it will also spread out beneath it, forming a little bead which you remove later.

3. Install the glazier's points. Although the time-honored little metal triangles are still used, you'll find several different styles of points today, some of them easier to use. And you'll find some simplified methods of using them (see photos). Points spaced about 8″ apart will do the job on large panes, two to a side on smaller pieces of glass.

4. Soften up some more snakes of compound and press them into position. Then take your putty knife and, holding it as shown in the photograph, smooth out the bevel. Do not move the knife too fast; a slow trowelling movement produces the smoothest bevel. There should be a small ribbon of excess compound *on the glass* beyond the corner of the knife, as well as on the frame itself. This is assurance that the bevel is complete. The two little ribbons are easy to pull off without touching the bevel.

Old putty that has become brittle may not need to be removed entirely, but flaking sections should be cleaned to firm material with a glazier's chisel. Smooth glazing compound into the cavities and paint.

5. Paint. Although some manufacturers of glazing compound approve the idea of painting immediately, it is no doubt better to wait a few days, to let the compound firm up and "skin over." The degree of convenience should be your guide in this decision. When it would be a nuisance to wait, you might want to go ahead and finish the job, particularly if you are using a latex paint. On the other hand, when you do a reglazing job on a storm window that doesn't have to go back on the house immediately, the wait would be worth the bother.

The most vulnerable areas of windows are the lower sills. Begin repair by scraping away loose paint down to bare wood, a two-handed job.

Sand rough spots with medium grit sandpaper, feathering edges of old paint to blend with bare wood surfaces. Follow up with fine sandpaper for a silk smooth surface.

Finish sill with good quality primer and interior paint. A properly painted window has 1/8" overlap of paint on the pane. Use of masking tape assures a straight edge.

WHERE DO YOU WORK ON A WINDOW?

It's no fun, and it's not particularly safe, glazing a window at the top of a ladder. There are a half-dozen or so up-and-down trips, hanging on with one hand or with a knee hooked over a rung. And the tools you drop, not to mention the glass.

Of course, the problem disappears with storm sash. You take the window down, reglaze it, and put it back up. But what about regular windows? Fortunately, they are usually covered with screen or storm sash, thus protected and rarely broken. But when they do go, is it much of a job removing a window? Probably less of a job than you think. Many experts balance the removing window versus the ups-and-downs of doing repairs with the window in place this way:

If it's a ground floor window that you can reach from a step-ladder, leave the window in. If it's a second story or higher window, calling for an extension ladder, take the window out.

How to remove a window. You can always remove a sash, either upper or lower, from inside. The way you do it depends on how old the house is and how antiquated or up-to-date the windows are.

Starting with the oldest, there is a flat molding, called the "stop" that runs from the window sill to the top of the window frame, on either side. It forms the channel for the lower sash to ride in, teamed up with a square member called the "parting strip." On the far side of the parting strip is the channel for the upper sash, formed by the strip and an outside molding.

If you remove the stop on one side, you can lift out the lower sash. Then, if you remove the parting strip on the same side, you can lift out the upper sash.

Important: Virtually every window has sash weights (if they're old enough) or spring-powered counterbalances. In the case of weights, you'll find that the sashcords are fastened into the side edges of the sash by means of a knot fitted into a slot. Lift out the cords and tie a loose overhand knot in each to keep it from being pulled into the window frame by the sashweight. The spring-type counterbalance is usually fastened to the bottom of the sash by means of some screws

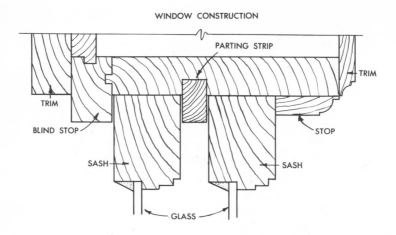

Components of a window construction are illustrated in this drawing. The window sash slides up and down in channels formed by the stop and the parting strip, the parting strip and blind stop.

through an L. When you remove these screws, the L will start to rotate. That is because the adjustment tension of the spring is set by twisting the L when it is installed. Do not let the L spin free. Instead, let it unwind slowly and count the revolutions. That way, you'll be able to rewind the spring to the same tightness when you replace the window.

Since the stop has no doubt been painted over and is therefore stuck on, you probably have to work at it with a fairly broad chisel or a pinchbar. If you pry it loose from the back, that is, in the channel, any mars or scratches will be less visible than if you work from the front edge.

The parting strip is usually bedded in a groove in the window frame. Like the stop, it should be removed with the prybar applied to the outside, to minimize the damaged look.

In newer windows, the entire construction may be different. On both sides of the frame you'll find a metal or a plastic molding that forms the channels for the two windows and includes the counterbalancing mechanism. This device is only lightly fastened to the frame, often with a nail at the top and a staple at the bottom. If you remove the window stop and

188

those fasteners on one side the entire thing slips out of the frame, freeing both upper and lower sash. All you have to do is take out the counterbalance screws, and the sash is free to go into the workshop where it's handy to work on the broken glass.

FAULTY WINDOW ACTION

Older windows, riding in wooden channels, are often hard to operate, because of the wood-against-wood friction. Even worse, sometimes, is wood-against-paint friction, and that is why it is standard painting advice never to paint in the channels. The worst kind of sticking comes when a paint job virtually glues the window in place. Conversely, a window is sometimes too loose.

Hard-riding windows can usually be loosened up with an application of stick lubricant, candlewax, or spray lubricant. Be sure to treat the edges of the window stop and the parting strip, as well as the bottom of the channel.

Paint-stuck windows. They'll usually break loose if you pound along the sides of the sash with the heel of your hand. It may be necessary, also, to use a screwdriver or small prybar at corners of the sash, prying against the frame to break the paint layer. Follow this with lubrication. In extreme cases, remove the window stop on both sides and jiggle the sash loose. (Metal or plastic window channels are, of course, never painted, nor do windows mounted in them very often stick.)

Air-leaking windows. These let in a lot of cold, and they should be weather stripped. As with doors, check the leakage when the wind is blowing against that side of the house, feeling along the edges and top and bottom and "meeting rail" for drafts. Building supply outlets sell special weather stripping for windows. The most common forms are metal, light and inconspicuous. When you install a strip on the back side of the lower sash meeting rail you never see it, yet it cuts down air leak between the two sashes. A strip on the bottom of the lower sash seals off the leak between it and the sill.

Rope-type weather stripping can be used around windows, and it is especially effective when the gap is large. Nailed to the lower *outside* edge of the lower sash, it will cork up any space between it and the sill. When air leaks at the edges of a window, you can seal it off by nailing strips snug against the outside of the sash frame.

Windows that rattle. Either because of shrinkage or wear, rattling windows are loose in their channels. You can tighten up the lower sash by removing the stop and renailing it closer to the sash. The proper spacing is about the thickness of a postcard, loose enough to slide, but not loose enough to rattle. It is more difficult to silence a noisy upper sash, because the parting strip can't be moved, and in some cases neither can the outside molding. The easy way to silence an upper sash is by cutting narrow strips of felt and cementing them to the back side of the parting strip.

WHEN A SASHCORD BREAKS

The counterbalancing systems of windows sometimes go bad, whether they are the modern spring-powered kind or the old-fashioned sash weight variety. Fixing the modern kind is simple. Fixing the old-fashioned kind is so difficult you may decide to convert to more up-to-date version.

When a window has a sashcord it works this way. The cord fastened to the edge of the sash, in a slot, rides up the inside of the frame, over a pully mounted in the frame, and disappears. Inside the frame the wood is fastened to an iron casting, a weight which helps you raise the window and helps hold it open at the top.

Over a period of time, the sashcord wears. And it may break. It or its function must be replaced. To do this, you must get into the frame, where the weight is.

If you'll examine the channels the sash rides in, you'll discover that near the bottom, there is an access method provided in one form or another. It may be a wooden insert. It may be metal. And it may be painted over so many times that it is all but invisible. When you remove it, you can reach in and pull out the sash weight. Next, remove the window (use instructions above) and you have both ends of the sashcord available, one tied to the weight, one inserted in the slot in the sash.

To replace the cord, whether it is broken or merely badly worn, cut a length of new cord the exact length of the old one. Slip one end over the pulley at the top of the window frame. By feeding it into the frame and jiggling it, you should be able to make the cord fall to the opening near the bottom. If necessary, tie a piece of string to the cord and feed it into the opening at the top, with a weight tied to the end. Fish out the weight at the bottom, then pull the string through, drawing the sashcord with it. Tie the end of the sashcord to the weight. Slip the cord into the slot in the sash. Put things back together.

There are variations to this. Many homeowners living in older houses are replacing sashcord with a special sash chain you can buy at building supply or hardware outlets. It lasts longer. Another variation is spring-powered counterbalances building supply dealers have, replacing the cord idea entirely. They are easier to install than sashcords are to replace and your dealer can give you specific tips for working with the kind he handles.

How to modernize the system. Since you must go to the bother of taking the window apart in order to replace sashcords, and since it is shortsighted to fix one side of the window without doing the other, even though for some reason only one cord may need replacement, why not consider this idea.

At any good building supply outlet, you can buy the modern, metal or plastic glide-and-counterbalance units discussed above and solve a number of problems at one time. First, you end sticking problems; second, you end some weather stripping worries, and third, you get trouble-free counterbalancing.

The changeover is simple. You merely remove the stop and the parting strip. Cut the cord. If the pully in an old window interferes, remove it. Then, you slip the new system in place along with the sash, connect the counterbalance, and nail the stop back on.

The price of a pair of units is in the $5-$6 area, cheap enough for a modernization job that ends most window problems permanently.

MORE EFFICIENT WINDOW LOCKS

The standard window lock does very little to baffle a burglar who is very serious in his intent to break into your house. It's a simple matter of breaking out a small piece of glass, twisting the lock, and raising the window. Modern locks are available, however, that require a key and that are hard to jimmy since the keyhole is on the inside, where it can't be seen.

Generally, these locks are stocked by hardware stores. They install in the same way as the no-key kind, often using the same screw holes. They have a disadvantage, and it is one reason for the frequent ineffectiveness of such locks: You can't leave the window partly open for ventilation.

There is, however, a type of lock that differs from the standard, in that it goes at the side of the window. The main part, the bolt, of the lock screws on the top of the lower sash. The strike screws to the side of the upper sash, and *there are two strikes*. One of them goes a few inches above the other. Thus, you can open the window a few inches, but still lock it against further opening.

Lock that mounts on the meeting rails is similar to old standby, but has a key that makes it tough on breakers-and-enterers. Even if they break glass, they may not have time — or want to risk time — to remove screws. Block that event with one-way screws you can buy at locksmith or hardware stores.

New version of meeting rail lock mounts at the corner of the window, with strikes on the upper sash. It can be engaged with window closed, with lower sash raised, with upper sash lowered, or both opened slightly. Thus, there is ventilation plus security.

For dormer windows, a lockable handle replaces the old one. In some cases this may require drilling out old rivets and installing new ones to mount handle.

REPAIRING FAULTY SCREENS

Screens and screening are rarely subject to serious damage, and the problems they present call for a replacement more often than repair. The screening deteriorates. Moldings may rot away, even the frame may decay. All of these failings are likely to occur first at the bottom of a screen, where moisture lasts longest following rains, and where there may be accumulations of debris which encourage decay. For that reason, inspect screens, particularly at their bottom edges, once a year. Fortunately, you can usually take your time about repairs, when you find them. Screens are rarely a crisis problem.

Replacing defective screens. Although there are many different kinds of window screen designs, those requiring replacement of the screening are usually pretty old and pretty much of simple construction. The frame is a square molding.

The screen is held to the frame by means of tacks or more recently staples. The edge is covered with a delicate "screen molding."

In some cases there may be a groove under the screen molding. The screening is pressed into this groove by means of a "spline" which may be metal or wood. This system is excellent, because the spline not only holds the screen securely, but its action helps draw it tight.

The exact design of the screen will become apparent, of course, as you dismantle it to replace the screening. First, carefully lift off the molding. Use a small pinchbar or chisel. Apply the lift at the exact point where brads or staples occur, holding the molding down. Otherwise, it is almost sure to splinter. Then take out the tacks or staples holding the old screen. If it is a spline design, and the spline is metal, you may be able to lift it out intact and reusable. Wooden splines are almost sure to come out in pieces. If this is the case, and if you want to use the spline system on the new screen, you'll have to cut some splines to size from wood scrap.

New materials. Now being used for screening are fiberglass, aluminum, and plastic, which cost a trifle more, but whose permanence and ease of handling make them worth the small difference. When you buy the new screening, be sure the width and length are slightly bigger than the opening to be covered. This may make it necessary to buy screen one size wider (usually no more than 6″) than you actually need. But if you don't have the excess at the edge, you'll find it almost im-

Always paint the sash and cross members before you install screening, both to protect the wood and to prevent the possibility that bare wood may show through.

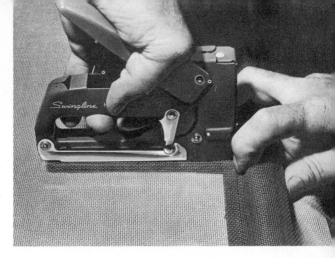

Staples are faster and handier than tacks in replacing screens.

possible to stretch the screen tight and smooth. There'll be nothing to hold on to.

There are no rules for putting new screen on a frame, but there are some procedures that make the job easier for most people. First, position the screen carefully at one corner, so that the molding will just cover it. Fasten it with one tack or staple at the corner and one an inch or so from the corner on both sides. This will anchor the screen firmly and let you stretch it tight.

Second, move to the adjacent corner on the longer side of the screen. Pull the material tight, really tight, and fasten it with the three-tack (or staple) system mentioned above. Then run fasteners along that edge, spacing them about 6" apart. Make sure that the wires of the screen run *exactly parallel to the side of the screen.*

Third, move to the other corner adjacent to the one you did first, pull the screening tight, and fasten it at the corner and every 6".

You now have the screen fastened on two sides, and the excess you'll need for handling is on the other two sides. It may be, also, that there are a few large wrinkles, waves, in the screening, running diagonally. They will disappear when you pull the material tight in the other two directions.

Fourth, move to the free corner. Pull the screening diagonally toward that corner until the wrinkles disappear and you can see that the threads will come into parallel with the frame. You will probably have to line this up pretty much by eye at first, since a certain amount of "sag" toward the center is inevitable. Then, as you run fasteners along the remaining

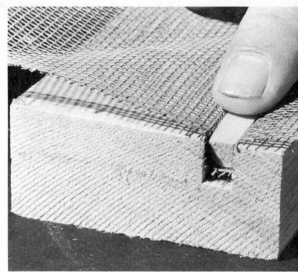

Principle of spline method of installing screening is shown in this mock-up. Spline is slightly smaller than the groove, and holds the screening slip-proof when it is pressed in place. The action of the spline tends to pull the screen tight.

two sides, you can apply the amount of tension required to bring the screening and the frame into parallel.

Fifth, nail the screen molding back in place. If it was badly damaged when you lifted it, buy new molding. *Paint it before you install it,* to save a lot of tedious cutting along the screen. When you're replacing a molding, if you use brads one size larger than the originals but no longer, they'll hold tight.

All that remains now is to cut off the excess screen, running a sharp blade along the edge of the screen molding.

Replacement with a spline. If the screening was originally held in place with a spline, you have two choices. You can replace it with a spline, or you can forget the spline and do the job with tacks or staples as outlined above. This may be the

It may not always be necessary to replace an entire screen. If the half on either side of the crossbar is okay, lift the molding, cut across the bar, and remove only the bad screening.

196

better choice if wooden splines were ruined when you took them out. If you decide to go with the splines, the procedure is a little different from that involving fasteners, since you can't use the same tightening techniques. Follow these steps:

First, position the screening at one corner so that it overlaps the grooves on both members of the frame by a distance about equal to the width of the grooves. Force the spline in on the shorter of these two sides. Start at one end and pull the material as tight as possible as you work the spline in progressively toward the opposite corner.

Second, move to the opposite side, where you have an overlap of screen to pull on. Make it tight beneath spline, then force the spline into the groove. You'll find that the action of the spline draws the screen up to its final tightness.

Third, force the spline into one of the remaining two sides, lining it up carefully with the frame.

When there's a cross member. Use a sharp knife to cut the screen across the cross member, leaving the fasteners holding that part of the material you'll leave in place. Lift the fasteners from the screen to be removed. These may be splines or tacks or staples, but there is normally never a spline across the cross member.

Lap the new screening over the old at the cross member, and do the rest of the job as covered above.

Repairing a hole. When a screen has a hole in it, but is otherwise in good condition, you can patch it with a small piece of screening as shown in the accompanying photographs.

1. Cut the hole into a true rectangle, cleaning up the ragged edges. Tin snips or even a pair of household shears will do this job.

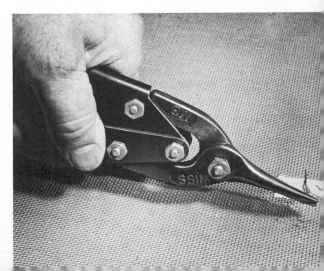

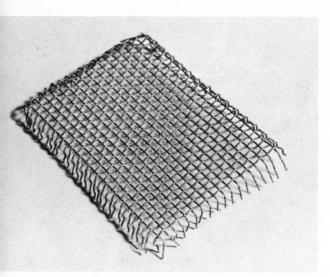

2. Cut a patch of screening material a little bigger than the hole, then strip away two or three strands on all four edges. Bend the resulting strand ends 90 degrees downward. An easy way to do this is over the edge of a table.

3. Lay the patch over the hole, and maneuver the strands through the screen. Then, bend the ends of the screen fibers, to hold the patch in place. It will be barely visible.

198

FLOORS AND STAIRS

FLOORS AND STAIRS are the most vulnerable of all home construction components. They are usually unsupported from below. They must withstand the ravages of traffic and the abrasion of dirt. They are the only surfaces of the house that are frequently subjected to the effects of detergent and water. The wonder is not that you may have to work on floors now and then, but that you don't have to work on them more often.

Some of the troubles a floor can give you involve construction, and apply to both wood floors and those covered with tile or sheet materials. They are covered later in this chapter. However, the most frequent repair jobs involve work on the surfacing materials and they will be discussed first.

HOW A FLOOR IS CONSTRUCTED

Standard residential floor construction involves these elements, shown in the accompanying drawings:

• Floor framing is composed of *joists*, which are usually 2 x 6, 2 x 8, or 2 x 10 (less commonly, 2 x 12) planks on edge. First-floor joists are supported at their ends by the house foundation, or by the foundation at one end while the other end rests on a beam located halfway between two foundation walls. (If a house is quite big there may be two beams.)

Second-floor joists are supported by outside walls and by the room partitions of the first floor.

• Also part of the framing is the *bridging*, which may be in the form of an X of light lumber nailed between joists, or pieces of the same 2″ stock as the joists, cut to length and spiked in a staggered row between them. The purpose of bridging is to prevent the joists from twisting, and to distribute the load more evenly between them.

• On top of the joists is the *subflooring*. This may be composed of 1 x 6 or 1 x 8 tongue-and-groove boards or of plywood, usually ⅝″ or ¾″ thick. Subflooring of boards is most often nailed at a 45-degree angle to the joists, a further contribution to the strength and uniform resilience of the floor.

Typical floor construction in a house. In some homes, the subfloor may be ⅝″ plywood instead of 1″ boards nailed diagonally. The beam may be a steel I-beam instead of doubled-up 2 x 6s or 2 x 8s. Second-floor construction is the same, except that the joists are supported by walls rather than by foundation.

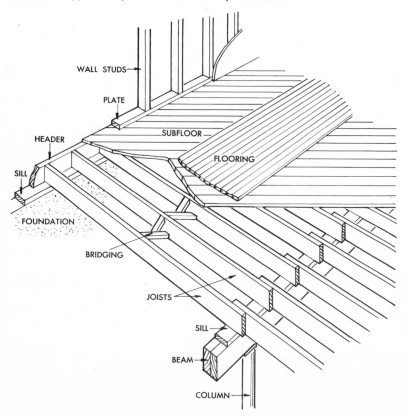

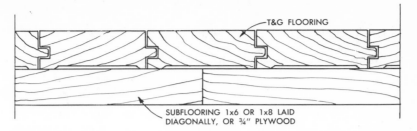

Cross-section of tongue-and-groove flooring laid on lumber or
plywood subflooring.

Hardwood flooring. When a finished floor is hardwood (most
often oak or maple and less commonly one of the southern
hardwoods) the flooring strips are tongue-and-groove. Flooring is always laid crosswise to the joists, with the rare excep-
tions you may encounter in unique situations in individual
houses.

Since the nails holding hardwood flooring down go through
the tongue, you can never see them, except perhaps at the
edges of the room, beneath the baseboard and shoemold.
The strips vary in length from about 2' to perhaps 10. Thus,
any "run" of flooring is composed of two or more pieces, except in rooms that are quite small. The ends of the strips are
machined true and square at the mill, so that there is rarely
any gap between two lengths.

Resilient flooring. The term "resilient flooring" is often used
to cover the entire range of tile, linoleum, vinyl "roll goods"
and similar materials. The floor gains no strength from resilient flooring materials, and therefore the underfloor usually
consists of two layers:

(1) The subfloor may be the same as for hardwood—either
boards or ⅝" or ¾" plywood.

(2) There is also another layer called *underlayment,* carefully nailed (sometimes with adhesive) to the subfloor. The
material is most often plywood or hardboard, usually ¼"
thick. Its purpose is to bridge and level off any irregularities
in the subfloor, but more important, to provide a smooth surface for the resilient material. This is necessary because all

201

resilient flooring tends to "follow the floor"—that is, conform to indentations, bumps, ridges, cracks, etc., in the material it is laid over.

These flooring materials are laid in a mastic or adhesive that is troweled on the underlayment, usually with a toothed spreader that automatically measures and uniformizes the mastic.

Block flooring. One of the increasingly popular recent forms of flooring is hardwood in blocks that is laid much the same way as resilient tile. The blocks may be several side-by-side strips of regular hardwood flooring, or they may be squares of plywood faced with oak or some other hardwood. The blocks are grooved on two sides, tongued on the other two. Thus, when they are laid, the units lock together.

Although block flooring can be put down over a plywood subfloor, it is standard practice to use an underlayment over a board subfloor. The reason for this is to minimize—even eliminate—the chance that unevenness in the support of the boards would coincide with the joists in the block flooring and produce a rocky floor.

With the general character and construction of floors made clear, what are the problems you run into—and their solution?

WHEN A FLOOR SQUEAKS

A squeaky floor indicates that one or several of the structural elements covered above is letting a little slack into things. As a result, two boards rub together and produce the annoying squeak. It may be between two flooring boards; it may be between a flooring and a subflooring board; it may be between a subflooring board and a joist; it may be between a joist and the beam it rests on.

The first step is to find the squeak. You may have to listen with your ear close to the floor, or you may have to go down to the basement. Get some member of the household to activate the noise while you chase it down. To pinpoint it exactly, try laying your fingers gently across the floorboards. Quite often you can feel the vibration.

The cure depends on the nature of the construction parts involved in the squeaking.

• If the noise is caused by a friction between two framing members that are not exposed—presenting no esthetic problems—hammer some nails or spikes into the joint to stop the movement. Just in case the nails may not kill the motion altogether, squirt some oil in the crack.

• If the noise is caused by friction between flooring and subflooring and you can get at it from below, drive three or four screws up through the subflooring into the flooring. Predrill for the screws, because that flooring is hard. Select screws about a ¼″ shorter than the combined thickness of the two flooring elements, so you can be sure the points won't come through above. Draw them up tight, even using a screwdriver bit in a brace to make sure the two layers of the floor are held tight and motionless.

• You may find that the subfloor has warped upward, leaving space between it and the joist, resulting in a squeak when weight is applied above. Handle this problem by screwing a cleat (a length of 2 x 2 is good) flush with the top of the joist, just under the offending subfloor area. Then run screws up through this cleat into the subfloor, pulling it down against the top of the joist. As you make final turns on these screws, ask someone to stand on the floor above, to help make things tight.

• When flooring boards rub together, you may be able to quiet them by screwing from below—as covered in the above paragraph—provided you drive screws into both of the offending boards.

• Squeezing glue between boards that rub together and squeak will usually stop the friction. Use the kind that comes in plastic bottles with a nozzle, and force as much glue into the crack as you can, so that it will work into the tongue and groove. Keep off the floor until the glue dries.

• Lubrication is one of the simpler methods of eliminating squeaks in floorboards. Since the floor is finished with a relatively impervious material, you can actually squirt oil between the boards. Any that remains on the surface wipes away. Or you can use powdered graphite.

• A wood-swelling material (Chair-Loc is one brand name) squirted into the crack between squeaking boards swells them into such a tight fit that the squeak is eliminated — unless, of course, the crack is too wide in the first place.

In some cases, you may find it necessary to nail or screw from the top to silence a squeaky board. If you do, try to find some hardened steel flooring nails. Building supply dealers usually have them, although a hardware store may not. You can use ordinary nails — 8-penny finishing nails — if you pre-drill through the oak with a bit slightly smaller than the nails. (They'll bend if you try to hammer them through oak.) It's best to drive the nails at a slight angle, and it's even better to use them in pairs, driven at opposite angles. This gives the best grip. Countersink the nails and fill the holes with wood plastic that matches the finished wood. Spot-stain the patches to make a better match, if necessary.

When you do squeak therapy with screws, you may want to use a plug cutter to obtain little disks of the same wood as the floor, to cement into the counterbored screw holes. Again, spot stain the plugs to match.

REPAIRING DAMAGED FLOORBOARDS

It is not easy to remove and replace hardwood flooring, because the boards are tongue and groove not only at the edges, but also at the ends. Each board is locked in with its neighbors. For that reason, plus the difficulty of matching a new piece of flooring to an existing floor, it is almost always best to approach repairs with an eye toward patching, rather than replacing. Taking this approach in stages . . .

• Sanding and refinishing a damaged area is one of the easiest repair methods. The sanding, whether done by hand on a small area or by machine, should be blended into the surrounding surfaces. Be sure to avoid straight-line margins which would be more conspicuous than random curves. After you've graduated down to fine sandpaper, it may be necessary to blend and mix pale stains of the proper color to match the existing floor. Remember that the final hue will be the result of the stain, if any, plus the floor finish you use, since both contribute color or intensity to the wood.

• Filling scratches or dents in a floor is essentially the same as it would be in any wooden surface. At well-stocked paint stores you can buy wood filler of the plastic wood type in a variety of colors. One of them may be the color you want. If not, use the "natural" filler, and stain the patch when it is hard and smoothly sanded. It's a good idea to apply some of the filler to a "test" surface, so you'll have a place to experiment with stains.

• Wood patches are better than plastic wood when the scratch or gouge is large and deep. With a router or chisel and mallet, cut out the damaged area ¼″ or so deep. Then cut a piece of flooring the right size and thickness to fill the depression. If you make the patch from a piece of wood with a grain that closely resembles that of the floor, it will be inconspicuous when it is sanded and stained and finished to match.

Replacing a floorboard. Should you find it necessary to put in a new piece of flooring, it is easiest to replace an entire board, even though the damage may be confined to a small part of the strip. There is no neat and clean way to get the damaged board out. One technique is to run a portable electric saw down the middle of the board, set to cut exactly the depth of the board. Then, you can pry the two strips out. Be careful not to damage the adjacent board. If you don't have a saw available, removing the board is just a matter of chisel and mallet.

To insert a single board in standard floor, saw off the lower lip of the groove and the tongue of the adjacent board. This lets the board fall into place after you fit the tongue into the groove of the other board.

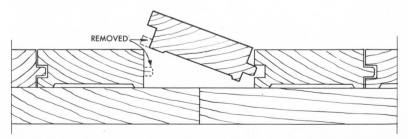

REMOVED

Once the strip has been removed, use a chisel to cut the *tongue off the end* of the board at one end of the gap. Use a plane or table saw to *remove the bottom lip of the groove* off the replacement board. Cut this board the required length, *leaving the tongue end intact.* In other words, cut the scrap off the end of the new strip that has the groove in it.

To put the replacement strip in, slip the tongued end into the groove at the end of the opening. Press or pound the board into position. Since you have removed the bottom lip of the groove on the new piece, and since you have removed the tongue at the end of the cavity, the new strip will seat down on the subflooring.

You'll probably have some fairly heavy sanding to do, bringing the new piece down flush. Then custom-stain and finish the new wood.

The techniques used for handling a single board translate easily into work on several boards, with this difference:

After the first piece has been sawed or chiseled out, you will be able to use a pinchbar under the tongue edge of succeeding boards, to pry them up from the subfloor, applying the bar at the nailing points. When you have loosened the board enough, pry it up in the middle and saw it in two. Then finish ripping the two halves out.

When you put the new strips in place, start at the edge of the opening which has the flooring with the tongue. Cut the replacement pieces to length, and nail them in place through the tongues, the same as the original pieces were nailed. Sand, stain, and finish.

Replacing block flooring. The specific type of block flooring determines the specific methods of replacing damaged units. If your floor blocks are made up of actual strips of flooring, you may be able to remove a single strip and replace it, following the methods covered above. If it is made of plywood blocking, the entire square must be replaced, of course.

Owing to the tongue-and-groove design of these blocks, removal requires these steps:

1. Using a portable saw, make a cut diagonally from corner to corner, in both directions. Be sure to cut only as deep as the thickness of the block.

2. With a chisel or prybar, lift each of the triangular sections at the center of the block. They'll break loose, and let you disengage them from the tongue-and-groove joining at the edges.

3. To insert a new block, you must first rip off the tongues and the bottom lip of the grooves. This will let the square settle into the opening. Some modifications of the size may be necessary. If so, use a plane.

4. Apply adhesive or mastic and press the new square in place.

As with other wood floor repairs, it will be necessary to experiment with stain colors in order to match up the new block or strip with the rest of the room. Some block flooring is prefinished. When this is the case, you must find a block of the same finish. Color differences, then, will be those resulting from aging and weathering of the floor—perhaps not great enough to be critical. You may, however, be able to bring them closer together by brushing on a thinned coat of dark oak varnish stain, then wiping it off selectively and carefully until the remaining film provides just the right amount of coloration.

When a floor is old and badly worn and damaged, you'll find it almost as easy to put down a new floor—right on top of the old—as to make repairs. The techniques for handling block flooring and resilient floor tile are shown in accompanying photographs.

REPAIRING RESILIENT FLOORING

Damage to floor tile, linoleum, and similar materials is always repaired by replacement. That is why it's a good idea, if you have such a floor put down—or put one down yourself—to save the trimmings, ends, or extra tile. It's just about impossible to go back to the floorcoverings store a few years later and buy materials that will match.

About the only tools you need to do resilient floor repairs

HOW TO LAY BLOCK FLOORING

Block flooring may be composed of short lengths of regular hardwood flooring, like these tiles, or it may be of plywood. In both cases the pieces are tongue-and-groove, easy to lay.

An underlayment of plywood or hardboard makes the new floor level. Nail sheets every 4″ along the edges, every 8″ throughout, using roofing nails.

Lay out experimental rows of blocks in both directions to determine the best spacing. Then mark a line at the edge of the row, a few feet from one wall.

Spread the adhesive over all of the area on one side of the line, and lay the blocks in that area. This way, you have a clean place to stand.

Then, with the newly laid floor to stand on, turn around and do the other part of the floor. Be sure to follow instructions on the mastic, and be sure you snug the squares close together.

The rows at the end of the room will have to be cut to fit. The final step: nail the baseboard and the shoe mold in place. They must not be nailed tight on the flooring or they'll interfere with normal expansion and contraction. Use a matchbook cover as a spacer.

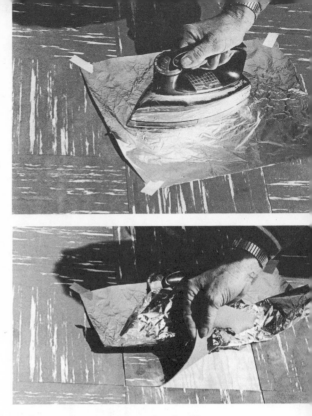

Remove a damaged floor tile by taping a sheet of aluminum foil over it, then heating the tile with a flat iron.

When it is hot, you can peel the tile from the floor. If any adhesive remains, scrape it up before applying new adhesive for the replacement.

are a linoleum knife, a broad spatula, and a notched adhesive spreader. And, the family flatiron. To lift damaged tile, do this:

1. Spread a piece of aluminum foil over the tile, and run a hot iron over it until it softens.

2. Slip the broad spatula under the edge of the tile and lift and scrape it off.

3. Continue to apply heat to the adhesive which remains on the floor where the tile was, and scrape the area clean. Try to make it absolutely smooth, or the roughness will show through the new tile.

4. Spread mastic or adhesive with the notched spreader, and put the new tile in place.

Patching damaged linoleum or other roll goods calls for basically the same techniques, but first you must make a patch that will be a perfect fit for the cutout area. To do this, position the patching sheet over the damage. Be careful to match up patterns, if any. Hold the material firmly in place and cut it to final size and shape with the linoleum knife. As you do this, let the tip of the knife go through the patch, and mark the exact shape of the piece on the floor.

210

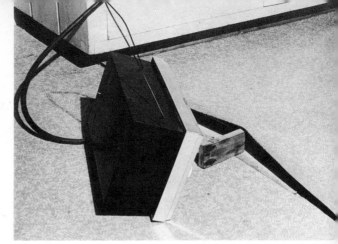

Seams often lift in linoleum installations, and water soaks the underlayment. Before you trowel in new adhesive, dry the crack thoroughly by directing a small electric heater at it, or a hair dryer. Vacuum out any debris, then glue the material back down.

Set the patch aside, and continue cutting the flooring material, following the line "scribed" by the knife. When you have cut through the resilient material, use the aluminum foil and hot-iron stunt to remove the old linoleum. Clean the area up, spread the adhesive, then put the patch in place.

If you discover a big difference in the color of the new piece of linoleum or the new tile, chances are the old floor has an accumulation of wax and cleaning materials. Try scrubbing the entire area thoroughly with some such strong cleaning agent as dishwashing detergent. This will take the old flooring back to its original surface, and although the match may not be perfect, it should be fairly close.

WHEN A FLOOR SAGS

There are probably very few suspended floors in the world without some degree of sag and a small amount is nothing to worry about. However, when the sag becomes severe, it indicates structural problems that may not be limited to the floor itself—and not measurable by a little unevenness under foot. The sag may signal the need for some serious bracing and reinforcing from below.

As the accompanying drawing shows, the stiffness, firmness, rigidity of a floor is provided by the heavy joists, on edge. The subfloor helps to distribute load over two or more joists, but does relatively little to make the floor strong. Further, the flooring itself contributes little to the strength of the floor.

Therefore, floor sag is always due to downward flexing of the floor joists. The reason for the bend may be excessive weight above, the inevitable "droop" over a period of time, or a warping in the lumber that occurred as it dried. This is the key to bringing the floor back to plane; the joists must be straightened, then either supported or reinforced so that they will stay straight.

When a sag in the floor develops slowly over a period of time as often happens, you may not notice it until one day is seems that a table or chair is standing at an angle. When you make that discovery, check for the exact location of the sag this way:

1. Stand furniture to one side and roll back the rug.

2. Use a board 8′ or 10′ long with an absolutely true edge. Check it by sighting down the length. Position the board over the suspected sag. Mark the spot on the floor where the sag is the greatest—that is, where the space between the board's edge and the floor is greatest.

3. Turn the board 90 degrees as a further check to find the low spot.

The reason you must find the precisely lowest spot is that you must apply the corrective forces to that spot, from below. Once you have located it, determine some point of reference common to the room you're in and the room or basement or crawl space below. You do this as a means of locating, from beneath that same lowest spot in the floor sag.

How to use a floor jack. To raise the sag in the floor, you need a heavy-duty jack. If you're working in a crawl space, a regu-

Telescoping jack-post comes in the form of two heavy tubes that fit together, held to the required length by a pin. There are flange plates for top and bottom, and a heavy threaded rod that unscrews from a socket to extend lifting pressure.

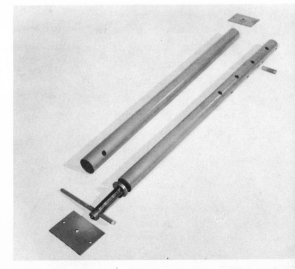

lar contractor's jack will do the job. You can rent one at any well-stocked rental center. If the sag is over a basement, the regular jack will be too short. Instead, use a jack-column— often called a "Tel-e-Post." This device can be adjusted to any normal floor-to-ceiling height, and is equipped with 6″ or so of heavy screw drive. Here's how to set either of the jacks up for business:

1. First, you need a firm base. If you happen to be setting up on a concrete floor, this is no problem. If, however, it is a wooden floor, you must establish a "bridge" across four or five of the floor joists. To do this, lay two, three, or four lengths of 2 x 6 or 2 x 8 on top of each other, across the floor joists. Be sure they run crosswise of the joists of the floor you're standing on. This bridge will distribute the force of the jack over an area large enough to support it.

2. Next, you must provide a similar form of bridging across the sagging joists above, spanning three or four or more, depending on the degree and the spread of the sag. Usually a length of 4 x 4 works for this bridging, and it is relatively easy to handle, compared to a lamination of 2-by-stuff.

3. Position the jack between the two bridges and snug it up, to hold the upper bridging in place. Be sure it is vertical.

You are now ready to start screwing the jack upward, applying the pressure needed to raise the sag.

Important: Do not force all the sag out of the floor at one time. If you do, it may cause cracks and ruptures that will be a tough job to fix. Tighten the jack about ¼″ a day, until things are raised far enough. Although it is true that this may cause some inconvenience—if the jack has to stay in a living area for several days—it is still preferable to the damage that may arise from jacking too far too fast.

As the jack rises, it gradually pushes the joists back up to where they belong. It is good practice to continue the operation until the floor has been raised a bit too high—that is, until there is a slight upward bow. This anticipates the inevitability that things will settle back a little when the jack is removed. However, *if the jack can be left in position as a column* (see over) the slight over-raise is not necessary.

Telepost or floor jack should be capped with three or more 2 x 6s or 2 x 8s, bridging at least three floor joists. This distributes the load and reduces the chance of damage to the floor as you jack it up to remove a sag.

Making the correction permanent. In order to prevent the sag from coming back, you must either reinforce the joists while they are in the raised position, or establish some sort of support from below, to hold the joists up where they belong.

The standard procedure when the joists must be reinforced is to select some 2″ planks the same width as the joists, and spike them to the joists involved. If the sag is relatively small and the load is not great, you can usually do the job with a single plank for each joist. For greater rigidity, put a plank on both sides of the joist which runs through the middle of the sagging area.

Select these planks carefully, avoiding large knots. Be sure they are straight, although a slight edgewise bow is not undesirable since you can often spike it in place with the bow up and gain a little counter-sag force.

Force the planks up hard against the subfloor, and spike them into the existing joists with 16-penny spikes spaced the width of the plank apart—first near the top, then near the bottom, in a zigzag pattern. Cleat (bend over) the nails where they come through the joist. Then remove the jack.

If it is possible to leave a vertical support in place to hold the sag up permanently, do so. It is the best overall answer. When the jack is one you rented, you can usually replace its function with a post cut about $\frac{1}{8}''$ longer than the distance between the floor and the bridging across the joists. This can be a 4 x 4 or a pair of 2 x 4s spiked together—or heavier timber if required. Sledgehammer it into place, then remove the jack.

You should treat this post with a wood preservative, if it rests on concrete or on any other material which might invite decay. A good way to apply the preservative is to pour it into a pail or any kind of container that is big enough and stand the post in it for half an hour or so. Let it drain.

The common practice with a Tel-e-Post is to leave it in place, where it acts as a steel column. Although you can replace it with a lally column or a wooden post, there is hardly enough saving to compensate for the bother.

Important: If you live in an old house—old enough so that it has wooden posts in the basement—it may be that sagging is caused by the gradual disintegration of one or more of those posts. You can be sure that this is the case if there is a sag in the floor near the location of a post. It is good foresight to replace all such posts with steel lally columns or post jacks.

Handling small sags and dips. There are times when a sag covers a relatively small area—hardly more than the distance between two joists. When this is the case, the problem is usually caused by a sharp warp or dip in the joist which runs across the middle of the sag. And it is usually impossible to jack up the joist to remove it.

Instead, cut a half-dozen or so wedges, quite flat in pitch, from a scrap of 2″ stock. Slip the points of the wedges in between the top edge of the joist and the subfloor, some on one side, some on the other, where the sag occurs. Tap the wedges in, starting with those nearest the middle of the sag and working alternately toward the ends. This operation will gradually lift the nails holding the subfloor to the joists, and raise the sag. If the subfloor seems reluctant to leave the joist, insert the flat end of a wrecking bar into the crack to get the separation started. Leave the wedges in place of course, after the floor has been brought up level.

SECOND-FLOOR SAG

When the sag is in a second floor, there are obvious additional problems. To begin with, the ceiling below covers up the joists. And the sag in the floor becomes, as well, a sag in the ceiling. Since the jack-and-reinforce techniques described above would require that you remove the ceiling, there are some decisions to be made.

1. Is the sag in the ceiling an eyesore—highly noticeable? If it is, correction of the sag must involve removing the ceiling material.

2. Is the sag bad enough so that the ceiling is cracked? If it is, perhaps removing it and replacing it wouldn't be a bad idea anyway.

3. Is the ceiling sag no bother—just the floor above? If this is the case, there may be a method of correcting it without jacking it up. See the next question.

4. Is the floor above a regular hardwood floor, or does it happen to be a form of tile or sheet goods that could be removed—or replaced? If it's the latter, correcting a sag may be a relatively small job.

When the ceiling must be removed. This job will be messy, if the ceiling is plastered; much less so if it is plasterboard. First you must remove the ceiling. See Chapter 16 for the way to tear out either plaster or plasterboard and replace it. While the ceiling is open, handle the sag by whichever of the techniques applies in the situation. Be sure to spread the load of the jacking operation over several floor joists by building a "pad" of 2 x 6s or 2 x 8s under the jack.

Repairing a sag from above. When the sag in a floor over a ceiling does not call for correction of the ceiling itself you may be able to tackle the problem from above, and if you can, there are several advantages. Not the least of these is that you don't have to ruin the ceiling. And you don't have to clutter up the living space below with jacks and other paraphernalia.

The basic technique for repairing the sag from above is to take up the floor, fill in the depression with vinyl patch and other materials, as discussed below. The difficulty of the job depends on the nature of the floor. Generally, it is hard to take up wood flooring—although it can be done. And it is relatively easy to lift linoleum or tile.

Earlier in this chapter we described the basic techniques for taking up wood flooring and replacing it when it is damaged. Use these same methods raising flooring when your job is to correct a sag. If you work carefully, you may be able to save most of the strips and use them again.

To correct floor level, you must remove the flooring over the entire area that is depressed. You must first establish which way the tongues on the strips face, because you must lift the boards by prying up under the tongue edge where the nails are. Then, work "tongue-wise" across the sagging area.

When the area is bare, cut a piece of lumber with an absolutely straight edge to a length that will reach across the spot, in both directions—two pieces if the space is oblong.

Obtain some epoxy autobody repair material. Mix it according to directions, and spread it over the depressed area, using the straightedges to make sure you are bringing things back up to level. When this epoxy has hardened, check it with the straightedges. Use a chisel or heavy scraper to knock off any high spots. Mix more epoxy if necessary to fill low spots. Work for a surface as true and level as possible.

Then replace the flooring boards you took up, adding new strips as necessary to replace any that were damaged. The final step is refinishing the floor, and it may turn out to be just as simple to do the whole thing, instead of attempting to make the worked-over area match, if it has many new boards.

If the floor is one of the resilient materials, see the steps outlined earlier in this chapter to lift it. You won't need the extra complications of epoxy patching material under a resilient floor. Instead, use the vinyl patching material sold normally for spackling at lumber or hardware outlets.

REPAIRS YOU CAN MAKE ON STAIRWAYS

Stairways are complicated, not only because they are made of many small pieces, but also because many times they are constructed to fit special situations. In addition, there are several different methods of stairbuilding—some of them done on the job, some of them in millwork factories. Some stairways are simple saw-and-nail joinery; some involve elaborate routing and rabbeting and mortising. Nearly always, the joinery is covered with moldings. Most of the time, a finished stairway is sealed off below.

For all of these reasons, repairs to stairs depend a great deal on your own diagnosis and ingenuity. The basic principle is to notice carefully how you take things apart so you can put them back the same way.

We'll begin with the basic construction:

Stairs are composed of *treads* that you walk on, *stringers* that support the treads, and *risers* that close the spaces between the treads. (In some functional stairs, the riser is omitted.)

In the simplest construction, the stringers are cut out in the zigzag step pattern, the treads rest on top of the horizontal surfaces, and the risers are fastened to the vertical faces. In more sophisticated stairway construction (usually done at the factory), the zigzag is mortised into the stringers, and the treads and risers are inserted in the mortises. It is common with this construction to rabbet the back edge of the tread into the riser, and rabbet the top edge of the riser into the tread above. A stairway constructed like this is all but indestructible, and replacement of parts requires the trickery of a professional.

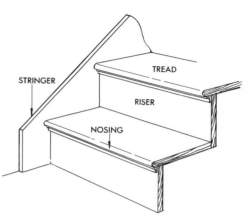

These are the main components of a typical stairway. In this model, the risers are joined to the treads with butt joints. A stairway can also be built by rabbeting the treads and the risers, as shown in the following drawing.

Squeaky stairs. Have someone activate the squeak while you pinpoint its location, both by sound and by feel. The friction that causes the noise may be at any joint in the tread-riser-stringer complement, but it is most likely to be between the tread and the riser. The simplest and surest way to get rid of it is to depress the tread as far as it will go, then drive two or three finishing nails through it into the riser. Be sure the nails go in at an angle, for maximum resistance against the tread rising. You better drill a hole through the tread, which is most surely oak and hard to drive a nail through. Sink the nail heads and fill the holes with plastic wood.

If the riser is rabbeted into the tread, and if you don't want the patched nail holes in the tread, you can do this job another way with a lot more bother. Remove the molding beneath the lip of the tread. Predrill holes slightly smaller than the nails at an upward angle through the riser into the tread. Drive the nails. Replace the molding.

When the stairs are open below, you can take care of the squeak by gluing and screwing a strip of wood to the back of the riser, up snug against the bottom of the tread.

If the squeak occurs where the tread joins the stringers, the easiest silencing method is powdered graphite or some other lubricant. However, if the stairs are open below, you can screw-and-glue a cleat at the joint. Or, when the tread is mortised into the riser, tap in some small wedges to tighten the joint.

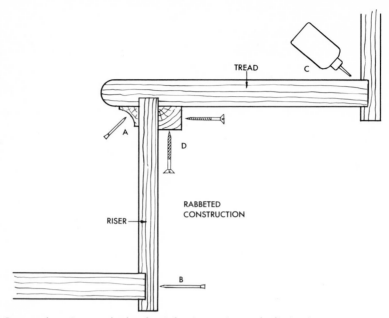

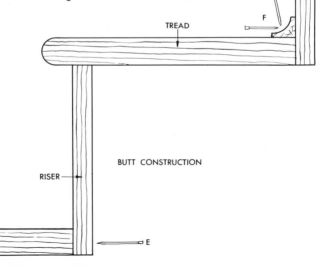

Best and easiest methods of reinforcing stairs and eliminating squeaks in rabbeted and in butt construction. A. Remove molding and drive nails diagonally through riser into stair tread. B. If steps are available from below, drive nails through riser into the back edge of treads. C. Squirt glue into the joint where tread sinks into riser. D. Screw and glue a cleat in the joint of riser and tread if available from below. E. Nail through tread into riser, angling nails for maximum holding power. F. With brads and glue, fasten a molding into the corner of tread and riser.

Replacing treads. When stairs are built in simple butt-joint manner, it is easy to replace a tread should one become worn or damaged. Simply pry the step off. Get a piece of stair tread at the lumberyard, cut it to length, and put it back. Finish it to match.

Things are harder when the stairway is built with mortises in the stringers, but the job can be done. Bore a hole in the middle of the tread, then use a keyhole or similar saw to cut the tread in two. Now you can pry and lift the two halves out.

Cut a piece of stair tread exactly to this length: *the distance between the stringers plus the depth of one mortise in the stringer*. Cut the rabbet in the bottom, positioned the same as the rabbet in the old tread.

By inserting one end of this new tread in the mortise in one stringer, and fitting the rabbeted joints together, you can seat the tread into position — except that the other end will not be in the mortise. So, slide the tread toward that end until it is centered, halfway into the mortise at both ends. Nail it in place, replace any moldings, and finish the new wood to match.

16

WALLS AND CEILINGS

FORTUNATELY, VERY LITTLE ever goes wrong with the internal components of walls and ceilings. The wall studs are heavy 2 x 4s, ceiling joists are even heavier 2 x 6s, 2 x 8s, or even 2 x 10s. With blocking between studs to make them even more rugged and bridging between joists for the same purpose, walls and ceilings are pretty permanent.

The story is different, however, with the surfacing materials that go on walls and ceilings. They are, in some cases, pretty delicate. It isn't hard to punch an accidental hole through a wall. Moreover, owing to the wide expanse of wall or ceiling surfaces, there are always problems with expansion and contraction and settling. The brittle, nonflexible materials used for walls develop cracks with annoying regularity. Often, you must make the same repairs several times, until the house finally settles into its permanent shape and position.

STANDARD WALL AND CEILING CONSTRUCTION

Walls are built of studs which run vertically. At the floor, there is a "sill" into which the studs are spiked. At the top of the wall there is a "plate." Spikes go through the plate into the studs.

The plate forms the support for the ceiling joists, which usually run across the narrower dimension of the room. In both cases, the framing members normally are spaced 16″ from center to center.

The wall and ceiling facing materials are fastened to the studs and joists, in one or another of these constructions:

• Wood lath, less and less common in new construction, is almost sure to be found in older houses. Lath is rough-sawn wood about 1½″ wide, about ⁵/₁₆″ thick, nailed across the studs or joists with deliberate spaces between the strips. When plasterers trowel on the first coat, it works into the cracks and provides an excellent link with the lath. There are usually multiple coats of plaster—a rough coat or two which builds the wall up level, then a finish coat or two of finer plaster producing the final smooth wall.

• Plaster lath is a sheet material formed of plaster between heavy sheets of paper. The construction crew nails the units of plaster lath to the wall and ceiling members, and then the plasterers go to work.

• Drywall construction is the increasingly popular use of large sheets of plasterboard, designed so that the only actual plastering required is treating the joints and the nailheads with a "joint compound."

Basic tools and materials you use for making repairs on walls and ceilings are a wide spackle knife, linoleum knife to cut plasterboard surfacing, chisel to remove loosened plaster, hammer, nails, joint cement and joint tape. Resin-coated nails are best, and they should be a size larger than those used originally on a plasterboard wall.

Spackle and patching knife are easiest to use if you round the corners of the blade slightly. This keeps the points from digging in, and gives you a smooth surface, easy to finish off with sandpaper.

The type of wall treatment has a bearing on the kinds of damage the wall or ceiling is most likely to suffer, and on the methods you'll find it easiest to use in their repair. For example, cracks are most likely in plastered walls which are extremely brittle and intolerant of shifting and settling. However, they are so rugged that you aren't likely to break a hole clear through them into the inside of the wall. Plasterboard, on the other hand, very rarely cracks (except at the joints). But you could ram the corner of a table into the wall and punch a hole clear through the surfacing. Another problem that often needs attention is "nail popping," caused by vibration and by wood shrinkage upon aging.

REPAIRING CRACKS IN PLASTER

It is much easier today to fill plaster cracks than it was a short time ago, and the reason is new materials for the job. Many of the old time-consuming and messy preparation steps can be bypassed entirely, because modern patching paste and powders have greater adhesion, longer working life, and different setting characteristics.

Several factors influence the choice of patching materials, and among them is cost. When a patch calls for a fairly large volume of material, something like plaster of Paris is cheap — and it works well in large volume. Smaller repairs may call for water-mix powders with special working characteristics, such as the Muralo product called "Spackle" or Durham's "Rock Hard Water Mix Putty." However, typical plaster cracks and blemishes are easiest to repair with ready-mixed spackling-patching materials of a vinyl formula, such as that produced by DAP and several other manufacturers. Adhesion, working life, and workability of the vinyl formulas make them extremely effective except when repairs are so extensive as to make cost a factor. Methods of working with each of these materials are discussed below, under the conditions where they best apply.

Most useful forms of patching materials are water-mix putty or spackle, plaster of Paris powder, and vinyl paste spackling compound. The vinyl material, ready-mixed, is easiest for most home repairmen to use, although it is most expensive. Plaster of Paris is cheapest.

Fine cracks. Some extremely fine cracks will disappear under a coat of today's thick acrylic wall paints. However, when they reach the width popularly called "hairline," run over them with vinyl patch and a putty knife. The photographs show the best method of handling the knife, which must be flexible. If you shop for one at your hardware store, test several for flexibility to be sure the one you pick will bend properly under fairly gentle pressure. When a knife bends in this manner, it squeezes the patching materials into the crack, filling it completely. It is a good idea to round the corners of the knife slightly, with a file or stone. A blade this shape tends to blend the patch off smoothly at the edges, while a sharp corner may produce a groove that calls for still another application of the patching material.

There are usually three stages in simple crack patching:

1. With firm pressure that bends the knife, force the patch deep into the crack.

2. With minimum pressure—with the knife almost straight—scrape the excess material off the surface.

3. With medium pressure, "trowel" the patch smooth.

As with all wall and ceiling patching jobs, you must go over the area with sandpaper after everything is dry, to produce final smoothness. And, in some circumstances, it may be necessary to give the patched area a texture to match the surrounding area. Techniques for this are described later in the chapter.

It is not necessary, as is sometimes recommended, to widen or enlarge a small crack when you work with vinyl patching materials. And it is not necessary to dampen the crack. The vinyl material has good adhesion and dries even in very small quantities.

Vinyl patch in wider cracks. When there is a serious settling or shifting of the wall or ceiling, resulting in extensive cracking in widths up to perhaps the diameter of a pencil, you can use vinyl patch and the methods covered above. However, you may find that the vinyl material shrinks slightly as it hardens, making a double application necessary.

Anticipating this, make the first application with the trowel blade well bent to force the patch deep. Then trowel off the excess vinyl patch. With a damp cloth, wipe off all the material on the surface adjacent to the crack. This leaves you with a smooth area to work on when you make the final application.

Preparing severe cracks for patching. When cracks in plaster are severe—both wide and extended—there is often damage to the adjacent material. Examine both sides of the crack for plaster that may be loosened from the lath, or finish-coat plaster that may be loosened from the base coat. Chip all the loose material away, right down to *plaster that you are sure is sound* and well bonded to the lath or the base coat.

If it is your plan to use plaster of Paris or another of the economical cementitious products for the patch, you can help make sure the new material will stay in place if you undercut the edges of the area, using an old chisel. That way, the patch fills under the lip and is "keyed" in place.

As a final step, before applying the patch, dampen the edges of the damaged area. This improves the bond of plaster of Paris and similar materials, and eliminates the chance that the patch may harden poorly because of insufficient water.

Mixing powder patching materials. There are some time-saving, money-saving tricks for mixing powder-form patching materials:

• Use a square pan, such as a cake pan or a tray from the photographic darkroom. The reason for this is the ease with which you can lift material from the tray against one of the straight sides, vs. the problems of scraping the square-end trowel up a rounded surface.

• Do not add the water to the powder. Instead, sprinkle the powder over the surface of the water in the pan. This technique serves as a sort of gauge as to the amount of powder you need, since it settles into the water. Keep sprinkling until there is no free water—and no dry powder. A little stirring then gives you a good mix.

• Estimate the volume of the damage to be patched, then use the amount of *water* it would take to fill that void. Add powder to the water, and you'll discover that you have very little material left over.

Best way to mix a powder form material is to judge the amount needed, and pour that amount of water in a square pan. Sprinkle powder over the surface uniformly, until the water has absorbed all it will take. Then stir. Straight side of the pan makes it easy to scrape up a knife-load of patch to apply to the wall.

• Read the instructions on the powder can very carefully, not only to find out tricks for using the specific patching material, but to find out what its working life may be. Some powders set hard in half an hour or less. They cannot be softened, but must be thrown out. Others, owing to special formulation, may stay in working condition for several hours. If you are working with plaster of Paris or another of the quick-setting powders, you can extend the working life by adding a little vinegar to the mixing water.

Applying the patching material. It is almost never possible to patch a large crack in a single operation. Part of the problem is the volume of patching material involved and the difficulty of troweling it smooth the first time. In addition, there is sure to be a certain amount of shrinking and fissuring, which must be caught later.

These are the steps that have proved easiest, working with a powder-mix material:

1. Glob the patch into the opening with an across-the-crack motion of the knife, working to fill the crack as completely as possible. Don't worry about a little messiness.

2. Working *with the crack*, apply pressure enough to bend the knife as you draw it along, forcing the patch in. Make repeated passes along the crack.

3. Now go over the area using the knife as a scraper, and remove the excess material.

4. Make one more pass along the crack, smoothing things as well as possible. It sometimes helps to *dip the knife in water* for this phase of the operation.

If you were lucky, the surface is now smooth. If not, let it set. Then sand off any high spots, and go at it again with patching plaster to fill any small remaining low spots. You may want to switch to the handier and easier vinyl material for this last stroke.

If the wall or ceiling you are working on is smooth-troweled, your patch will show very little if at all when it is painted. However, if there is a texture in the plaster, you must work to match it. There are several methods of doing this — all of them pretty much hit-or-miss. All must be done before the patch sets hard. Try stippling or brushing with a paintbrush or whiskbroom. Wiping with a coarse cloth or a piece of towel-

BASIC STEPS IN PATCHING ORDINARY CRACKS

1. Apply the first coating of material with strokes across the crack in both directions, to work as much patch as possible, as deep as possible, into the opening. Work fast if you are using one of the powder-mix materials with an early setting time. With vinyl and some powders, there is less hurry.

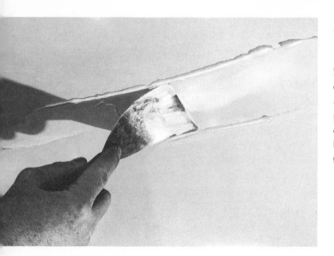

2. Force the material into the crack firmly. Best way is with a flexible knife and enough pressure to produce a bend as shown here. If there are hollows, pick up some of the furrow at side and trowel in.

3. Using the knife as a .scraper, pick up the excess patching material alongside the crack. This helps avoid too much overthick area that has to be sanded down.

230

4. After the first application has hardened, come back with a touchup finish application. You can, if you wish, use economical powder materials for the first filling, then switch to easier working vinyl patch for the finish coat.

ing produces a different type of texturing, somewhat akin to the deliberate rough troweling plasterers sometimes leave. If the surface must be pebbled, you can usually make it match by painting with "sand" additives paint stores sell for mixing into wall paint. In some cases you may want to "sand paint" the entire area.

PATCHING DAMAGE IN PLASTERBOARD

Although plasterboard does not often crack the way plaster may, it may give you trouble in other ways. Sometimes the taped joints fail, and must be retaped. Nail popping is fairly common. And there is the tougher problem of a hole completely through the surface.

Nail popping. When plasterboard is installed, it is nailed along all the studs or joists. The nails are "dimpled"—that is, hit with one soft blow after they are driven home, so that there is a depression on the board. This depression is then filled with the standard joint cement. If the nails loosen, as they may when the dampish wood of new construction dries out, they push off their cement cover.

It is not enough merely to hammer them in. They will quite likely loosen again. Instead, pull one of the nails and take it to the hardware store or builder supply outlet. Get some nails the next size larger—preferably coated. Replace popped nails with these larger nails. Then trowel the dimple smooth with joint cement.

BASIC STEPS IN PLASTERBOARD JOINT TREATMENT

1. Glob on a thick layer of joint cement along the seam or crack. Work in distances of 6' to 8' or less, so you can move to the next step before the material starts to dry.

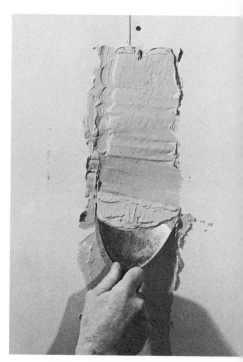

2. Apply a length of joint tape over the cement, centering it carefully and pressing it into the layer. The tape will pick up moisture and swell slightly. That accounts for the wrinkle (below wrist) as the knife forces the tape smoothly deep into the cement. You may have to lift the tape ahead of the knife, if it swells too much.

3. When the tape is imbedded, go over it with cement and make sure that it is all covered, so that no paper shows. This is important, but take pains also not to let the layer of cement get too thick, or you'll create a ridge. Depressions shown in this photo disappear with the next step.

4. Final trowel-on of cement should be thinned very slightly if it has started to thicken in your container. Skive it off on both sides (only one side is shown here) so that it comes down to zero at the edges. Finish the job with sanding when the cement is dry.

233

Loose tape. Plasterboard joint tape does not usually loosen unless it is soaked with water, and rarely then, unless it was improperly imbedded in joint cement when the board was put up. The first part of the repair process, of course, is to remedy the cause for the water. Then, as the accompanying photos show:

1. Rip the tape from the joint, deliberately going beyond the area of actual damage, if possible. Make sure that all the tape is removed that will come off.

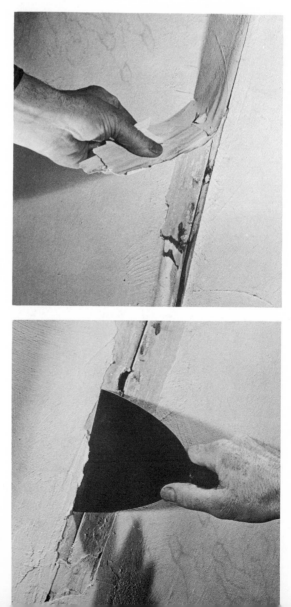

To replace plasterboard tape, tear off the loosened tape as far as it will come free, in both directions. Prod along the joint in search of bubbled tape, which indicates that more of it should be dug off. Use your knife at both sides of the crack, making sure that all of the loosened and deteriorated cement is gone.

2. With a spackling knife, work along the joint, removing any joint cement that is loose or flaking.

3. Tear—don't cut—a piece of new tape the right length. Rough, torn edges are least conspicuous.

4. Run a bed of joint cement along the crack, and press the tape into this material. Then use the knife to smooth the tape and force it into good contact with the cement, all along the patch.

5. Finish the job with a layer of cement troweled over the tape, thick enough so that you cannot see the tape, but not so thick as to leave a pronounced ridge. This final cementing must extend laterally from the tape a few inches, and be skived down to zero at its edges.

If texturing is necessary, see the suggestions described previously.

PATCHING HOLES IN PLASTERBOARD

The difficulty with patching a hole in plasterboard is that there is no back-up for the patching material. The accompanying photographs show a method of overcoming this problem. Use this trick if the hole is not too large — say within the limits of about 8″ by 10″. You may want to mix up an inexpensive batch of patching powder to fill the majority of this depression, then finish it off with plasterboard joint cement or vinyl patch.

When a hole is bigger than about 8″ by 10″, use a different technique:

With a saw, enlarge the hole as far as the two adjoining studs or joists. Keep the cuts at right angles to the framing members. If it happens that there is a joint in the board at one side, break the material free. At the other side—or both if there is no joint—use a chisel to cut the plasterboard *right down the middle of the joist or stud.* This leaves you with a rectangular hole.

Now cut a piece of plasterboard to fit the hole, nail it in place, and use standard tape-and-joint-cement techniques to finish the job.

HOW TO PATCH A BREAKTHROUGH IN PLASTERBOARD

1. First cut the hole to a more or less rectangular shape, using a keyhole saw. Undercut two opposing sides, so that they bevel back under the board. Cut the other two sides so that they are beveled on the front. This trick keys the patch against movement into the wall or out.

2. Cut a piece of plasterboard about 2″ bigger than the hole. Punch two nail holes through it, and loop it around a scrap of wood as shown here.

3. Insert the plasterboard through the hole, into the wall, and then snug it up tight against the back of the plasterboard by twisting the stick until the cord is tight.

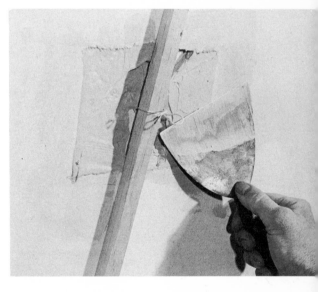

4. Fill the depression with patching plaster, working around the stick and the string. Get as much plaster in place as possible. Then, let it harden. When it is hard, cut the string away and patch the rest of the area.

5. Sand off any high spots, and finish up with a final application of patch.

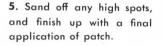

WHAT TO DO ABOUT EXTENSIVE DAMAGE

If, because of something serious like a fire or extensive water damage, a large part of a wall or ceiling must be repaired, it may be simplest in the long run to cover the entire area with a new material.

For example, acoustical tile is easy to put on a ceiling, and it is no longer available only in the polka-dot pattern that once seemed somewhat inappropriate for residential use. Today's tile patterns are tasteful and beautiful—and they are effective factors in the control of sound. Installation is simple, since the lightweight tiles go up with daubs of mastic.

When large-scale damage makes a wall repair seem hopeless, you'll find it simple to apply an entirely new surface, using ⅜" plasterboard. With this thickness, it is not always necessary to replace (or fur out) door and window trim, because there is enough "reveal" to maintain a good appearance.

And, of course, there is always paneling, when it is appropriate. Modern thin plywood materials with every conceivable wood and finish as the face—or hardwood simulations—can be put up in a day or less, covering damage and adding to the appearance of a room at the same time.

MAJOR DAMAGE MAY CALL FOR
A COMPLETE NEW SURFACE

Construction shortcomings let water in over this "bow window," making patching a nightmare because of repetition. Final decision, after the bad flashing was fixed by a carpenter: Cover the area with a new surface.

Masonite is a good material for this operation, because it is rugged enough to be handled—and easily cut to fit. You could use plywood or plasterboard.

Cut out enough material on the square to cover the area. Lay it out in front of the situation, and transfer the shape to the hardboard. Mark it with chalk.

Handy saw for cutting shapes is the popular homeshop saber saw. Be sure to work with the material face down, so the roughness of the cut is on the back—that is, above, when you put the material overhead.

If there is final fitting to be done, use a block plane along the edge of the hardboard.

Nail the material in place with finishing nails into the joists or other framing members. Sink the nails.

Spackling compound, wood plastic, or other patching material fills nail holes and any other joints or openings, before you paint the new surface.

New ceiling of acoustical tile was the solution for extensive damage to the ceiling in this room. Installation is simple; the tiles go up with daubs of mastic.

17

ROOF REPAIRS

DAMAGE TO A ROOF—even if it is small in itself—is often directly responsible for tremendous damage inside the house. It doesn't take much of a leak overhead to make ceiling plaster fall, floorboards warp, wallpaper peel off, and more, during a three-day rain.

Since a rainy day is about the worst kind of an environment for roof repairs, there is a well-founded adage in the world of home repair; the right time to fix a leak in the roof is *before it starts to leak.*

This is an even greater truth in view of the fact that a small leak may exist for years without revealing itself in the form of dripping water. Meanwhile, it is letting moisture into the inner structure of the house, causing mildew and decay where you can't see it until, one day, something caves in.

As with any other phase of preventive maintenance, anticipating roof troubles before they start must depend on careful periodic inspection. And, of course, you must know what to be on the lookout for.

All roofing materials deteriorate, although some of them go faster than others. Rain, hail, sleet, snow, heat of sun, freezing weather, wind—all these have their effect. Add the damage done by tree branches that overhang the roof. (Rain-carrier repairs are covered in Chapter 18.)

HOW TO WATCH FOR DETERIORATION

You can do a fairly worthwhile inspection job, of a fairly new roof, from the ground. Use field glasses if you have them handy. But you must go up on the roof if there are indications of trouble.

Wooden shingles. Cedar shingles follow a set pattern of color change from the day they are laid. To begin with, they are a light reddish brown. This color fades, at first, until the shingles are a silvery gray. This is caused not only by bleaching of the natural pigments in the cedar, but also by the way some of the colorants dissolve in rain water and leach out.

From the day the shingles have turned their lightest (usually the first year) they start to darken, taking on an increasingly deeper gray color. Eventually, they become a gray so dark it turns quite black when the shingles are wet.

The thing to watch for, in your inspection from the ground, is differences in color change, variations from the norm. If a patch of shingles shows a color unlike the surrounding area, the reason is usually an accumulation of moisture under the shingles. You can check on this by watching the roof dry, as it dries after a rain. If there is an area that stays darker in color — that is, wet-looking longer — it is fairly certain that there is water under the shingles. This water may be causing no damage; it may never cause any damage. But the area becomes suspect and should be checked periodically.

As a wood shingle roof starts to age, there are other things to watch for:

• Cupped or dished shingles usually take their form from water beneath. They dry faster on the outside, and the wood shrinks. Cupping also may be caused by the use of inferior-grade shingles, a few of which may slip into the job even when top materials are specified.

• Splits in shingles may be caused by too much space between them, by improper nailing, by widths that are too great. Aging and weathering contribute.

• Worn and weathered shingles are merely showing the ravages of time. However, the wear may be greater in some

DEFECTS TO LOOK FOR IN WOODEN SHINGLES

Among the most serious defects is a split in a shingle directly over the joint between two in the next row.

Shingles as badly warped, cupped, eroded, split, and mildewed as these (and of a low grade, in the first place) may have to be replaced, although spraying with wood preservatives may give them added years of leak-free life.

Erosion shows up best at the base of a row. Shingles shown here have lost about $3/16''$ of thickness.

These shingles, brittled by age and showing other typical signs of deterioration, have been walked on—and the broken shingle shows the type of damage that results from trafficking over an old roof. That explains the use of cherry pickers to work from.

Less common is insect damage, always out of sight back in the overlap of the shingles. Sometimes you can detect it when sawdust-like bits of wood wash out from beneath the rows.

Composition shingles show their age and deterioration mainly through alligator-like crazing. This means the shingles are brittle; a strong wind could break the flaps loose, unless they are cemented down securely. Roof spraying specialists can rejuvenate shingles like this.

shingles than others. Most often the shingles that are cut "flat to the grain" erode faster than those which expose the edge grain of the cedar. It is easy to check the actual amount of weathering a shingle has undergone by examining it *close to the butt of the shingle just above it.* There will be little or no reaction to the weather at the exact point where the shingle emerges from the one above it. But, there will be a sharp "dip" to the new, worn level — a good indication of the amount of wood that has weathered away.

Composition shingles. A composition shingle is formed of a "felt" of asphalt-and-fiber, on the surface of which there are granules of a mineral material. These granules give the shingles their fire resistance — and their color.

Deterioration comes slowly, in several ways. The base gradually decomposes, eroding away under the elements, with the passage of time. The granules may, as a part of this decomposition, gradually loosen and wash away. A certain amount of brittleness may develop with time, causing the shingles to break away in small pieces. And, if the wind is violent, the flaps may raise and tear loose. Finally, there may be a change in color — partly because of fading of the coloration in the minerals, partly because the minerals wash away.

Composition shingles tend to deteriorate in a rather uniform degree, owing to the homogeneous nature of their construction. All the shingles on a given exposure usually need replacing if any of them do. And, one exposure (south or west) may need replacement before areas subjected to less abuse from the weather (north or east).

However, there are examples of physical damage that may make replacement of a single shingle unit necessary.

IF YOU GO UP ON THE ROOF

Two things to remember when you go up on the roof for repairs or for examination:

• You can damage the roof rather seriously tramping around on it after the shingles have aged enough to be brittle. Therefore, keep your traffic to a minimum.

• You can damage yourself—especially if it's a two-story house. Older roofs grow more and more slippery, especially composition shingles with granules that are coming loose.

Be careful. Wear rubber soles. A roof is dangerous *if you find it unnerving to walk up or down it without using your hands to make a quadruped of yourself.* It is not how steep the roof actually is; it's how steep it seems to you.

If you find the roof uncomfortable, use the trick (see photo) of hanging a ladder over the peak, working up and down it on both sides, then moving it along to the next position where work is necessary.

Even when the roof is not particularly steep, and you don't mind working on it, try to keep the ladder you came up directly below where you are working. If you should lose your balance, you'll have a chance to grab it before you go over the edge.

One more thing: Do not climb over the end of a ladder onto the roof. Make sure there is enough ladder extending above the eaves so that you can climb the ladder high enough to step off the side. The danger involved here is not so much the chance that you'll fall climbing off the ladder to the roof. Instead, you're likely to fall trying to get back on the ladder if it doesn't extend far enough past the eaves so that you can mount it safely from the side.

This ladder trick makes roof work safer. Clamp two stubs of 2 x 4 to the rail, just below a rung, angled to hang over the ridge.

THE BASIC REPAIR DECISION

There are three stages of roof deterioration, when your objective is to prevent serious damage to your home.

1. You may be able to replace a few shingles and put things back in shape again.

2. You may be able to contract for a rejuvenation job.

3. You may have to call in a roofing contractor and have the whole thing done anew.

When wear is extensive, what you hope for is the second procedure. Both wood shingles and those made of asphalt composition can be given new life — enough to make the investment truly worth while. The technique most often used is to spray a wood preservative on cedar shingles, a solvent on composition roofing which softens asphalt, giving it new life. The men who do the job work from cherry pickers, and properly never put a foot on your roof. You can find a roof renovator in the yellow pages.

Since the men who do renovating are interested in a successful job (most of them guarantee their work), they will not ordinarily work on a roof that is too far gone to be revived by their services. For that reason, it is almost the best idea to call on one for an estimate and an appraisal. His decision may determine for you the need for a new roof.

So effective are life-extending treatments for roofs that you should consider a treatment for a new roof, if you have the job done over completely or if you are living in a fairly new house. The use of Cuprinol or Pentox or other preservatives based on pentachlorphenol can double the life of wood shingles, and sometimes more than double their life.

If you want to increase the life of composition shingles, many authorities recommend two coats of a high-grade acrylic house paint sprayed on the roof. Such paints as Moore-Guard, Lucite, K-100 and other acrylic formulas will dry over asphalt (an oil paint won't) and add protection for the house itself. Don't overlook the opportunity to pick your color, if you have this job done — or do it yourself. Most home experts these days vote for white or quite light colors on the roof, as a means of cutting down on the amount of heat your attic picks up on a sunny day. On the other hand, you may decide on a color that enhances the looks of your house — or the whole neighborhood.

HOW TO REPLACE WOOD SHINGLES

Since every row of shingles must overlap the one next below it, they must be laid from the bottom up. The men who built the house and roofed it started with a double row at the eave line. Then they laid the next row, and the next, and the next, until they reach the ridge. (In actual practice, this may be done in the form of a pyramid or triangle, in order to increase efficiency and to allow two men to work as a team.)

Principles of proper shingling are shown in this layout. No crack lies above another crack. Each shingle overlaps the one below it by slightly more than half its length, so that there is actually double overlap at the thin upper end of the shingles. This is why you must buy replacement shingles of the same length as those already in place.

The nails in each row are driven high enough in the shingle so that the next row above overlaps it. This prevents water from leaking through the nails because each nail is overhung by the shingle above it. While this is as sound a method of construction as you can think of from the standpoint of weatherproofness, it makes replacing shingles a little difficult. The accompanying photographs help to illustrate the procedures. (They were shot on a "staged" roof, owing to the difficulties of making photographs on an actual roof.)

First, dig out the damaged shingle, using a chisel to split it into narrow strips. If it was nailed properly, there are two nails up there under the next shingle, usually a little less than one quarter of the shingle's width in from each edge. Therefore, all the narrow strips will pull out easily except those which may happen to have the nails through them. Keep at it until everything splits free.

Pick out a shingle that is the proper width, or rip a wider one to size. It should fit easily between the two adjacent shingles, ideally with about ⅛″ of space on each side.

Shove the shingle up into the space where it is to go, until the thin end hits the nails. Give it a couple of taps so those nails make two marks at the end. Pull the shingle out, and use a saw to *cut two slots parallel to the edges* at the point where the nails made their marks. The length of these slots should be just enough to let the shingle slide past the nails into position, but no longer. One way to make sure the slots are the right length is to check them against one of the scraps of the old shingle that has its nail mark in it. Another way is to slip the shingle into position when the slots are about right and continue cutting until they are.

There is an alternative method of handling the problem of those nails. With a metal-cutting blade in a keyhole saw, or with one of those little hacksaw blade holders (see photo) you can work up under the butt of the shingle and cut the nails off. You must hold the saw so that it cuts fairly close to the surface, or the nails will still give you trouble.

In order to fasten the new shingle in place, you must break one of the basic rules of roofing and drive a nail that is exposed to the weather. It should be one nail, in the middle of the shingle, just a little above the butt. To keep this nail from becoming a leaking spot, put a dab of roofing cement or other calking material over its head.

Another method of securing the shingle in place is with a mastic-type adhesive. Spread a thick "sausage" of mastic on the bottom of the shingle. Keep the butt elevated as you push it in, then press the shingle down to bring the mastic into contact.

REPLACING A DAMAGED SHINGLE

1. Split shingle in the middle of this picture puts a crack right over the joint in the row below. It should be replaced.

2. Use a chisel and hammer to split the shingle into strips you can pull out.

3. Shove a new shingle up into place until its end strikes the nails that held the shingle you removed. Then saw a kerf parallel to the shingle edges where each of the nails made its mark. This lets you shove the new shingle into place, the slots riding up the nails.

4. An alternate method of getting past those nails is by hacksawing them off close to the surface. This, however, is not as simple as the method covered above.

5. When the new shingle is in place, drive one nail through it in the center, 1" or 2" up from the butt.

6. Make that nail weatherproof by putting a dab of roofing calk, or other weatherproof calk-patch material.

Repairing a larger area. If you discover damage to an area covered by many shingles, you use the above splitting technique only for those along the top row of the damage. The rest of the shingles can be ripped off any old way. An excellent tool for the job is a square-nose shovel or spade. Shove it under the butts and pry up. When the shingles are all off, use a hammer or wrecking bar to pull the nails.

In this operation, be careful not to damage the roofing felt. If you do dig through this — or if it is in bad shape anyway — replace it, slipping the new stuff under the edge of the sound felt at the top and edges, letting it lap over the felt at the lower side of the repair job.

When you buy the shingles for this repair work, one thing is important: *they must be the same length* as those used on the house originally. Otherwise, gaps will develop as you lay successive rows. Sometimes a building supply dealer will have a "broken" bundle" of shingles and will sell you a handful. On other cases, you may have to buy an entire bundle, which might be the best idea, all in all. You can store them away for the next time you need to work on the roof.

Now you're in the shingling business. To keep the new shingles lined up, obtain a straight length of 1 x 4 or so, long enough to reach completely across the repair area. Position it against the butts of the shingles on the sides of the patch. Use a chalk or pencil to mark a line across. The butts of the new shingles go along this line.

Start at the bottom. *Making sure that you do not put one joint over another,* fit a row of new shingles across the lower edge of the patch. Use two nails to a shingle, each one in from the edge a little less than one quarter of the shingle's width. These nails go in a row crosswise, that will be covered by an inch or two of the next course of shingles. You'll discover that each nail goes through the shingle it is holding in place, and also through the thin end of the shingle below it. Thus, each nail goes through two shingles, binding them together, sound and weathertight.

Continue to use the straightedge, so that the butts line up properly. At the top of the patch, split out the shingles and fit in the new ones as described above.

WORKING ON COMPOSITION SHINGLES

Composition shingles are just about completely homogenous, as compared to wooden shingles which vary considerably from one to another. That is why a composition roof is likely to deteriorate uniformly from gable to gable and ridge to eave, except for physical damage caused by wind or abrasion. Like wooden shingles, however, composition roofs suffer the most deterioration fastest on southern and western exposures, compared to eastern and northern. Keep this in mind when you inspect the roof.

These roofs are further "unitized" by the form of the shingles, which are usually in strips, rather than single. In addition, they may be designed to interlock in ways that make them more weathertight.

Because of these factors, it is rarely necessary to replace more than an occasional flap, torn loose by the wind or other stresses. In these cases, you do not remove anything, and you can often make use of the loose flap, if you can find it.

To begin with, if a flap is raised, but not detached, use roofing cement to fasten it back down. There may be a little separation at the crease; in that case, smear some cement along the crack.

Even if a flap is completely detached, you can replace it by cementing it in place and filling the crack.

Damage caused by strong winds raising the flaps of composition roofs is just about eliminated with special dabs of adhesive. After installation, the overlapping shingle bonds to the adhesive patches. If you have flap-raising troubles with your roof, you can buy a special cement that seals them down, applied with an ordinary calking gun (*right*).

Easiest method of replacing a missing flap in composition roofing is to slip a piece of aluminum or copper or galvanized steel into the roof, in place of the flap. See text for methods of replacing an entire composition strip.

When a flap is lost completely, the best method of repair is to cut a piece of sheet metal (copper, aluminum, or galvanized) more or less this size: twice the height of the flap plus 2″, by the width of the flap plus 4″.

Slip this piece of metal into the space left by the missing flap, with its edges under the adjacent shingles and shove it up until its upper edge is under the next shingle above.

Cement the metal in place, and cement the adjoining shingles to it. If the spot is conspicuous, paint it a camouflaging color, using a coat of primer followed by housepaint or exterior semigloss enamel.

Repairing larger areas. Should you find it necessary to replace an entire composition shingle unit, or more, try to save the job until a hot day, so that the shingles are at their most flexible. You can, except in quite cold weather, soften a shingle area with a heat lamp or photoflood in reflectors.

You will usually be able to raise the heat-softened shingles above the damaged strip far enough to get at the row of nails. Use a pinch bar to pull them. The strip may still be held by nails farther up under the shingles above, but those nails are so close to the edge that you can pull the strip loose.

Now, use the old strip *as a pattern to cut out notches* on the new piece where those nails near the edges were located. This will let you slip the new strip up into position. With the flaps still raised, you can drive new nails. Come close to the old nail holes, but try to miss them so that the new nails get a good grip on the new wood. Finish up by cementing down the flaps.

254

WHAT TO DO WHEN A ROOF REALLY LEAKS

When you discover that a roof leaks, it is most often because you discover the evidence of it in some living area of the house, in the attic, or in some under-eave area. It would be normal to expect the leak to be directly above the evidence. This is just about never the case, since the water had to run down a few rafters and along the underside of some roof sheathing and so forth, before it came to light. For this reason, the location of a leak *in the roof* bears little relationship to the location of the leak below. Instead, all you know for sure is that the leak is *uphill* from the place where it shows up.

The first move toward finding the leak is to make a careful search—while it is leaking—for the path the water takes. Examine sheathing, framing, and other construction members uphill from the place where the leak shows up. Trace it, if possible, to its origin.

If you can't do this, here is a trick:

1. Establish a point on the roof directly over the leak inside.

2. Pull a garden hose up on the roof and start soaking it down beginning at the point you estimate to be over the trouble area inside. If there is any doubt about being directly over it, start soaking the roof at a point several feet below as a safety measure. Conduct this soaking over a width of perhaps 10'.

3. Gradually—very gradually—raise the soaking operation. A row of shingles at a time is a good gauge.

4. Post an associate inside, ready to note the very first sign of water coming through to the inside surface, with instructions to let you know the moment it does.

5. When he gives the signal, make a note of the point to which your roof-soaking has progressed. It will be very close to the point where rain water is entering your house.

It is important to move upward with your soaking very, very *slowly*. Otherwise, the first sign of a leak may actually come from water that you sprayed on the roof a distance below, but which took a little while to make its way through.

With the general area of the leak now established, begin examination of the roofing material, in search of the cause. Replace shingles and roofing paper as covered above in the discussions of wood or composition, as the case may be.

As the relative complexity of the foregoing may indicate, the job of locating and repairing an active roof leak is not one of the simplest home repair jobs. If your home is fairly new, the man who built it may feel it within his range of responsibilities to give you a hand with a leak that quite likely may be his fault. If your home is older, you may decide that it would be wiser and easier and safer to call in a roofing specialist.

RIDGES, VALLEYS, AND FLASHING

Thus far in roofing repair techniques, the problem has been with a single roof plane. There also are ridges, valleys, and flashing. They represent only a small part of roofing area, but they can bring up special problems since their job is always to bridge the gap between two non-continuous surfaces. Here are the ways:

• The ridge is the peak of the roof, always there unless the house happens to have a single-pitch roof.

• Valleys occur between two downward-sloping roof areas. A gable, for example, produces a valley on either side.

• You find flashing where a roof meets other construction areas. A wing on a house, a single-story element against a two-story house, a shed roof off a wall of the house—these and similar construction elements usually produce a situation where the roof meets siding or other exterior wall material. Flashing is also the means of joining the roof to a chimney.

These elements of a roof do not present problems very often. The unusual problems involved in their construction invite special attention from the craftsmen who build the house. Because it is harder to do the job, the job is usually done better.

The standard method of handling ridges in original construction is with the same material that is used for the entire roof. That is to say, in a composition roof the ridge between

The metalwork above a chimney that emerges from a pitched roof is called a "cricket." Be sure to examine it when you check the roof for damage. As shown here, the pieces of roofing are missing which should cover the exposed triangle. Also, check where the cricket is mortared into the chimney bricks and tuckpoint new mortar in if necessary.

one plane and another will be formed of composition material. Most often, a wood-shingle roof will have wood as the spanning medium from one plane to another.

Valleys and flashings are different. In these situations the cross-over material is most often metal—aluminum, copper, or galvanized steel. The metal is bent to form a sort of trough down which water runs. Since the trough extends up beneath the shingles (or siding, in the case of flashing) there is little chance of a leak. The shingles or siding shed the water into the trough, where it sluices rapidly down to the eaves. When there is trouble, it is usually due to deterioration of the metal trough or blockage due to debris.

Repairing ridges. The ridge of a roof has things easy. All the water it must handle is the immediate rainfall on it. No water drains to it. It is at the top. Therefore, the ridge rarely needs work unless there is damage from branches of trees or other physical damage. On a wood-shingle roof, the ridge is most often a pair of boards, usually nailed over the tops of the final row of shingles. If, because of damage or weathering, these boards need to be replaced, it is a simple matter to rip them off and replace them with new stock. You'll probably eliminate the need for ever doing the job again if you flood the boards with wood preservative on sides, edges, and ends before you put them in place—with aluminum or galvanized nails.

257

Damage to the ridge of a roof is most likely due to branches or trees. Cut them back, patch with trowel-on cement.

The ridge of a composition roof is composed of a row of composition shingles, laid astraddle the ridge, overlapping each other with the nails of each shingle covered by the next.

When any of the segments are damaged, it is easy to raise the corners of the next shingle, lift the nails, and remove the defective material. As with run-of-the-roof shingles, it is easiest to do this on a hot day, or with the warmth of a heat lamp to soften the composition.

REPAIRING FLASHING MATERIALS

It is not often necessary to replace flashing completely. Most of the time, the damage is due to rust or erosion of the metal. Occasionally you may find joints separated, probably because of the stresses caused by ice freezing.

Rusted flashing. When a flashing material is galvanized steel, found especially on older buildings, there is certain to be some rust. Check your flashings to see, and if you discover any brown coloration that would indicate rust, buy a can of good quality metal *primer and topcoat in latex.* This should dry fast enough so you can get the job done quickly.

There may be spots where the metal has rusted through, or nearly through. Cut patches of the same kind of metal large enough to cover such spots with an overlap of 2″ or 3″. Carefully bend the patches to conform with the curve of the flashing. Use heavy paste-form roof patching cement to fasten the patches in place. If, in your judgment, the rest of the flashing metal indicates a considerable amount of deterioration, use a brush-on roofing cement to coat it completely, including the new patches.

258

Aluminum and copper flashing. Flashing made of these metals is not subject to rust in the same way as galvanized steel, and for that reason does not need repair so often. However, the life of both can be prolonged by a coating of paint. Check with your paint dealer for a primer specifically recommended for these metals; some primers are not intended for use on copper or aluminum.

Important: If you patch holes in copper or aluminum, be sure to use copper or aluminum. Do not use steel or iron. If you do, you'll set up a situation in which electrolysis will cause rapid decomposition of the metal.

Repairing joints. Copper flashing usually has soldered joints; galvanized steel sometimes does. However, crimping is common on galvanized steel, and it is always used on aluminum. Either way, when a joint separates, the two elements may pull apart far enough so that an overlap patch is necessary.

The easiest roof repair job is done with a calking gun and a tube-form material that has enough body to form a good bead. You may want to use a putty knife to trowel the material smooth after you've gunned it into place.

When the joint is widely separated, cut a patch of the same metal and cement it in place, as discussed above under Rusted Flashing.

WHERE FLASHING JOINS NON-ROOF AREAS

The standard method of installing flashing at points where roofing meets another material involves the "overlap" principle of shingling itself. The metal, bent to fit in place, extends well beneath the shingles. It is installed first, then shingles are laid over it.

On the non-roof surface, the flashing extends well beneath the siding or other material. Again, the metal is positioned, then the siding is nailed over it. Any repair work involves only replacing the siding material, making sure the flashing is secure beneath it.

When the non-roof material is brick, the problem is tougher. The flashing extends under the shingles, but it is bent and mortared into the bricks, whether they be structural or chimney bricks. Because of temperature changes from hot sun to freezing, the mortar often loosens between the bricks where the flashing goes. Although this can be repaired by chipping out the loose mortar and troweling in new, it is better to use a flexible calking material. Its flexibility stands a chance of longer survival than the brittleness of mortar. Be sure to chip away all loose mortar before calking.

The plumbing vent. One more area where a roof may give you trouble is around the plumbing vent—that stubby length of 3″ or bigger pipe that sticks up through the roof a few inches. Its purpose is to prevent air-locks and blockage in the plumbing system. The most common type includes a collar and flange that fits around the pipe, under the shingles above, and over those below.

Now and then, owing to expansion and contraction of the plumbing "stack," the collar may come loose from the pipe. If it does, trowel-on roofing cement makes a simple repair.

The stack (air vent) of your plumbing system may spring a leak, which is easy to repair with brush-or-trowel roofing patch.

HOW TO KEEP
RAIN-CARRYING EQUIPMENT
AT WORK

LIKE YOUR ROOF, your gutters and downspouts are out of sight, and for that reason so often out of mind that they go neglected. Minor, easy-to-fix damage or deterioration grows until simple repair becomes complicated.

That is why rain-carrier maintenance and repair always begin with an inspection twice a year.

WHAT TO INSPECT

Every fall after the leaves have fallen and every spring when it warms up, make an inspection of the system from a ladder. You are looking for these things:

• Collected debris that not only interferes with free movement of the water but can also contribute to corrosion. There should be relatively little debris if you have taken the wise precaution of installing *leaf guards over the gutters*. These guards are screens in one form or another that you slip under the lowest row of shingles. The screen covers the top of the eaves trough. Any leaves or other debris of a sizeable nature sluices over the screen, while the water passes through and down the system. Leaf guards are more effective than simple sieves at the top of each downspout, because they keep the entire system, not merely the downspouts, clean.

• Rusted areas in the inside of the gutters, which should always be repaired as soon as possible, before the extent of the damage is so great that a whole section may have to be replaced.

• Evidence that pools of water have dried in the gutters, instead of running on down the system. Take a whiskbroom along the gutters if they are quite dirty, and look for the long oval-shaped area of encrusted sediment that indicates repeated pooling and drying.

• Mechanical failures show up in several ways. Joints may be forced apart by frost. Hangers may be loosened by the weight of snow and ice or water during a downpour. Downspouts may have separated from their connections at the ends of runs. This doesn't happen often when the joints are riveted, and therein lies the answer to repair. Force the joints back together, and use sheet metal screws or rivets to make them strong enough so it won't happen again.

• Paint failure on the outside of the gutters and downspouts is, of course, visible from the ground. However, there may be deterioration of coatings on the insides, too. You can't find it if it's inside downspouts where you can't see, and where it is quite rare, anyway. But you'll save work and money if you can catch finish failure on the inside surfaces of gutters. It is standard and sensible practice to brush-coat the gutters with roofing cement every year or so. This is simpler than taking care of the corrosion you may encounter if gutter linings go bad.

• A less common but serious type of rain-carrier damage is the downspout split by entrapped water that freezes and expands. When this happens, downspouts are finished and must be replaced.

The specific repair and maintenance techniques for each of these problems are covered below. It will be easier for you to handle them, however, if you first run down the mechanics and engineering of rain-carrier systems.

IMPROPER DESIGN
CAUSES QUICK DETERIORATION

Peeling paint is often a sign of more serious troubles. In this corner, with two roof areas above it, there should be a downspout. Overflowing water has contributed to paint failure in this area.

The streaks down over this gutter are a result of run-over, caused by a low spot in the middle of a run which is too long in the first place.

One downspout (off the picture to the left) has the job of handling all the runoff from the dormer at the right plus all the roof—and it's too much. There should be a downspout where the stub-end empties into the gutter.

KINDS OF RAIN-CARRYING EQUIPMENT

Gutters are made in two basic shapes: half-round, and "K" style, the kind with the square back and the ogee front. Downspouts are round and rectangular with rounded corners, sometimes plain and sometimes with corrugations. The elements are aluminum, galvanized steel, plastic, copper, or wood (except downspouts), as well as some less common materials not often used residentially. Although the K style is growing more and more popular, you still find a lot of half-round on older houses. If the older house is old enough, you may find both K and half-round, along with a wide variety of hangers, joints, corners, and caps, not to mention a number of different shapes in the downspouts.

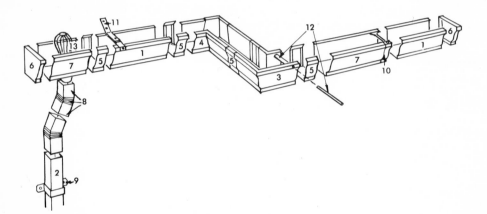

Modern rain-carrying equipment is composed of slip-together components, both in the K style shown here and in half-round. You can buy any of the elements individually for repair, and replacement, or for a new installation.

1. Gutter.	7. Outlet section.
2. Downspout.	8. Elbow.
3. Outside corner.	9. Pipe band.
4. Inside corner.	10. Clip-around hanger.
5. Slip-joint connector.	11. Strap hanger.
6. End cap.	12. Spike and ferrule hanger.

13. Squirrel cage.

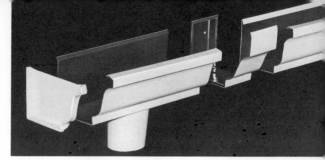

Slip-together elements make rain-carrying systems easy to assemble. Virtually any repair can be done by replacing a part, in K style as shown here or in half-round.

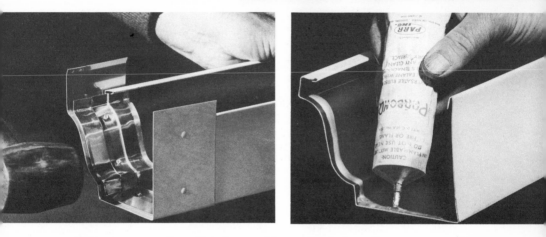

Units are a snug fit, calling for a rubber mallet to force them together. Gutter cement must be used to insure a watertight joint. Be sure the rivets or screws you use are of the same metal as the gutter and connector.

For this reason, it is not possible in this book to cover every style in every system, but it is possible to present repair guidance that can be *translated to any situation*. K style elements are used in the photographs, but the operations are the same if you are working with half-round materials.

The accompanying drawing shows the various elements of a typical rain-carrier system. The gutter and the downspout come in lengths of 10' and longer, up to 30' in some cases. All of the elements slip together with special fasteners as shown in the photographs (there are similar slip connectors for half-round).

If you decide that the best method of repair is replacement of a length of gutter or downspout—or part of a length—or of one of the connectors, corners, or outlet sections or caps, you may want to take the damaged element to your building supply dealer and have him give you what you need to replace it. What he gives you may not be identical in appearance, but it will be identical in performance.

265

Important: Do not mix other metals with galvanized iron elements. If you do, you may run into excessive corrosion due to electrolysis, that is, galvanic action that takes place when iron or steel is in contact with another metal. This applies to rivets, fasteners, and other elements. Use steel with steel, aluminum with aluminum. If circumstances suggest or dictate the use of plastic with steel no electrolysis will result, as long as the fasteners, etc. are steel.

It has been the experience of many homeowners that wooden gutters are inefficient because of the relatively small channel compared to the exterior size. When wood gutters begin to check, split, peel, and rot, it's time to think of replacing them with one of the other materials. Putting up a whole new gutter is no more than a one-man job, since the elements are so light in weight (particularly aluminum) that one man can handle them, even up at eave height.

Wooden gutters are difficult to repair. The photo above shows how an end cap of wood can be nailed over a rotted gutter end. Wood rot like that at the joint of two gutter pieces (*below*) is so difficult that replacement with a metal gutter is easier.

BASIC RAIN-CARRIER ENGINEERING

Rain-carrying systems are based on the convenient fact that water runs downhill. As long as there is a continuous downward pitch, the system will deliver the water. However, the more water the greater the pitch must be, or the greater the size of the eave troughs must be, or both. To stay within workable limits, these guidelines have been set up for rain-carrier installations.

• You need a downspout for every 500 square feet of roof area.

• You need a downspout for every 20′ of gutter. In other words, if a run is much longer than 20′, it should be high in the middle, with a downspout at each end.

• You need ½″ of pitch, that is, downward slope, for every 20′ of gutter run. A full inch is better. There are reasons for this. First, the pitch should always be steep enough to carry water to the downspout rapidly. Otherwise, it may fill the trough and run over.

Second, the movement of the water should be strong enough to carry along normal dust and dirt in the gutter. Third, the pitch should be enough to eliminate puddles and pools of water between rains, since lingering wetness means more corrosion and rust.

• Downspouts should have as few bends, elbows, as possible, since the curves increase the chance that leaves and other solids washing down the system will clog things, blocking the movement of the water.

• At the foot of every downspout you need some means of delivering the water away from the foundation. This may be splash blocks, deliberate grading, or underground piping. If you don't have it, the buildup of water is likely to produce basement leaks and deterioration of foundations.

It is reasonable to expect, although not at all a certainty, that the builder of your home followed the engineering principles when he put up the rain-carrying equipment. However, if performance fails repeatedly, it may be necessary for you to modify the system.

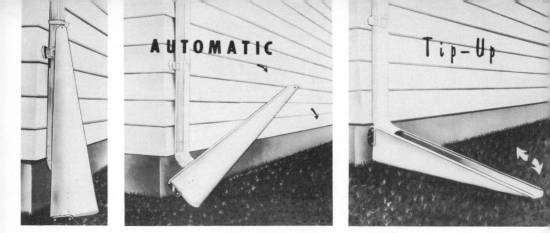

"Rain drains" are available for attaching to bottoms of downspouts to carry water away from foundation walls. Some are made of flexible plastic, and roll out on lawn when water flows. Some reroll automatically, other must be rerolled by the homeowner. *Courtesy of Chapiewsky's, Inc.*

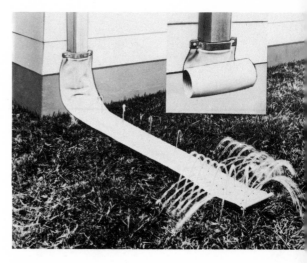

Metal downspout extensions stay up when the system is dry, fold down with weight of water when rain falls. Other types are manually operated. *Courtesy of Chapiewsky's, Inc.*

REPAIR AND MAINTENANCE TECHNIQUES

Although some rain-carrier repairs are as simple as painting, there are others which may invite consideration of this question:

Is it better to fix the element involved, or to replace it?

For example, a split downspout can be repaired by some such method as applying fiberglass and sealer over the crack, or riveting on a metal patch. But it's a lot of work, and your time might serve you better if it were spent replacing the downspout, a simple job. On the other hand, a rusted spot in the middle of a long length of gutter might be more efficiently repaired than replaced.

Always keep in mind the simplicity of the system, the relative ease with which elements can be removed and replaced, plus the most important factor of all: Replacement parts with modern pre-finishing techniques will quite likely outlast your repair job.

Peeling paint. All too often, paint starts to come off the rain-carrying system of a house before it fails on the rest of the house. Metal is, or used to be, hard to keep painted, largely because the key to success is proper priming, and priming is often carelessly done. After all, it doesn't show. Today's pre-primed metals and, in fact, today's better-sticking primers, make the job easier and more permanent.

When gutters and downspouts show only here-and-there failure, the best thing to do is repaint the bad areas. Then, if paint starts to peel in other places, you have a pretty good indication that the entire system may need refinishing, sooner or later.

Handle the spots that are peeling this way:

• Use a putty knife or similar tool to peel off *all the paint* that will come loose around the area. Examine the gutter or downspout for several feet on either side, to be sure that there are no bubbles or other indications of failing adhesion. If you find them, scrape away the bad paint.

• When you have scraped away all loose and flaking paint, use medium sandpaper to "feather" the hard edges of the sound paint, so they won't be unsightly when the job is finished.

• If the bare metal shows loose or flaking rust, use a wire brush to remove all that will come off.

• If the bare metal shows no rust, but is instead relatively bright, use a multi-solvent liquid like Wil-Bond or Liquid Sandpaper on a rag to wipe the surface of the metal. The purpose of this step is to remove any substances from the surface that foil good painting and to provide better adhesion.

• Use a specific primer for the first coat, not an ordinary paint. Some modern paints are labeled "self-priming" and give excellent service, ordinarily. However, remember that you are working on what seems to be a problem area. Buy a can of specific primer for that first coat. There are excellent latex-base primers with relatively short drying time, if you want to use one to make the job go faster. Feather out the paint at the edges, to avoid an abrupt line.

• Use either latex house paint or a trim paint in your color for the first coat, feathering it out. If the patch looks all right, you can save the second finish coat until it is time to paint the entire house again, if that day is not too far in the future.

The same fundamentals apply to repainting large areas of the rain-carrier. However, with a lot of scraping, sanding, painting, and ladder moving to do, you might want to investigate the possibility of taking down the gutters. Some systems have eave troughs suspended by means of hangers that "unclip" in one way or another. If it looks easy to take them down, easier than all the ladder work, do it.

Rusted metal. Rust on the outside of gutters and down-spouts is always related to failure of finishes, as covered above. If it becomes serious, it is because it was not attended to in a sound preventive maintenance program.

Rust inside the system is different. A fairly serious problem of corrosion may develop in a single season. Repairing it is different, too, since you are interested in protection, not good looks.

Modern rain-carrier materials, among the quality lines, are treated with rust inhibitors both inside and out. The best method of handling rust, therefore, is to maintain these inhibitors: good paint on the outside and a good continuous film on the inside. As you make your semi-annual inspections, watch for indications that the inside of the gutter is starting to go. When you make that discovery, get in there with a brush and a can of paint-on gutter cement. Be sure to bring the coating up the sides of the gutter to the edges.

When you find actual rust, the methods of handling it depend on how bad it is. Can you wirebrush it, then coat it with gutter cement? Or is the rusting so bad that the metal is weakened? If the latter is true, you have three choices: First, you can patch the area with metal and cement. Second, you can replace that part of the gutter which is actually damaged. Third, you can replace the entire element. The methods of doing all three are covered below.

APPLYING A PATCH

• Get hold of a piece of the *same style and size and metal* gutter as that you are repairing, about a foot longer than the area to be patched. Trim the flanged or "hemmed" edges off this material, so that what you end up with is a piece of metal the shape of the gutter. (Actually, you could buy a piece of flashing or other sheet metal and bend it to shape, but it's harder to do.)

• Press the patch into position. It will not fit perfectly, since you are asking its *outside* size to nest *inside* the existing gutter. You will find it simple to make a few minor adjustments in some of the bends and curves so the fit is quite good, however.

• While the patch is in position, drill holes in it for sheet metal screws that will hold it in place, eventually.

• Remove the patch. Lard the area with gutter cement. Put the patch back, and drive the sheet metal screws from the outside on the front and bottom, from the inside on the back.

• End up the job by carefully coating the patch — especially its edges — with cement.

This job is so simple that actually replacing part or all of an element is unnecessary, unless the rust has gone through the metal and no kind of patching would make it look decent.

Important: It is a temptation to use heavy aluminum foil for the patching material. This is okay if you happen to be working on damage to an aluminum system. But, if the system is steel, you may cause corrosion problems (electrolysis) unless you take certain precautions. Make sure that the coating of cement forms a *complete "insulation" between the metals.* Do not use fasteners, but instead bed the foil in a heavy layer of cement, then cover the foil with another layer.

SPLICING GUTTER WITHOUT
A SLIP-ON CONNECTOR

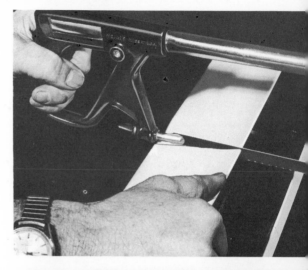

Cut gutter easily with a very fine-tooth hacksaw by working quite flat to the surface and sawing over the far edge of the metal. Rotate the gutter as you finish the cut on each side.

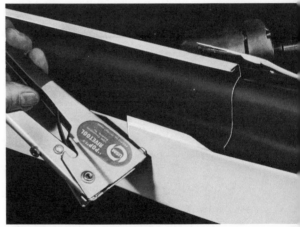

Use square-nose pliers to un-bend the hem and the nose on the gutter on one side. Then fit the other piece inside. Use plenty of gutter seal between the two, then fasten with pop rivets or sheet-metal screws. It is best to put fasteners in bottom first, to pull joint tight.

Apply seal to the joint both inside and out. When it is dry, paint the joint to match the rest of the system.

Inserting a new piece of gutter.

• Use a hacksaw or tinsnips to cut out the damaged length of gutter.

• Buy a piece of material about 3″ longer than the piece you cut out.

• Using the techniques shown in the photographs, fit the new piece by slipping it too far into one end, then sliding it back into the other end until the spacing is even at both ends. Use gutter cement and sheet metal screws or pop rivets, as shown.

You may not be able to find a dealer who will sell you less than a 10′ length of material. When that is the case, you will probably discover that at least one end on the new piece will match up with an existing joint and possibly both ends, if your system happens to be built up of 10′ units.

Replacing a unit. This solution is the easiest of all. Take out the screws or drill out the rivets that hold the piece in at both ends. Remove any nails. Put the new length in, using cement and using the same screw and rivet positions with the new fasteners.

THE PROBLEM OF GUTTER HANGERS

When you replace more than a couple of feet of gutter, you are sure to run into one or more hangers, which are usually spaced every 32″ or so. Some hangers wrap around the gutter, some clip around, some fit inside in a manner that makes them demountable. You loosen them, take the gutter down, then refit them around the replacement. On top of this, some installation may have nails through the gutter into the fascia or rafter ends or some other element of the eave construction.

It is not necessary to match the hangers (it may in many cases be impossible) as long as you match their function. Check at your building supply dealer, who will handle several styles, for the one that is easiest for you to use in your situation. As with any element you are replacing, it is a good idea to take a hanger to the lumberyard, show it to the dealer, and let him give you one that will work for you.

BASIC TYPES OF HANGERS
FOR EAVE TROUGHS

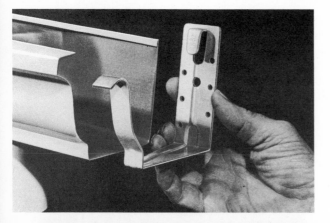

Fascia clip is typical of hangers that fasten to the fascia board at the eaves. If the fascia is not vertical, wedges of the proper angle make this and similar types of mountings effective. A great advantage of the fascia clip is the ease of adjustment up and down on the board for proper pitch.

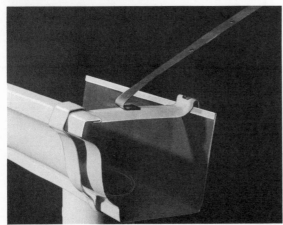 

Strap hanger fastens to the roof itself, and is not dependent on eave design. Properly installed, the strap is under a shingle (raise the flap to nail it), not on top of the roof, as at right.

Easiest kind of hanger to use is the spike and ferrule. The ferrule, actually a metal tube, molds the edges of the gutter and the proper spacing. Spike must go into a solid member, preferably a rafter end.

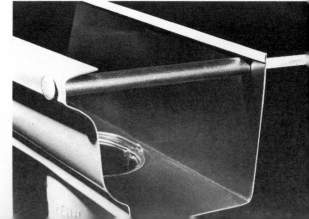

CHECKING THE SYSTEM FOR ADEQUATE PITCH

Although it isn't particularly inviting work examining the rain-carrying equipment during a rain, you can come out to the same place by hauling a garden hose up the ladder on a sunny day. Make these checks:

• Let the water from the hose trickle into the gutter at the high end of a run, that is, at the end opposite the downspout outlet. When there is a downspout at both ends of a gutter run, it means that the high spot is, or should be, in the middle. This is the case when a run is much longer than 20′. If it is much longer than about 40′ there may be three downspouts, one at each end, and one in the middle. There will be two high spots, too, half way between the ends and the middle. Not all rain-carrier installations follow this rule, and the result may be overflowing, because the run is so long that the roof sends too much water down for the trough to handle.

• Check for puddling by letting the hose trickle into the gutter until the water has made its way to the downspouts. Remove the hose. Wait until the water movement has stopped, i.e. until it is standing still in the trough. It is simple, then, to watch the water dry. If it leaves stretches where the water stands, you know that the gutter should be raised at those points.

To correct these low spots you must modify the hangers that are involved. Start by laying in the trough a strip of straight-and-true 1 x 2 or 2 x 2 lumber long enough to span the low spot. The sag of the gutter will show beneath this board. It must be raised until the space between board and gutter disappears.

The exact method of doing this will depend on the kind of hangers and the method of installation involved. First, of course, you must remove any nails that occur in the sagging area. Then, you must either raise the hangers or increase their tension, depending on their design. If spike-and-ferrule hangers are used, pull the spikes and redrive them. Some hangers may have slip-joints intended specifically for such adjustment. In some others you may have to twist a wire suspension or crimp one that is a strap of metal. Whichever method your system dictates, use it to pull the gutter up until there is no longer a sag beneath the straightedge. If it is necessary, add new hangers.

It is important in all this that the fasteners at each end of the sag remain in place, to hold firm that part of the gutter which is in proper alignment.

INSTALLING A NEW RUN OF GUTTER

It is by far easier to install a new gutter run than to repair an old one. The steps involved are these:

• Take down the old material carefully enough so that you can assemble it on the ground. On a driveway, walk, or level stretch of lawn is the best place to do it.

• Lay out the new material beside the old, making it exactly the same length, with outlet elements in the same places.

• Join the pieces, using cement and rivets and connectors, as shown in the accompanying photographs. The replacement is now ready to be hoisted into position.

Establishing the pitch. Keep in mind that the ideal pitch is at least $1/2''$ for each 20′ of run and that an inch is better. Here's how to establish the pitch:

1. Tap on a nail at the high end of the run, as high up on the fascia as convenient. (In some cases there may be no fascia, and the nail will have to go into a rafter end or other element.)

2. Fasten a length of mason's line or other slim but stout cord to the nail.

3. Move to the low end of the run and draw the string tight.

4. Hang a line level (less than a dollar at any hardware store) on the string. Adjust the string up and down until the bubble in the level is properly centered. *Important:* The string must be drawn tight enough so that any sag is negligible.

5. Measure down 1″ from the point where the level is true. Drive another nail.

6. Make the line fast and taut between the two nails.

7. By snapping the line or marking with a pencil, indicate the slope of the gutter along the fascia or other board or

To determine the correct slope for your gutters, tie a chalk line to a nail driven into the fascia board and, using a line level, adjust the line until the bubble is centered. Then lower the line 1" for a run of 20', or slightly less than $\frac{1}{8}$" in a 2' span.

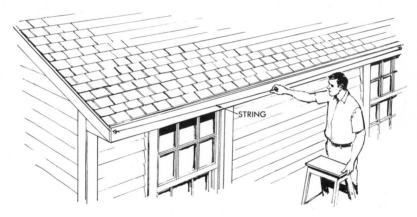

When the chalk line is secured at the desired slope, pull it out at the center and let it snap, marking a line on the board.

If you replace the gutter spans by yourself, suspend far end first on a circular wire held by a nail, then attach your end along chalk line.

If you need to repair roof gutters held by nails and ferrules, pull out the nails with a vise-grip type plier using a twisting motion. Hammer claws will dent the surrounding gutter rails.

boards. This is the line which the edge of the gutter must follow.

Again, the type of fasteners you use must depend on the style of your eaves. But, since you don't have to match up with anything, pick a type of hanger that is easiest to install.

WHEN DOWNSPOUTS CLOG

If you use leaf guards or screens properly, chances are you'll never have trouble with clogging downspouts. Any debris that gets through the guard will be small enough to wash away. But, if you do find that a spout isn't draining:

• Do not try to force the impediment on through with a broomstick or something similar. That way, you'll only pack it tighter.

• Use a plumber snake, from the top or bottom or both, as a means of digging the impacted debris loose. Combine this operation with a garden hose on full force, so hydraulics help you with the job. (Sometimes the bathroom plunger can move debris in downspouts.)

BASEMENTS AND FOUNDATIONS

Concrete is one of the world's most abundantly used construction materials, and it is often described as being "easy as mud-pie" to work with. Keep in mind, however, that there are essential guiding principles necessary to the success of concrete projects.

First, concrete and most other cementitious products *set* hard. They do not *dry* hard. In fact, it is a little recognized phenomenon that concrete will harden under water. The mix must be kept moist until the hardening and curing are well along. For standard materials, this means three or four days, although there are special formulas that set much faster, even in minutes. (See Special Cement Patching Materials below.) Regular concrete doesn't reach its ultimate hardness and strength for about four weeks. In critical situations it is important to keep the material damp for that period of time, which explains the stretches of newly poured concrete highway you so often see covered with straw or a plastic film, to retain moisture.

Once concrete or mortar has been mixed with water, *if the water evaporates before the mix hardens, it will never harden.*

Since you are working with relatively small quantities in repair and maintenance work, and since small quantities tend to dry quickly, this is an important fact to keep in mind. After the initial set, keep patches damp either by spraying them with a fine mist of water or by laying or hanging wet burlap or the equivalent over them. (When you use ready-mixed materials check the instructions carefully for any special moistening operations.)

The importance of maintaining moisture makes it virtually impossible to use ordinary concrete or mortar in any situation requiring a thin layer. When it is troweled out as thin as $1/2''$ or less, the bond with existing materials is almost certain to be poor, and the chances are great that it will dry and powder without setting. (There are special materials intended specifically for thin-spread use, as discussed below.)

MIXING CONCRETE AND MORTAR

Concrete is composed of cement and a homogenous mixture of sand, pebbles, and stones or crushed rock. The latter are called "aggregate," and the material is broken down by size. "Coarse aggregate" is stones or crushed rock up to 1″ in diameter. "Fine aggregate" includes sand and pebbles that will pass through a $1/4''$ screen; this is sometimes called "pea gravel."

An ideal mix has these proportions:

• Enough coarse aggregate to fill the space involved.

• Enough fine aggregate to fill the voids (spaces) around the stones in the coarse aggregate, plus about 10 per cent.

• Enough sand to fill the voids in the fine aggregate, plus about 10 per cent.

• Enough cement to fill the voids in the sand, plus about 10 per cent.

• Enough water to produce a proper working consistency, which will be a little wetter for pouring, a little dryer for trowel application.

Sand mix is a mixture of sand and cement only. It is the proper material to use when a crack or other defect to be repaired is small.

If you were involved in a project the magnitude of Boulder Dam, you'd operate on the fill-the-voids formula above, to avoid overusing the most expensive of the ingredients, cement. For your around-the-house repair work, this is the formula most often recommended:

3 parts gravel.

2 parts sand (or a bit more, depending on the nature of the coarse material).

1 part cement.

There are three elements of caution:

• All the sand-gravel-stone ingredients must be clean. "Washed" is the word masonry material suppliers use. The reason is that any fine silt, clay, or other soil materials coating the coarses or fines — or intermixed with them — occupy space that should be filled with cement. The result is loss of strength.

• No coarse ingredient, no small stone or crushed rock fragment, may be bigger than one-half the thickness of the final job. In other words, if you were filling a depression or a crack with a minimum dimension of 1″, no element of aggregate should be bigger than ½″. In fact, many experts recommend that for cracks up to 1″ wide, *you use sand mix, with no coarse aggregate at all.*

• All elements must be thoroughly intermixed, so that the cement, sand, fines, and coarses are an absolutely homogenous mixture.

Important: Even when you buy the extremely convenient and efficient premixed cement products such as Sakrete, you should mix them at the job, to insure this homogeneity. Such bagged materials may have a tendency to jiggle into layers during transportation, with the coarses gradually migrating to the top. Therefore, when you open a bag of Sakrete, don't feel safe dipping out a shovelful and mixing it with water. It is better to empty the entire bag (on a driveway or sidewalk) and mix it thoroughly with a shovel or hoe until you are sure it is uniform. Then, use what you need and shovel the rest back into the bag. *It is not necessary to do this the next time you dip into the bag,* because the ingredients won't stratify while the bag is standing in storage.

Mixing techniques. You mix concrete as well as sand-mix on a mixing board about 4' square, in a wheelbarrow, or in a mortar box if you need only a small amount. The steps are the same in any case.

1. Thoroughly intermix the sand-pebble-gravel ingredients until they are uniform. Then spread them as smooth and level as possible, in as thin a layer as the mixing container or board will permit.

2. With a shovel or trowel (depending on quantities involved), turn the material over several times, with a lifting, sifting action. Then mix it horizontally in both directions.

Important: Cement is gray; aggregate is normally brown. Keep mixing until the color is uniform, until you can no longer see streaks of gray or brown.

3. Now form the mix into a crater or dish, heaped up in a doughnut, hollow in the middle.

4. Pour a little water in this crater. The exact amount of water cannot be predetermined, because there is no useful method of figuring out how much moisture is in the sand to begin with.

5. Scrape the mix into the water from the sides. Add more water as necessary, mixing carefully. Scrape more of the mix in; intermix it thoroughly; add more water if necessary. Repeat this until all the mixture is wet.

THE SIMPLE STEPS IN MIXING CONCRETE

1. Whether you use a mixing board, the driveway, or a mortar box (as shown here) the first step is to spread the aggregate in a level, uniform layer. Then spread the proper amount of cement (see text) evenly over the layer of sand and gravel.

2. Intermix the aggregate and the cement thoroughly by chopping, lifting and sifting, and furrowing in both directions. Watch the color of the mix, and when it is uniform (no gray cement streaks and no brown sand streaks), it is well mixed.

3. Scoop a hollow in the middle of the mix and pour in a small amount of water. It is best to add water gradually rather than pour it in all at once, risking putting in too much.

4. Scoop the mix in from the sides of the hollow and puddle them together. Use lift-and-plop motions of the trowel, along with slicing and chopping. Bring in more dry aggregate. If you need more water, add it slowly.

5. When the mix is right, it will stand in a mound with fairly straight sides, without slumping and without draining water out at the bottom. Meanwhile, light strokes of the trowel will bring water to the top, as shown here.

Four kinds of aggregate are symbolized in this photo. For large repairs, you use "1" con mix," which includes all these ingredients. For smaller openings, the 1" stones at the left are omitted, and it becomes "½" con mix." When the crack is fairly narrow, patch it with "pea gravel mix," omitting the stones entirely. For the smallest kinds of damage, omit all the gravel and use only the sand.

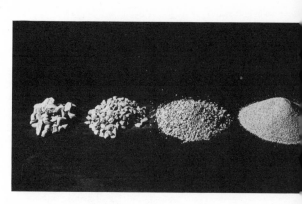

How wet? There should be just a bit more than enough water to fill the voids in the mix. If you work gradually, especially as you are gaining experience with the specific batch of sand, gravel, etc., you'll notice the point where a stroke of the trowel across the top of a heap of mixture will produce a smooth, watery gleam. The gleam may disappear in a minute or two. Another trowel stroke will bring it back. This is just about right.

Keep in mind that a mix intended for use in a vertical situation, such as a wall crack, must be a bit thicker than one for a floor repair, which you can afford to mix a little wet so it will "puddle."

If you should happen to add too much water, you'll notice that it tends to pool in depressions. It is best to dry the mix by adding a small amount of dry sand only, mixing it carefully. It is usually not necessary to add any more cement unless you find that it takes a lot of sand.

Ready-mixed concrete. Mixing a batch of Sakrete or similar material does not involve the addition of cement, of course, since it is already there. But you should mix it carefully and add the water gradually, the same as with concrete you mix yourself.

Never forget that problems in masonry repair are caused by improper preparation, mixing, and application in the first place. Special care with repairs can help avoid a repeat problem.

CONCRETE IN LARGE QUANTITIES

Although the vast majority of mortar and concrete needs for repairs involves only small quantities, there may be times when you'll need the worksaving, timesaving services of a cement mixer. You can rent one in just about any community, powered either by a gasoline engine or an electric motor.

Figure your needs in cubic feet, then check with a masonry supply concern and buy a mixture of sand, pebbles, and gravel sometimes called "con mix." It comes in grades with 1" coarse aggregate or ½" coarse aggregate. If you're faced with the job of filling a fairly large cavity, buy the bigger stuff. Buy also, a bag of cement for every 5 cubic feet of con mix, for the standard proportion is 1 part cement to 5 parts con mix, and a bag of cement is exactly 1 cubic foot.

Mixing concrete in a cement mixer is simpler than hand-mixing, because of the thoroughness of the machine.

• While the mixer is running, shovel in five units of the sand-gravel mix. Usually the shovel itself works as a measure.

• Let the gravel work in the mixer for a minute or two, until it becomes uniform.

• Add the cement. Give this mixture long enough so that it is uniform in color—no gray streaks of cement, no brown streaks of sand and aggregate.

• Add water with a hose, gradually. When you have the right amount, the mixture will form globs on the blades inside the mixer, but the globs will slide off when the blade rotates to the top. You'll notice, too, that the rattle-bang of the stones against the mixer walls disappears and the noise becomes a swish and plop when the right amount of water has been added.

When mixing is complete, dump the load into a wheelbarrow to be transported to the job. Don't shut off the mixer without emptying it if you can help it; if you do, the mix settles to the bottom, throwing the tub off balance and often making it hard to start the rotation again.

After you dump the load—unless you'll be mixing another right away—hose out the mixer while it is running, to prevent residue from hardening and sticking to the metal of the blades or tub.

SPECIAL CEMENT-PATCHING MATERIALS

For ordinary basement floor and wall repairs requiring a cement mixture, it is cheapest to use standard ready-mixed or mix-it-yourself materials covered above. This is particularly true when large quantities are involved, on account of cost.

There are, however, certain jobs, and certain crisis situations, which call for special materials. And today's market is full of formulas containing chemicals that give you performance far different from that you get from ordinary cement mixtures of concrete or mortar. Here are some of the most useful.

Hydraulic cement. This material is a modification of ordinary cement-based mix, but it hardens in just a few minutes. It is the right material to use when a foundation or floor is actively leaking running water. (See below.) You may want to use it for many small repairs, because of its convenience. But it is expensive. A can the size of a 1-pound coffee can costs $2 or more.

Specific instructions for mixing and use are printed on the container of any hydraulic cement you buy, but some generalizations may be of value. First, the stuff sets so rapidly that you must not mix more than you'll use in about three minutes. Second, it is not normally recommended for cracks less than ¾" in width or depth. Third, it is intended for use more like putty than cement: It must be pressed into place with a minimum of troweling or rubbing.

Air-drying cement. This material defies the law that says you must keep a patch wet. It is not truly a cementitious product. Unlike regular cementitious products, it will not set under water. This product handles like sandmix, and dries hard in a few hours. (An example is Patcho, made by Roxseal, Long Island City, N. Y.)

Expanding cement. The usefulness of this material comes from the phenomenon of expansion during curing. Once it has been applied, and after the initial set, the cement expands. It forms a tight plug in cracks or holes, although it is not intended for use in an active-leak situation. Most major cement manufacturers produce "expansive cement."

Special patching materials include Top 'n Bond, intended for surface smoothing right down to a thin edge, hydraulic and patching cements that harden in minutes and are essential for active leaks, and plastic materials such as Epoxite, which is not a cementitious product at all. Rather (*below*) it is a bag of plastic jelly and a bottle of hardener, intended for sealing very fine holes.

Surface coating. Some cement products are intended specifically for use in thin layers, or as a topping material. Examples are "Top 'n Bond," part of the Sakrete line, and "Thorocrete." The mix can be used about as thin as you can trowel it, and special polymers in the formula produce a bond in situations where ordinary cement would dry and turn to powder. It can be used, also, for ordinary patching where a sand mix would be appropriate.

Paint-on sealer. Products like Thoroseal mix with water to a thick paint consistency and go on with a brush. They seal walls that may be transmitting moisture through the concrete. They go over concrete block, almost entirely eliminating the block-and-mortar pattern. You can also use them for small patches when regular patching materials aren't available.

Epoxy sealers. Not actually a cement product but very useful in wall and floor patching are epoxy materials such as Boyle-

Trowel types you find handy in masonry repairs: 1. Mason's trowels in two sizes, the smaller usually most workable in repair work. 2. Tuck-pointing trowel, used to apply mortar to cracks or joints between blocks or bricks. 3. Short and wide plastering trowel used for applying concrete or plaster. 4. Longer, slimmer plastering trowel used for smoothing.

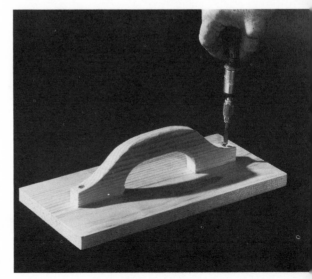

Wooden float produces a sand-textured surface, as opposed to the perfect smoothing of a steel trowel. Make a float as simply as this, with a scrap of 1 x 6, a cutout and rounded handle, and two screws.

Handy tools for cleaning up cracks before you add new material are: 1. Mason's hammer with a chisel-like end used for chipping and in masonry replacement, for breaking brick or block. 2. Coarse, heavy carborundum stone for grinding away unwanted cement or mortar. 3. An ordinary cold chisel and two special chipping chisels, for working loose material out of cracks, and for shaping a crack for proper repair.

This is a hawk, used for holding a batch of repair material up against a vertical surface so that you can scrape it off and into a crack. Make it from a piece of plywood about a foot square, with a 5" length of closet pole or equivalent for a handle, fastened on with a screw. Hawk shown has an aluminum top, easier to use, easier to clean.

Midway's "Epoxite." You buy a bag of jelly-thick plastic and a bottle of activator, mix them in the can, and brush them over areas that leak, *but not while they are leaking.* The material must go on dry surfaces. Generally speaking, the epoxy materials (at something like $6 a quart) are not intended for *filling*, but rather for *sealing*. It is recommended that you fill cracks and openings with hydraulic or with ordinary cement, then use epoxy as a sealing topcoat.

289

BASIC BASEMENT AND FOUNDATION REPAIRS

Repairs of damage or deterioration in basements and foundations fall into two classifications: the dirty, difficult, messy jobs that involve leaks, and the mud-pie jobs that involve only dry cracks, mortar failure, etc.

These are again divided by two questions: Can the repair be done from the inside, or must it be done from the outside? Is the repair above the surface of the ground, or should the earth outside the wall be, properly, dug away?

When the latter situation exists, you may be wise to turn the whole business over to a professional, because there can be a lot of labor involved.

Cracks and other voids are easy to fill, and small leaks are easy to plug, as discussed below. However, there are considerations beyond mere repair.

• If a crack opens again after you patch it, and it seems to be a continuing repair job, you can be sure that there are structural shortcomings which should be attended to. Study the area to see if you can determine the reason for and the seriousness of the problem. For instance, if a wall bulges or seems to skid at the base or at a corner, or if a crack reappears at the top of the wall, you can be sure that there are undue pressures from the earth outside. You need a contractor to take care of the problem.

• If a wall leaks pretty generally, not merely in one place, the call may again be for the contractor, because the man who put in the foundation probably did an inadequate job of waterproofing the outside surface of the wall. To take care of the situation, somebody may have to dig away the dirt, clean the wall, apply asphaltic waterproofing (or plastic) and shovel the dirt back in place. Carefully—to avoid cutting the protective film.

• If a basement tends to leak all along the base of the wall, it's a good sign that there is a "head of water" producing excessive hydrostatic pressure, and it may be necessary to dig down and install drain tiles along the footing, which should have been done in the first place. This lets the water drain off without building up such great pressure at the base of the wall.

However, an attempt should be made to make the required repairs in a simple way first, without inviting in the expense of an outside contractor.

THE RIGHT WAY TO FILL A CRACK

While working with concrete is simple, there are some critical steps involved in simple crack patching, some of which are not often adequately emphasized.

Fine cracks. When cracks are ¼″ wide or less, it is difficult to handle them with regular cement mortar, because of the drying problem and the difficulty of working the patching material deep enough to fill the space completely. It is sometimes advisable to chip and chisel these cracks until they are wider. *It is much simpler to use a special material intended for small cracks.* Special-formula fine sand mixes, such as Patcho and E.Z. Perma Cement, can usually be worked into small cracks without the need for chipping. (Be sure to check the label to find out whether the material must be kept wet for how long.)

The technique of using these materials, normally covered in excellent detail on the labels, involves simply knifing and troweling the mix deep into the crack. If you jiggle the tip of the trowel along the crack after it is nearly filled, you can be fairly sure that the fines of the mix have worked to the depth of the crack. When you've worked in all the patching material the crack will take, trowel the surface smooth. After the initial set, you can use a whiskbroom or other tool to simulate the texture of surrounding material.

Patching wider cracks. Although the special-formula materials work in larger spaces, you can save money by using ordinary sand mix or pea-gravel mix that you stir up yourself or buy already mixed. These are the steps:

1. If necessary, widen the crack to at least 1″. Avoid

"dished" or beveled edges that would result in a thin-edge patch, subject to drying before setting. It is sometimes recommended that you undercut the edges of a crack, to form an inverted V. Although this "keys" the patch into the existing material, its major function is to avoid a thin spread of concrete or mortar. Actually, a square-cut edge will do this. When it is difficult to chip a crack to the desired shape, you can avoid trouble by filling it with ordinary materials to within ¼" or so of level. Then, finish off with a material such as Patcho, Top 'n Bond, or Thorocrete, which will harden even at a feathered edge.

2. Be sure that all loose or crumbling material has been chipped loose. Clean out dust, particles, flakes with a broom.

3. Saturate the crack with water—thoroughly. Let it absorb all it will. Mop up the excess.

4. Mix a cream-thick batch of pure cement and water, "neat cement" and water, as it is sometimes called. Swab or brush this mixture on the presoaked crack. *This is an important step, very often overlooked.* Its purpose is to condition the crack ideally to accept the patch with a perfect bond.

5. Lay in the patching material, taking pains to work it into the depth of the crack. Be sure there is a little too much so that you can puddle it in place.

HOW TO PATCH A CRACK
IN A CONCRETE FLOOR

1. With chipping chisel and hammer, knock loose all fragments of concrete at the edges of the crack. At the same time, widen it to a minimum of ¾". 1" is better. Cut the edges square, or undercut them. In no circumstances leave a V edge.

2. Brush and flush the broken chips and fragments from the crack. If possible, use a garden hose to make sure the crack is clean.

3. Dampen the inside surfaces of the crack, if they have not already been dampened in the flushing.

4. Prepare a surry of cement and water about the thickness of paint. Brush this "bond coat" on the surfaces of the crack. Its purpose is to provide a better bond than you'd get applying the patching material directly to the dampened concrete. Since the patch must be placed while the bond coat is still wet, have the material ready.

5. Fill the cavity with the mixed concrete and puddle it with the trowel, to make sure that it works into all the spaces. There should be a slight mounding of the material, as insurance that the crack is full with no voids.

6. When you have worked the mix well into the space, use the trowel as a "screed" and scrape off the excess.

7. Use the trowel (or a wooden float for a "sand" finish) or smooth the patch and make it match the surrounding surface. Keep the patch damp for three days, unless the material is one of those with special ingredients (see text). *Photos courtesy of Master Builders.*

6. Screed off the excess with a steel trowel or wooden float. The float will give a sand-textured finish.

7. If you want a smoother finish, dress the patch with a steel trowel. Or produce the texture you want with a whiskbroom or other tool.

Important: It is absolutely necessary to keep the patch wet for at least three days, unless it happens to be one of the special materials. Read the label. As soon as the patch has set hard enough so that it will not wash away under a fine spray, dampen the entire area. Do this two or three times a day, unless you devise some means of cloaking the patch with wet burlap or the equivalent.

Cracks on vertical surfaces. The processes involved when you patch a vertical crack are the same as for cracks on the horizontal, but there are some differences in technique.

Unless the quantities are so large that economy is a factor, use hydraulic cement or one of the other quick-setting materials. This reduces the chances that your mix will sag out of the crack while you are applying it or before it sets.

1. Start at the bottom of a crack that runs vertically or on a steep slant. Work the patching material in, progressing upward, so that each addition is supported by the concrete below it.

2. Work with as thick a mix as possible, that is, with as little water as possible. This will help prevent sagging.

3. Although you must wet down the area and you must use the application of neat cement and water, let the surfaces dry a little more on vertical patches than you would on horizontal work. This also helps keep the material in place until it bonds and sets.

In extremely difficult situations, you may find it necessary to position a board or a piece of plywood over the crack, holding it in place with braces slanting up from the floor or even reaching across the room. This board should cover, as snugly as possible, the entire crack except for an opening at the top. Through this opening, ladle the patching cement in small trowelfuls, tapping on the board to encourage the material to

HOW TO PATCH VERTICAL CRACKS
IN CONCRETE BLOCK

1. As with any crack, chip away loose material. Work beyond the apparent limits of the crack, to be sure you remove defective masonry that might come loose later.

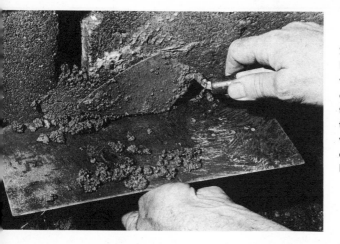

2. Mix the repair mortar as heavy as possible, that is, with a minimum but adequate amount of moisture. Use a trowel or hawk to support the mixture against the wall while you shove it into the crack. *Important:* Start at the bottom and work up.

3. After the heavy mixture has set slightly, use a thinner mix (with a little water added) to trowel the patch smooth. Keep it wet for three days, unless you are using a quick-setting material that doesn't require prolonged wetting.

settle to the bottom. When the patch thus applied has set, you can smooth it with one of the materials intended for thin-layer use.

Don't forget to keep the patch damp for three days or more, to be sure the concrete sets properly.

HOW TO REPAIR MORTAR JOINTS IN BRICK

1. Clean out loose or cracked mortar with cold chisel or screwdriver.

2. Remove all loose mortar by flushing with hose or with stiff brush and water.

3. While joint is still damp, fill with mortar. Use a tuck-pointing trowel to press the mortar firmly in place.

4. Scrape off excess mortar and finish joint to match rest of wall. After about five minutes, brush across joint to remove excess mortar on surrounding brick and finish again.

Patching water leaks. If you have a leak in basement wall or floor that dries up periodically, giving you a chance to work on it between floodings, the same techniques apply as are covered above. It's best to use hydraulic cement or an expansive cement, because of their extra sealing value.

When a leak is present all the time and must be patched wet, pick a hydraulic cement and follow these steps:

1. Chip away existing material until the crack is at least 1″ wide and deep. This is critical, because a certain amount of volume is necessary for the patching material to do its job. Be sure to cut square or undercut; do not cut a V-groove.

2. Use a garden hose and water pressure to flush away loosened masonry and dirt.

3. Mix the hydraulic cement with just enough water to produce a consistency similar to that of glazing compound or putty. Mix a small amount, since it must be in place within three minutes of the time the water is added. Experience will tell you—with each repair job—how much hydraulic cement you can mix and apply in three minutes.

4. You do not "grout" hydraulic cement, that is, you don't count on it flowing into the crack. It must, instead, be pressed in, either with your palms or a float. Do not use a troweling action. Just press it in, glob by glob. Prolonged contact with the material will dry your skin; use gloves, or be quick to rinse your hands after use.

5. Keep hydraulic cement patches wet for at least 15 minutes. (Read the label; the wet period may vary from product to product.)

ACTIVELY FLOWING LEAKS

You can patch a leak in a basement wall or floor that is actually pouring a stream of water, using hydraulic cement. The trick is to study the crack in search of *the point at which the pressure is greatest.* After opening and undercutting the crack, start at the ends, and gradually work the cement in, glob by glob, until the only remaining unfilled space is that where the water runs most vigorously, where the greatest pressure is. Work to make this final opening as small as pos-

When a leak in a basement wall is pouring water, use hydraulic cement to plug the hole. After mixing the cement, hold it in the hand for a minute or two until it's dry, then shape it to match the shape of the hole. Press it firmly in place and hold it until it has set. Shave off excess with trowel before the cement hardens.

sible, consistent with the pressure and the amount of water. Finally, mix a batch of hydraulic cement large enough to plug the remaining hole. *Do not apply it immediately, however.* If you'll hold this mix in your hands for a minute or two, you'll feel it turning slightly warm and it will give the appearance of drying a little. Shape the glob to match the shape and size of the final hole. Press it firmly in place and hold it there for a few minutes, until it has set. Then, if necessary, use the edge of the trowel to shave the excess material off, before it finally hardens.

WHEN A WHOLE BASEMENT WALL LEAKS

Sometimes a leaky basement wall doesn't confine itself to specific cracks, but seems to leak all across its surface. This condition makes itself evident in dampness—a beading of water droplets—over all or most of the wall. This condition, however, may indicate condensation of moisture from over-humid air in the basement instead of a water-permeable wall. If cold water pipes in the basement tend to drip, if there is a damp feeling to metal surfaces, be suspicious of condensation. One way to check it out is to stand a piece of glass tight against the wall in contact with the concrete, and leave it there overnight. In the morning, if the glass is dry but the wall back of it is wet, you know that it is not condensation.

Treatment of a "bleeding" wall is almost the simplest of all wet basement techniques. It hinges on a cementitious paint product such as "Thoroseal" that mixes with water and goes on with a brush. The slurry you paint on is white and the wall is not only dry, but it is a gleaming white. Homeowners often use Thoroseal to treat a wall that doesn't leak, just to get rid of the banality of a concrete block or concrete basement wall, and to brighten the area.

The slurry flows into the pores of the concrete, poured or block, and seals them against transmission of moisture.

Important: A cementitious product such as Thoroseal cannot bond to paints or other coatings. Therefore, if you have a leaking wall that has been painted, it may be necessary to sandblast the entire surface. This is most often a job for professionals. If the area is small, you may be able to clean it up with a water-wash paint remover (such as TM-4), taking special pains to scrub the surface clean with a stiff-bristle broom as you rinse off the remover. Even so, sandblasting is a more certain procedure.

PAINT ON WATERPROOFING MIX TO SEAL A WALL

1. Special cement formulas such as Thoroseal can be used for small mortaring jobs as well as brush-on coating. Here, a cove is troweled along the base of a wall, as the first step in waterproofing and decorating a wall that tends to "weep."

2. Critical step in applying brush-on coating is prewetting the wall. Good way to do this is to spray a few feet ahead of yourself as you work along the wall. Fine spray dampens without excessive runoff.

3. Big fiber-bristle brush is the right tool for applying cement paint (although a pushbroom does a fast job if the area is big). Apply the material first as though you were troweling it into the depressions. This insures a good fill.

4. Then, with less pressure on the brush, "tip off" the application, leaving it smooth as shown here. Tipping off must follow rather quickly after the initial application, before material starts to set.

Leaks at the base of a wall. Standard construction procedures invite a weak point where a foundation wall rests on a basement floor. The builders lay the slab for the basement floor. Then they lay up block or set forms and pour the basement walls. If the concrete floor is "green" and clean, the bond between the floor and wall may be a perfect joint. Given a little time lag or a little dirt, it may not be.

That is one reason why many basement leaks are at the juncture of wall and floor. The other reason is that the hydrostatic pressure is greater at that level than at any point above.

To reinforce and repair the joint between wall and floor, be sure to pick a strongly adherent material, one that utilizes sand only, rarely any coarse aggregate. Combine these critical materials with all of the concrete-mix precautions of this chapter.

To be doubly sure of adhesion, you can buy additives for concrete (such as "Acryl 60" made by Standard Dry Wall) that you mix with water. Such extra adhesion is important when you are working a base-of-the-wall leak and don't want to chip excessively to provide a physical bond for the batch.

Leaky basement addenda: A basement doesn't leak if the entire job of design, engineering, and construction of a house was well done. However, there may be inadequate drain-away of the spill from rain-carrying systems. There may be improper pitch toward basement and foundation walls, so that water flows to the house, down the foundation, and forms pressure at construction joints which they may not be able to withstand. It may be that a house was built on a piece of land with a water table so high that the basement or crawlspace is sitting in a sea of water at least during the wettest part of the year. Although there is nothing you can do about the water table, a landscape contractor can usually modify the pitch of the land in a way that lets surface water drain away.

SMOOTHING ROUGH CONCRETE SURFACES

When a basement floor or wall is rough, due to scaling or other imperfections, the only feasible method of making it smooth is with one of the cement materials especially formulated for extremely thin application. For example, "Thoro-crete," the acrylic-modified cement made by Standard Dry Wall, can be spread only ⅛″ thick or less and still perform properly. Top 'n Bond does the same job.

Floors. Go over the surface carefully with a stiff broom and if you note any scaling concrete, clean it down to sound material with a hammer and chipping chisel. If there are oils, paints, or other dirt on the floor, use a strong detergent to remove them. Hose the surface thoroughly with plenty of water. Keep it damp as you apply the surfacing material, but without puddles of water.

Follow these steps:

1. Mix a thin slurry of the surfacing material, and apply it with a heavy bristle brush or a push broom, as a bond coat.

2. Mix the trowel coat fairly thick, in quantities you can apply in about half an hour.

3. Apply in a layer just thick enough to level the floor, while the brushed-on coat is still wet.

4. Use enough trowel pressure to force the surfacing into all depressions, but do not overtrowel. Typical surfacing materials tend to foul the trowel. Keep it clean by rubbing it frequently over a wet cloth.

Specific instruction sheets for thin-use materials vary. Read them carefully, since some of the methods recommended may run contrary to standard concrete procedures.

Walls. Smoothing a rough concrete or concrete block wall is easy to do with brushing-consistency mixtures of Throseal, Top 'n Bond and similar products, applied this way:

1. The wall must be free of paint, oil, and other materials that interfere with bond. Chip away any loose or loosening bits of masonry.

2. If there are fairly large depressions or cracks, fill and trowel them smooth and level. Give these fills time to set, depending on the material used.

3. Mix the brush-on surfacing materials in a quantity you can apply in no more than thirty minutes.

4. Hose the wall down with clean water. Let the water drain until the surface is damp, not wet.

5. Use a big fiber bristle brush and apply the coating in a swabbing motion that lays on a smooth coating. (See photos.) The action of the bristles both spreads the material and "trowels" it into depressions. The brush marks will show, as there is no "leveling" that you'd expect from paint, so take pains to produce an attractive texture. The best appearance usually comes from an every-which-way brushing.

The application of Thoroseal and similar surfacing materials waterproofs a wall. If water presents a serious "weeping" problem, many experts apply a coat to the lower half of the wall, where seepage pressure is greatest. Then they coat the entire wall, thus double-coating the surfaces that may need it most.

20

TILE AND COUNTERTOPS
IN BATH AND KITCHEN

THE TILE USED IN bathrooms and often kitchens, and the plastic countertopping used in both kitchen and bath are among the most troublefree and durable of all household construction materials. The major problems come from failing adhesion with either tile or the "decorative laminate" used on counters and, now and then, walls. However, a tile is broken occasionally—someone may put an over-hot pan on the counter top—and the damage calls for patching.

THE MECHANICS OF WALL TILE

You find more ceramic tile than any other kind, although there is a lot of plastic tile and some enameled metal tile around. The latter are nearly always held in place with a mastic; ceramic tile may be in mastic or actually bedded in plaster. For ceramic tile there is a material called "grout" that fills the spaces between the tiles. Plastic and metal tile, being thinner, makes use of the mastic as a grout. Either way, the purpose of the grout is to seal the wall and make it watertight.

Although it takes experience and practice, few handymen have to handle tile set in plaster. The convenient, attractive and long-lasting squares are easy to install, repair, and maintain — with three improvements on the old techniques:

• The use of a smooth, water resistant material such as asbestos board for a back-up.

• The use of easy-to-spread, waterproof mastics for adhesion.

• The use of plastic-based materials (instead of cement products) for grouting.

THE KINDS OF TILE YOU FIND IN A HOUSE

Three kinds of tile are ordinarily used around the house.

Glazed tile is the shiny stuff, usually white on the back, with the color and glaze only on the exposed area. This is the kind of tile you find on walls, in shower stalls, on back splashes, and sometimes on counters — anyplace where wear and abrasion are relatively small. Cleaning is wipe-up easy.

Quarry tile is the same clear through. The surface is not glazed. Instead, it is matte, tough, capable of accepting considerable rough traffic. It is used on floors, although sometimes you find it used on heavy-duty counters. (The name doesn't come from "stone quarry," but is rather a corruption of the French word for square.)

Pavers are heavier, often bigger tiles used on decks or patios, stoops, walks, and other extra-heavy wear areas. Because of their size and thickness, they are still most often laid in a concrete base, unlike the glazed and quarry tiles.

You find all of these tiles in a variety of sizes and shapes, including hexagonals. Sometimes the smallest tiles are called "mosaics." In the rectangular groups are matching sizes composed of a single square, two-square shape, and a four-square shape. These shapes work together in ashlar patterns, either in a single color or in several matching or complementary shades.

While standard wall tile, measuring $4\frac{1}{4}''$ x $4\frac{1}{4}''$, and the larger pavers, are normally handled as individual pieces, some of the smaller sizes are unitized into sheets, so that a fairly large area can be covered at one time. The methods of unitiz-

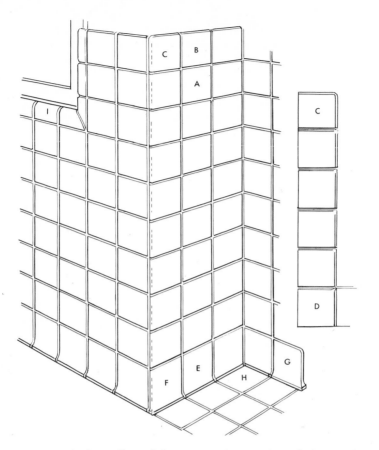

Ceramic tile for walls and floors comes in a variety of pieces:
(A) full tile; (B) surface cap; (C) outside corner, down; (D) inside
corner, up; (E) cove base; (F) left-hand cove corner or end; (G)
right-hand cove corner or end; (H) floor tile; (I) bullnose tile.

ing vary, but one common method is a group of small tiles
fastened to a sheet of heavy paper with a water-solvent glue.
Since the tiles are fastened to the paper, face side down, and
they are laid paper side up, all you have to do is soak off the
paper after the unit is laid and its adhesive has set. In another
form, a mesh on the back of the tiles holds them in unit form,
and the mesh simply disappears into the mastic when you lay
the tiles.

307

In addition to the tile forms you find around the house, there are coves for use at the floor, nosings for use at the top or edges of a tiled area, at inside and outside corners, and even three-plane corner for use where two walls and the floor meet. You may find that these special forms match the color of the tile, but quite often they are black, as a compromise which goes with all colors.

When replacement of tile is necessary, you can ordinarily find the shape and the color you want at a well-stocked tile outlet.

THE FOUR STEPS IN A TILING JOB

Whether you are doing repairs or installing tile over a wall area as a means of making it presentable, four steps are involved: a good sound base, proper adhesive, laying the tile, and a careful grouting job to fill and waterproof the cracks.

A base for tile. Since tile has little or no flexibility in its joints, the surface you put it on must be fairly rigid. On a floor, it must be *quite* rigid. Normally any standard wall is sound enough structurally. On an existing floor, there should be an underlay of plywood. The thicker the plywood is, up to 3/4", the better the subfloor. Use good-one-side plywood, not sheathing grade, because the irregularities in sheathing plywood may cause unevenness in the tile. In a bath or any other watery environment, the plywood should be exterior grade — waterproof.

If you discover much damage, a great deal of cracking in the grout between tiles, many loose tiles, it may be that the original underlay was inadequate. When this is true, repairs must include *new underlay* on top of the old, or the damage will surely come back. This means, of course, lifting the old tile with a stiff trowel or garden spade and replacing it with new, unless you are up to the tedious job of cleaning the old tile for reuse.

If the existing subfloor is of plywood, but perhaps too thin, you can usually make it firm and smooth enough with 3/8" or 1/2" plywood, nailed every 8" in both directions and every 4" along the edges. The addition of this much thickness to the subfloor will not ordinarily produce problems with bath fixtures, and you will find it possible to grout neatly where the floor meets the wall, even if there is a cove base in the room.

When the floor is a bath or laundry, etc., it should have a waterproofing-priming coat, a material you'll be able to buy at the same outlet where you buy the tile. These primers vary enough to make it important to read instructions carefully, to be sure you end up with a base which will not, in the future, soften and swell and give you repair troubles.

In severe moisture situations, such as a shower stall, the plywood base is augmented with a troweling of concrete at least 1″ thick, or with a sheet of 1/4″ asbestos board layed in a waterproof mastic. Provision must be made, of course, for the drain in either case. (Plumbing supply houses sell a "shower pan" of lead or copper, complete with drain hole and hardware, which requires only a cement-and-sand lining, then tile.)

Shower walls are at their best with a substrate of asbestos board, cemented in place. Not only is it an excellent surface for mastic-tile compatibility, not only is it resistant to water damage, but it also has excellent dimensional stability, shrinking and swelling only slightly with changes in moisture and temperature.

Ordinarily, counters in the kitchen or bath need only a firm plywood base, properly primed, for an excellent tile job.

Tile adhesives. Most paint and hardware stores and the mail order catalogs all provide mastics for tile setting. There are various kinds, ranging up to epoxies for maximum adhesion and resistance to moisture and chemicals. When you buy the adhesive, tell the tile dealer what sort of a base you are planning to put it on. He will recommend the required adhesive.

It's best to buy a toothed (or notched) spreader, although you can make one by filing teeth in a piece of 1/8″ hardboard. It is important for the teeth to be spaced according to specifications, for the mastic and to be the proper depth. On most

TRICKS THAT HELP MAKE LAYING TILE EASY TO DO

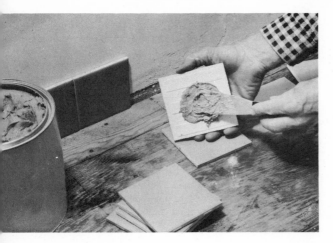

1. Start tiling a plain wall by laying a row across the floor, using a glob of mastic on the back of each tile. For proper spacing side to side on the wall, see the text.

2. Use a level to make sure that bottom row is absolutely horizontal. The space at the floor may not be exactly true—but that is better than having the courses up at eye level look crooked. Chips of tile, scraps of wood, etc., can be used to true the course.

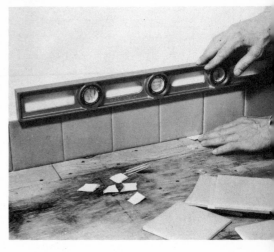

3. Since the rows should be truly vertical, too, make the courses at a corner true by hanging a plumb bob (or a spike on a string) and marking the edges. Cut the tile the right size to form a vertical but fit tightly into the corner.

4. If, however, there is a prominent window, a row of complete tiles should run across the bottom. In this case make that row the starting point, and lay tiles both down and up from it.

mastic cans you'll find a diagram of the proper size and spacing for the spreader teeth. If they are too big—or too small—you may spread too much or too little mastic for the best job.

Most mastics give you about an hour of "open time" during which you can lay tile in place, gradually spreading the adhesive ahead of yourself as you go, and adjusting each piece. When you work on a floor, don't "tile" yourself into a corner. Be sure not to walk on the new tile until the mastic has set the required length of time.

On walls, you must provide support for the tiles to keep them from sliding down the wall in the fresh mastic. This is taken care of automatically with some tiles, which have tiny ridges on adjacent sides, to hold them the proper distance apart. With other tile, you may have to improvise, as covered below.

Laying the tile. This is the easy part. Tiles should be firmed into position, but without too much pressure. Be careful not to skid them, or you may squeegee the mastic up at the edge. With individual tiles, it is best to place each tile on the edge of the previous one, then gently slide it off so that it slips into position without any skidding at all.

Blocks of tiles, unitized with paper, are flexible, much the same as a piece of plastic floor tile. It is simple to hold the far edge or corner away from the adhesive while you position the critical edges, then lower the free corner into place. Smooth and press the units with the palms of your hands and spread fingers.

311

5. Before you start to lay tile, be sure the base is ready. Sand high spots down, checking most carefully at the floor line, where plasterers may not do a finished job.

6. It is good practice to calk around pipes that emerge from walls, if there is space. This prevents the movement of moisture through the wall.

7. Pipes have flanges (against the wall on the two supply pipes, hanging down on the waste line) that cover the broken edges of tile. You'll find it easy to nibble tile with pliers, after you scribe the curve with a glass cutter. When the hole must come in the middle of a tile, cut it in two, then nibble the space out of the two pieces equally.

8. Final step is applying grout, a thin mixture of special cement and water. Rub it into the cracks with rubber-gloved hands, then use a window squeegee to remove most of the grout on the surface. Since it doesn't adhere to the glazed surface, you can wipe away the rest after it dries.

Grouting the tile. Tile, whether unitized or laid individually, should have about ¹⁄₁₆″ spaces, which are filled with a plastic or cementitious material that makes them watertight. Do not leave less than this amount of space. Do not leave much more. If you do you will get a poor grouting job. It is sometimes thought that you can increase or decrease the space between tiles as a means of making things come out right at the corners. This is not so. Accommodation for dimensions of the tiles vs. the dimensions of the wall must be made by cutting tiles at the corner to make proper fit. (See below.)

Standard grout comes in the form of a powder which you mix with water or in a premixed paste. There are grouts based on epoxy resins, as well as vinyl, which have the advantage of extra flexibility and elasticity, minimizing cracking between tiles. The methods for applying these materials vary from brand to brand; read the labels carefully.

To apply standard grout, you smear the paste over the surface of the tile, working it into the cracks. The object is to fill the spaces entirely. Any voids guarantee trouble later. After the grout is rubbed in thoroughly, an ordinary window squeegee is handy to clean off the majority of the remaining mastic on the surface. Then you "strike" the joints using some smooth, rounded end such as the handle of a toothbrush, leaving the grout slightly coved. While doing this operation, observe carefully the continuity of the grout, and fill in any voids that show up.

After the grout has hardened, the final step is to wipe it off the surface of the tiles, leaving them clean and smooth. An old turkish towel works well for this operation.

REMOVING BROKEN OR LOOSE TILES

You'll find it possible most of the time to salvage tiles that are loose. Use a chisel or screwdriver to pry them free. Then scrape or carefully chip away any mortar that may be clinging to the back of the tile. If necessary, use a weak solution of muriatic acid in water to remove the plaster, so that the tiles are clean. Meanwhile, remove any grout sticking to the edges.

FLOOR TILE OFTEN COME
IN UNITIZED SHEETS

Small tiles—square or in other shapes—usually come in sheets, held in proper spacing by a sheet of paper or a fine plastic net. This speeds the job of laying.

Basic step in preparation for new floor tile is reinforcement of the subfloor with an underlayment of plywood.

Underlayment gets a seal coat of waterproofing primer. Then, the mastic used for laying the tile is waterproof, too. Final step is grouting, as with wall tile.

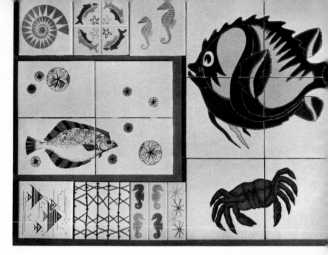

Typical of decorative tiles dealers handle are these sealife patterns. Although they are intended for sparking up a bath when it is first tiled, they can be used for repair work when matching tiles are impossible to find. The result is a sound tiled wall once more — plus the interest and color of the patterned replacements.

If a tile is broken you can go one of these routes.

• Use Duco cement to reassemble the parts.

• Take a scrap to the tile shop and ask the man to help you match it. Quite often a dealer will have a few old tiles in his junk box, and even if your house is old, there may be a chance that he can come up with the same color.

• Go deliberately after mismatch. You can buy units of tiles (see photo) that form picture-like decorations. If one of these would be appropriate, chip out the number of tiles necessary and install the decorative tiles. (On a relatively small wall, you could remove a hit-and-miss, Mondrian-like pattern of tiles and replace them with accent colors, making the whole misfortune seem deliberate.)

• Or, you can get hold of a tile that matches closely. From an inconspicuous spot (back of a door, down in a corner) carefully remove a tile. Use this tile for the conspicuous patch, and use the slightly mismatching piece in the inconspicuous place.

The next job is to restore the place where the broken tile came from. It must be the same level as it was originally, which means you have to spackle-fill some low spots with patching plaster. Using this plaster, adjust the depth of the hole so that the replaced tile is flush with its neighbors. When the patching plaster has set, apply mastic to the tile, put it in place, and grout when the time comes.

Replacing a larger area. When damage (usually water) causes a fairly large area of tile to come loose, it is usually simplest to restore the wall by using a piece of asbestos board cut to fit the opening. When you utilize this method, adjust the board for depth by troweling patching cement on the existing wall, if necessary. Fasten the asbestos board in place with nails into the wall studs, unless the space involved is so small that it doesn't span two studs. When this is the case, smooth the area with patching plaster at the right depth. Apply the asbestos board with mastic. Mastic the tile in position, then grout.

THREE STEPS IN REPAIRING
SERIOUS WALL DAMAGE

1. Leaks through plaster caused wall behind tile to deteriorate completely. For repair, the first step is fitting a piece of asbestos board into the damaged area. Then apply mastic.

2. Notched trowel spreads the mastic properly. Use of waterproof adhesive guards against repeat damage.

3. Position tiles and firm them into the mastic. Normally you can use the same tiles for repairs in damage of this sort, after they have been cleaned (see text).

HANDLING WALL-SIZE TILE WORK

When repairs or replacement, or new installation, of tile involves an entire wall, you must plan the layout of the units on the area. It would be convenient if you could start at one corner of a tiling job, working across and down or across and up, willy-nilly. You can't. There are certain features of a bathroom or kitchen or other floor or wall or countertop that dictate spacing, for example, soap trays, medicine cabinets, sinks, lavatories, tissue holder, etc., not to mention the height of a bathtub.

Nor do you want to end up in a corner or at an edge with a narrow row of tiles, while another corner has tiles full width. To avoid this, find the middle of the tile run. Using a tile as a gauge, mark tile widths across the span. If, at the end, the leftover is *less than half a tile*, you should lay the wall with a full tile centered at the middle. If the leftover is *more than half a tile*, a joint belongs at the middle.

This procedure works both laterally and vertically, whether you are working with unitized mosaics, standard wall tiles, or large pavers, on horizontal or vertical surfaces. The object is, insofar as possible, to "center" the tile job on its area, surrounding it with a "frame" that is as uniform as possible.

HANDLING THE PROBLEM OF
WALL-MOUNTED FIXTURES

You may want to dismount such items as wall-hung lavatories. If you do, tape up a piece of paper over the area where the mounting bracket was (*left*). Probe with a pencil until you find the screw holes. Mark the position of the paper, as shown here at 33" from the corner and 36" from the floor. That way you can reposition it after the tile is in place and use a carbide-tipped bit to drill holes for remounting the bracket (*right*).

To mount a recessed soap dish or similar fixture, leave four tiles (more if the fixture is bigger) out when you lay up the wall. Cut through the plaster in back, to allow the dish to recess.

Lay the dish face down on four tiles and pencil mark its shape and size in their exact center. Score along those lines carefully with the glass cutter. Try not to run the cutter beyond the corners. Then cut a crisscross of scoring in the area to be removed.

Use pliers (or nippers made especially for this kind of work) to chip out the space required for the fixture.

Coat the sides of the fixture with mastic and slip it into position. Clean away excess adhesive. When it has set, use grout to fill in neatly around the installation.

Working around a tub. The bathtub presents a special problem, since it is sound engineering to run a row of whole tiles at the top of the tub. In fact, standard built-in tubs have a lip which runs upwards at plaster level, so that tile can overlap it, making a watertight joint.

All of this dictates the height of one row of tile: the same height as the tub. From this row, you must lay tile down to the floor and up to wainscot height. (It is because the break at the ceiling may be awkward that a high wainscot is used, even in a tub-shower situation, with enamel on the wall for a short distance up to the ceiling above the tile.)

The simplest way to handle this problem is to nail to the wall a length of 1 x 2 exactly even with the top edge of the tub, and level. Lay the tile above this board. When the mastic has set beyond the sag point, remove the board. Prepare a series of vertical rows, adjusting them to exact height beneath the upper wall by cutting the tile which hits the floor, or the cove, if you are using one. Put these tiles in place in vertical rows, not horizontal, and keep the spaces proper ($1/16''$) by lifting each tile up beneath the preceding one. Cut tiles to fit for the bottom row. Thus, if there is any discrepancy—such as lack of parallelism—it will occur at the floor, where it is least conspicuous.

In a shower stall. Water plus steam makes the job tougher for tile in a shower stall, but hardly tougher for you. The best thing to do is to line the stall with asbestos board. Then, use an epoxy mastic and grout. You may find it interesting and easier to put in the ceiling diagonally, since it removes all of the problems of matching ceiling rows with wall rows.

SOME METHODS IN SHOWERS ARE DIFFERENT

Shower floor underlayment is reinforced concrete, made by placing a sheet of half-inch hardware cloth over the area, then cutting out a hole for the drain.

Then, a 2″ thickness of fine-mix concrete goes down, carefully troweled smooth. A wad of old rags in the drain keeps the concrete out of it.

On top of the troweled cement, sprinkle a thin layer of "neat cement"—with no sand. When the water has worked through this cement, lay out the sheets of tile.

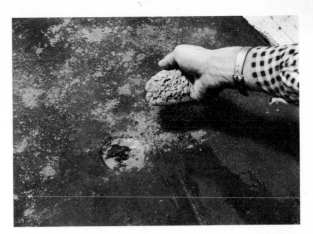

At the center, install the drain ring (which accepts the seive or screen). Then use glass cutter and pliers to shape final tiles to fit around the drain. Grouting comes last. Tile dealers sell special grout for shower stall use.

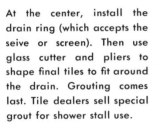

The walls of a shower stall go on last. If you lay the tiles (in mastic) on the ceiling diagonally, the effect is interesting, and you bypass the difficulty of having ceiling tiles line up with those on the wall. At the edges, use half-tiles cut on the diagonal.

HOW TO CUT AND SHAPE TILE

You need three tools to cut and shape tile—and they can be improvisations. Your tile dealer may loan or rent a tile cutter to you. Otherwise, buy a new glasscutter. To smooth edges you need a file or rasp; the variety called "bastard" is best. But, you can also use aluminum oxide sandpaper, about 80 grit, on a firm smooth wooden block. And, you need a pair of "nippers," a special breed of pliers with edges that come together on the front and back of a tile, producing a fairly clean break. But you can do nearly as well with an ordinary pair of pliers.

TWO STEPS IN CUTTING TILE

1. An ordinary glass cutter scores tile, so that you can break it by applying pressure as shown here, with the cutter mark positioned directly over a piece of wire such as a coat hanger. If you have much work to do, the tile outlet will loan or rent an efficient cutter that speeds the job.

2. Make the edges of the cut smooth with a rasp of the type labeled "bastard." It is most important to have the glazed edge smooth, so the grout will show an even line.

SOME TECHNIQUES ARE DIFFERENT
WITH PLASTIC TILE

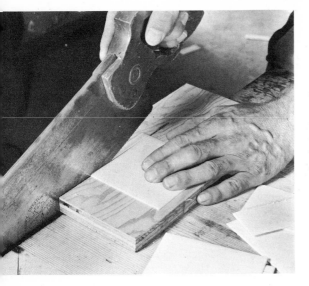

Plastic tile is easy to cut with a fine-tooth saw. Shown here is a cutting board formed of a single saw-cut in a piece of plywood. Position the cutting line of the tile over this slot, and your cut will be true and smooth.

Because plastic tile is easy to cut, you'll find it easiest to leave mounting plates, etc., on the wall and fit around them, rather than removing them and remounting when tile is in place.

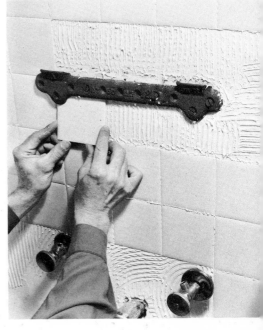

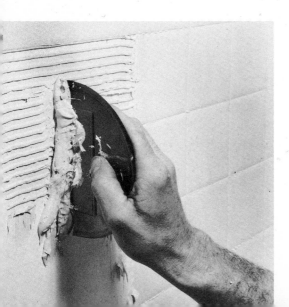

The spread of mastic back of plastic tile is a bit thicker than with clay tile, since the adhesive material is intended to ooze up between tiles, acting as a grout-like sealer.

Proper amount of mastic produces beads and strips between tiles, as shown here. Action here is placing the final cut tile in a corner.

Pencil eraser makes an excellent tool for smoothing the mastic between tiles. It gives you a neatly coved joint. When the smoothing is finished, clean away excess mastic on tile surfaces.

Straight cuts. Put the tile in the cutter, or lay a straightedge along it to guide the glass cutter. Score it sharply, the same as you would glass. Then position the score mark over a piece of wire (a coat hanger) and apply pressure on both sides with the heels of your hands. Click! Smooth the edges with the rasp or sandpaper.

Inside cuts. Sometimes it is necessary to cut a corner out of one or more tiles, as when you must surround a soap dish or some such. Score the lines of the shape carefully, making sure not to score beyond the point where the cut should be. Make a crisscross of score marks with the cutter over the area to be removed. Take the nippers and gradually chip out the crisscrossed unwanted area. Clean up the cut with rasp or sandpaper.

Important: Do not try to rush this job by taking bites that are too big, or you may cause the tile to break where you don't want it to.

With any cut tile, it is important mainly to have the visible edge smooth. When you grout, the joint will be neat and smooth, especially in view of the fact that the cut edge is most often in a corner or at the floor.

Spacing between tiles. Some tiles are produced with little ridges on two sides, to hold them the proper distance apart. In other cases, you have to provide the spaces, uniformly, yourself. An easy way to do this is to stock a couple of pounds of 6-penny finishing nails. Use two of them between tiles, point inward, and leave them there until the mastic sets.

REPAIR WORK ON COUNTERTOPPING

Most countertops these days are made of the rugged plastic materials called "decorative laminate," such as Formica and Micarta. They are rarely damaged, although misusing them as a cutting board will eventually destroy the surface. A hard blow with a pointed object may rupture the material by indenting the plywood it is normally mounted on. And, these materials are susceptible to scorching and burning.

Most repair work, however, is likely to involve recementing laminate which has come loose from the backing. Such adhesive failure is most likely to occur along an edge, where moisture may seep in. Although the adhesive is waterproof, the water may cause the fibers of the plywood base to loosen. When this is the case, of course, the plywood is certain to be waterlogged. Follow these steps:

• Lift the edge carefully and with a piece of wood about the size of a ruler or yardstick, continue to raise the material until you come to a corner.

• Raise the corner as far as you can without cracking the laminate, and prop it up with a stick.

• Leave it in this position until the area is entirely dry. You can speed up the drying with an electric fan, a photoflood, a hair dryer, or a little electric space heater.

• When it is dry, use coarse sandpaper to remove all the "whiskers" of wood fibers. Work as far back under the laminate as possible, but be careful not to let debris pile up in the crack, or it will result in an uneven surface.

• Use contact cement to put the material back down (see below).

Decorative laminate cuts readily with any type of hand or power saw, although saber saws tend to chip, even with a fine-tooth blade. When the cut is made, smooth the edges with an ordinary plane. A good way to hold the material steady is by clamping it between two boards, one end in the vise, as shown.

Patch a fairly large damaged area of laminate by cutting a piece of matching material big enough to cover the damage. Fasten it in place with double-faced "carpet" tape, then use it as its own pattern to cut through the laminate. Remove the cutout piece and put the new piece in place. Even with patterned laminate like this, it is usually possible to match lines in a way to make the patch inconspicuous.

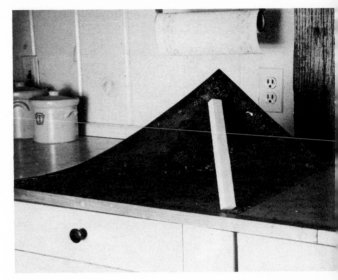

When the countertopping comes loose, it is usually due to water gradually soaking the backing. Before you glue it back, raise the laminate and leave it propped up until the backing is thoroughly dry.

PATCHING IN THE MIDDLE OF AN AREA

If the damage to the plastic laminate is not at an edge, but requires a cut-out patch, the first step is to visit the dealer to see if you can pick up a piece of matching material. Cut this material to size and fasten it over the damaged area with a double-face tape, most commonly sold as "carpet tape." Adjust the patch for the best match with the pattern, if there is one.

Use a linoleum knife to scribe carefully around the patch. If you are careful, using plenty of pressure, you can cut through for a perfect fit, although it will take many passes with the knife. When the damaged material has been cut all around, use a chisel or putty knife to break it out. Clean up the exposed base. If it is dented, use an epoxy filler to make it level. Then use the contact cement process covered below to cement the patch in place.

You can never avoid a certain amount of space around the patch, and there is danger that water will find its way through, possibly causing future troubles. Guard against this by grouting some Duco cement into the cracks, filling them completely. Wipe the surplus off the surface before it dries.

327

USING CONTACT CEMENT

Contact cement, a material familiar to many handymen, is unlike other adhesives in use and in performance. It sticks to just about anything in its liquid form; then it sticks to itself in its dry form. In use, you brush it on both surfaces to be stuck together, let it dry, then bring the two faces together.

The bond is instant. You don't have any adjustment period. If you are lifting a corner or edge, and the position is automatic, this is of no consequence, since the sheet can't get out of line. However, when you are working with a piece of loose laminate, follow these steps:

1. Cut a piece of the laminate to exactly the size needed for the repair.

2. Brush a coat of contact cement on the back of the laminate and on the base to which it is to be applied. In some cases it may be necessary to brush on two coats; read the instructions. These coatings must dry—but not too dry. They should be dry enough so that your fingers don't stick to them, but not so dry that they feel "varnish" hard.

3. While they are drying, cut two pieces of paper, each a bit more than half the size of the area. Newspaper works, but it's better to use a heavier material such as the "tagboard" stationery stores sell, or "poster paper" you can get at art shops. Lay these two pieces of paper over the area, so that *they overlap at the center* and cover the entire space.

4. When the cement is properly dry, position the laminate carefully over the space. It will not stick to the paper, nor will the paper stick to the base.

5. Place your hand on one side of the laminate to hold it in position. With the other hand, pull the piece of paper on the other side so that there is a space of about 2″ between them.

6. Press the laminate down along this space. It will adhere to the base, and it is now locked in position.

7. Pull the pieces of paper laterally, one at a time, rubbing the laminate into contact as you remove the paper. This prevents any undesirable buckling of the material.

8. When both pieces of paper have been removed, go over the entire area, pounding it with the heel of your hand. Try

PATCHING DENTS IN
PLASTIC LAMINATE COUNTERS

1. Mix a small quantity of epoxy filler (or auto body putty) on a scrap of aluminum, and trowel it into the dent with small spatula.

2. Force the patching material into the depressions with a putty knife, at the same time squeegeeing the excess off the surface. You can wipe away the remaining filler before it sets with a rag dampened with lacquer thinner — but don't wait until it sets. A small amount of smoothing with extremely fine sandpaper will not harm the laminate.

3. Mix a tiny amount of high quality enamel with tinting colorants to match the laminate, and "stipple" it on the patches.

329

to hit every square inch of the laminate to force it into contact, so it will stick and stay stuck.

Use the above cementing procedures for all work with decorative laminates, where you are patching in a small area or putting a new surface on an entire counter.

PATCHING SMALL DENTS

If a plastic laminate is ruptured by a hard blow, producing a dent, you can cut it out as covered above. But, it is easier to treat the damge the way you might handle a dent in your car. Use an epoxy filler.

First, chip out the broken laminate, and the damaged base, so that the hole is sound, the way a dentist drills out a cavity before he fills it.

Mix the epoxy filler and trowel it smooth, filling the depression completely. When it has set, sand off any high spots, if necessary, but be careful not to abrade the surrounding undamaged surface.

As a final step, use a high quality enamel of the proper color to finish the patch.

HOMEOWNER'S
4-SEASON
CHECKLIST

All through this book, the objective has been to recommend methods and materials for repairing the house you live in. It makes sense to anticipate damage and keep it from happening, or to catch it while it is minor, or to take care of it during the season of the year when repair is easiest. For an all-too-clear example, it is best to check the weather stripping on the front door during the summer, rather than wait until it starts leaking heat in the winter, promising more leakage when you have to leave the door open to work on it.

SAVE WITH INSPECTIONS AND PREPAREDNESS

Everyone who owns a home is sure to spend some time looking it over, both as an object of pride and as an investment worth some attention. From time to time, however, you'll be wise to go over the place with a fine-tooth comb (a pair of binoculars is an even better aid) in search of potential troubles or troubles that, although still small, are likely to grow.

In order to be able to make quick repairs as you discover them, it is wise to keep tools in shape and material on hand. Such items as glue, calk, epoxy fillers, solder, propane torch tanks, fuses, and the like should always be ready for that Sunday morning you find time for the job, but no retailers open to supply you with missing materials.

Take some time now and then to go over your tools and make sure they are in shape, and sharp. Check belts on power equipment often.

There are four times in the year when your inspections are most likely to reveal upcoming problems:

• The season change in fall when the heat of summer is over and temperature is dropping. Functions of equipment are changing and it is important to take preventative steps to protect against the ravages of winter.

• The dead of winter—when humidity is at its lowest and so is the temperature. This is the time when shrunken boards produce the widest cracks, when gaps in the insulation show up in bare spots on a snow-covered roof, when a heat-lagging furnace lags the most.

• In early spring when there is the first opportunity to check on freeze damage and other winter deterioration. Dampness, the major cause of deterioration in wood and masonry, is at its highest during this season.

• The heat of midsummer—when humidity is at its highest, along with the temperature. This is the season when mildew and rot show up and when insect activity is in full swing.

CHORES FOR THE FALL

As fall comes on, there are countless prevention chores you can take care of. Here are some of the important ones:

✔ Clean the leaves out of the roof gutters, after the trees are bare; don't leave them to mat together and clog the system. While you're up there, install wire-mesh leaf guards, if the system doesn't have them. Also install small wire cages in each downspout opening to keep vertical drainpipes (leaders) from clogging.

✔ Fix sagging gutter hangers or supports before they become worse. Repair small leaks immediately with asphalt roofing cement. Repair small leaks in joints, end caps with butyl rubber calking compounds. Look for leader pipes that may have pulled away from the bottom of the gutter. Force the pipe up under the downspout opening and renail the leader to the side of the house, adding an additional mounting strap or two if necessary.

✔ Examine calking at doors, windows, masonry-to-wood meeting places, etc. If you calk mini-damage now, you'll avoid the problems that magnify when water seeps into the construction and freezes.

✔ Look for raised nails in siding and trim, caused by continuously changing dimensions of the wood during summertime's variable humidity conditions. Replace nails with the next size larger—galvanized—before the whole board comes loose.

✔ If you have asphalt shingles, check to see if any have curled upward, split, torn, or disappeared completely. If they have curled upwards, cement them with a dab of roofing cement. When you notice a missing shingle, patch the area with a piece of metal flashing.

✔ If the furnace system hasn't had a professional checkup recently, call the furnace man and have him in to do it. In a forced air heating system, check the condition of the air filter in the plenum chamber. If you can't see a strong light clearly through it, the filter needs to be replaced.

✔ At least once a year, vacuum dust, dirt from behind grill openings, between radiator sections or fins. Also, once a year, remove cover from the thermostat and carefully blow out any accumulated dust or lint.

✔ Bleed the radiators in a hot-water system. Don't wait for an upstairs bedroom to turn cold in midwinter.

WINTERTIME CHECKS

✔ When winter sets in and there is snow on the roof, check for bare spots that indicate heat-loss areas. Also, take a look at the eaveline. You may discover a row of snow and ice at the edge of the roof, beneath the point where the wall hits it below. This condition is caused by the lack of heated area below the roof. Snow may fall on the roof, where even acceptable heat loss melts it. Then the water trickles down, but when it gets past the heated area, it freezes. This is called an "ice dam" and it may block the runoff of water sufficiently to produce leaks. For that reason, it should be removed.

✔ As snows melt in late winter, get up into the attic under the bare rafters and search for any dampness or tiny leaks that might be developing. Use a good light.

✔ Check all around the foundation for accumulations of snow and ice which might back up moisture behind the siding and trim. If you find them, shovel away. Small cracks in stucco and masonry should be repaired as soon as noticed, especially right before winter freeze-and-thaw periods might open cracks enough to cause large pieces to fall out completely.

THINGS TO CHECK IN THE SPRING

✔ Inspect the house interior at end of heating season. The drying effect of heaters may have opened old cracks in walls, ceilings, and aggravated squeaks in floors and stairs.

Don't just switch from storm windows to screens. Make the changeover an excuse for careful inspection of glazing and screening. Do the work that has to be done during the pleasant part of the year when you no longer need the storms, and don't yet need the screens.

✔ Examine all weather stripping.

✔ Take a look at the putty in every window. Use a ladder, or work by lowering the top sash and sticking your head out, then raising the lower sash. Loose putty is never easier to repair than when it is only local. Small patches go fast, because they are supported by sound putty on both sides. Since putty failure is usually caused by paint failure, and since small damage usually signals more to come, paint those windows this fall, if you can arrange for the time. And remember that the properly painted sash has the paint extending about 1/8″ onto the glass.

✔ Check out your spring and summer equipment, such as ladders, garden hoses, etc. Get the upkeep over with before you need them. Wood preservative *but never paint* is good for wooden ladders, since paint may cover up deterioration that makes the ladder weak and unsafe.

✔ Put on a rainsuit some April day when there is a downpour and watch the performance of your rain-carrying equipment.

WORKSAVERS FOR SUMMER

✔ Most decay and deterioration of wood takes place during the warmth and dampness of summer. Take a tour of the exterior in late spring, looking for exposed wooden surfaces in steps, porches, posts, and the like. Also check the siding of the house for areas where dampness might have seeped in. If painted siding is blistered or peeling, water seepage could be responsible.

✔ Carefully check under all eaves and other under-roof areas in early summer for evidence of bee or wasp nest activity. Knock down and spray any you find while they are small. Don't forget to expect the unexpected, such as blockage of attic louvers by mudwasps' nests.

✔ Make a trip into dark corners, crawlspaces, and other little-visited places to check on insect or moisture damage. You may find problems after a heavy rain that you never knew you had.

✔ Don't ignore the heating system in the summer. For instance, the dampness of a basement in summer may cause sheet-form insulation to come loose from ducts. Also, most motors, circulating pumps, and blowers of heating systems have oil cups which should be checked and filled with oil.

✔ After a bad storm, check with a carpenter's level to see if the walls are out of plumb. If there's damaged plaster, siding, or sheathing in the area you're checking, remove it and get down to the framing. Look for loose nails, split framing members. Go into the attic and check internal roof supports.

SOME THINGS TO CHECK ANY DAY OF THE YEAR

Not all troubles are seasonal. Some of them happen all the year around.

✔ Put a screwdriver on door hinge screws now and then. The constant action of the hinges always loosens screws a little, but if you tighten them before they loosen too much there will be no damage to the wood. This applies to kitchen cabinet doors, and other hinged fixtures throughout the house.

✔ Take a look at chromium drains and traps under sinks and lavatories. You may discover evidence of drying water, an indication that something should be tightened.

✔ Use a pair of binoculars to study your roof, particularly the day after a high wind.

✔ Note, every once in a while, the speed with which water drains from a sink or lavatory. Too slow? Now is the easiest time to take care of the problem, before it becomes a complete blockage. Same way with toilet tanks that don't fill rapidly enough (open that valve down below the tank) or bowls that don't empty fast enough (get out the plumber's helper now).

✔ As long as you're in the bathtub, anyway, examine the grouting of the tiles and the calking around the rim of the tub. They are easier to fix now than they will be when the tile starts to fall off.

✔ Prevent rust from spreading. Check for rust areas on furnaces, on galvanized iron gutters, downspouts. Remove rust spots with sandpaper, steel wool; wash surface with benzine or turpentine; repaint properly. Protect metal roofs and wrought iron with a coat of asphaltum paint.

✔ Inspect home electrical systems regularly. Look at cables, cords, plugs, switches. Replace insulation that's wearing thin, breaking off a cord. Repair loose, frayed wire ends that are under screws in the plug before they become dangerous.

✔ Close all possible entry holes (for rats, mice, insects, etc.) with wire screen, sheet metal — including holes under the roof. If you're closing your house for an extended period of time, cover the chimney with wire screening to prevent animals from entering.

As the man said in the Introduction to this book, "it takes a heap o' fixin'," but sometimes you can cut down the work by fixing things before they need it.

INDEX

INDEX